Routledge Questions & Answer

Criminal Law

2013–2014

Routledge Q&A series

Each Routledge Q&A contains approximately 50 questions on topics commonly found on exam papers, with comprehensive suggested answers. The titles are written by lecturers who are also examiners, so the student gains an important insight into exactly what examiners are looking for in an answer. This makes them excellent revision and practice guides. With over 500,000 copies of the Routledge Q&As sold to date, accept no other substitute.

New editions publishing in 2013:

Civil Liberties & Human Rights
Company Law
Commercial Law
Constitutional & Administrative Law
Contract Law
Criminal Law
Employment Law
English Legal System
Equity & Trusts
European Union Law

Evidence
Family Law
Jurisprudence
Land Law
Medical Law
Torts

Published in 2012:

Business Law 2012–2013
Intellectual Property Law 2012–2013

For a full listing, visit http://cw.routledge.com/textbooks/revision

Routledge Questions & Answers Series

Criminal Law

2013–2014

Norman Baird

Academic Director, QED Law Revision Seminars

Routledge
Taylor & Francis Group

LONDON AND NEW YORK

Ninth edition published 2013
by Routledge
2 Park Square, Milton Park, Abingdon, Oxon OX14 4RN

Simultaneously published in the USA and Canada
by Routledge
711 Third Avenue, New York, NY 10017

Routledge is an imprint of the Taylor & Francis Group, an informa business

First edition published by Cavendish Publishing 1993
Eighth edition published by Routledge 2011

British Library Cataloguing in Publication Data
A catalogue record for this book is available from the British Library

Library of Congress Cataloging in Publication Data
Baird, Norman.
 Q & A criminal law / Norman Baird. — 9th ed.
  p. cm.
 ISBN 978–0–415–53887–9 (pbk) — ISBN 978–0–203–08391–8 (ebk)
 1. Criminal law—England—Examinations, questions, etc. I. Title. II. Title: Q and A criminal law.
 III. Title: Criminal law.
 KD7869.B35 2012
 345.42076—dc23

2012029837

ISBN: 978–0–415–53887–9 (pbk)
ISBN: 978–0–203–08391–8 (ebk)

Typeset in TheSans
by RefineCatch Limited, Bungay, Suffolk

MIX
Paper from responsible sources
FSC® C004839

Printed and bound in Great Britain by the MPG Books Group

Contents

Table of Cases

Table of Legislation

INTERNATIONAL TREATIES AND CONVENTIONS

SECONDARY LEGISLATION

Guide to the Companion Website

http://cw.routledge.com/textbooks/revision

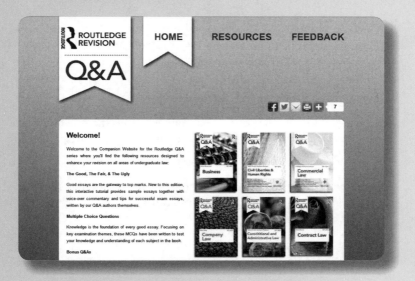

Visit the Routledge Q&A website to discover even more study tips and advice on getting those top marks.

On the Routledge revision website you will find the following resources designed to enhance your revision on all areas of undergraduate law.

The Good, The Fair, & The Ugly

Good essays are the gateway to top marks. This interactive tutorial provides sample essays together with voice-over commentary and tips for successful exam essays, written by our Q&A authors themselves.

Multiple Choice Questions

Knowledge is the foundation of every good essay. Focusing on key examination themes, these MCQs have been written to test your knowledge and understanding of each subject in the book.

Bonus Q&As

Having studied our exam advice, put your revision into practice and test your essay writing skills with our additional online questions and answers.

Don't forget to check out even more revision guides and exam tools from Routledge!

Lawcards

Lawcards are your complete, pocket-sized guides to key examinable areas of the undergraduate law.

Routledge Student Statutes

Comprehensive selections; clear, easy-to-use layout; alphabetical, chronological, and thematic indexes; and a competitive price make *Routledge Student Statutes* the statute book of choice for the serious law student.

Introduction

ANSWERING QUESTIONS IN CRIMINAL LAW

The purpose of this book is to assist students in their study of criminal law. It is not intended to replace standard textbooks but to complement them by providing illustrations of answers to typical examination and course assessment questions. It is anticipated that it will be of most use to students who have acquired a good knowledge of the rules and principles of criminal law but who still experience difficulty in expressing that knowledge when it comes to tackling questions.

PROBLEM QUESTIONS

Most examinations in criminal law include questions requiring candidates to analyse the liability of one or more parties in fictional 'problem' scenarios. These are designed to test knowledge of a limited number of offences and defences.

It is not always clear to students what exactly is expected of them when answering questions of this type. Common difficulties include tackling problems where some of the facts crucial to liability are not disclosed or where the authorities conflict, are ambiguous or are unclear.

Your aim should be to develop a systematic approach to answering questions well in advance of taking the examination. Well-structured answers are vital and it is hoped that the following guidance will assist you in learning how to do this.

ANSWER PLANS

Many candidates are reluctant to write a plan as they feel time is better spent writing the answer. This is a false economy. Structuring a plan will focus your mind, the issues raised will become clearer, and your thoughts will become better organised. Also, by planning your answer you will avoid overlooking important issues and wasting time on irrelevant matters.

STRUCTURING YOUR PLAN

Most questions raise issues concerning more than one offence and possibly more than one defence. Identify the offences and defences involved in the question.

Read the question again and check you have not missed any offences or defences raised.

Note any cases or sections of statutes that you think are relevant.

Put your notes into a logical order. Your plan should be designed to map the structure of your answer, identifying and organizing the issues raised by the question.

IDENTIFY THE OFFENCE

Your initial statement should always make it clear which offence you are considering. And so, you should start your discussion by writing, for example:

'It is proposed to consider Fred's liability for an offence of murder, contrary to common law.'

Alternatively use a heading:

'Fred's liability for murder, contrary to common law'

Be precise – use the proper name of the offence. For example, it is wrong to write, as many candidates do, that 'Fred will be charged with gbh'. There is no such offence. There are two major offences which require proof that D caused/inflicted gbh. They are 'causing gbh with intent' contrary to s18 of the Offences Against the Person Act 1861 and 'maliciously inflicting gbh' contrary to s20 of the same statute.

You should identify the source of the offence. If statutory you should specify the section and statute. If it is an offence contrary to common law, say so.

ANALYSING THE OFFENCE

Normally the most effective way of tackling criminal law problems is by dealing in turn with:

a.   issues relating to the *actus reus*, followed by,
b.   issues relating to the *mens rea* or *fault* and finally,
c.   the availability of relevant *defences*.

ACTUS REUS

1.   Define the *actus reus precisely*. Use the exact words of the appropriate statute or other authority. Do *not* use your own words.

      If you are not allowed to take statute books into the examination you should consider learning relevant parts by rote.

      If you are permitted to take statute books into the examination you should know the offences covered in your syllabus so well that you only need to use the statute book occasionally to check the precise form of words. There is no time in an examination to puzzle over the meaning of unfamiliar terms. Learn the statute before the examination not during it!

2. Address the issues raised by the question.

   If there is no need to elaborate on elements of the *actus reus* and then say so and proceed to consideration of the *mens rea*. If, however, there is some element of the *actus reus* that requires amplification identify the issue and explain and apply by reference to relevant authorities. Use your common sense here. If George has taken a can of beans from a supermarket shelf then make the point that the can of beans is 'property belonging to another' for the purposes of theft but do not waste time on an involved discussion of ss 4 and 5 of the Theft Act 1968. The examiner will not give credit for lengthy accounts of law unrelated to the issues raised by the question. The examiner will be interested, however, to see whether you understand and can explain the law concerning appropriation and consent as decided in *Gomez* (1992) and *Hinks* (2000).

3. If the facts do not permit a conclusive answer acknowledge that in your answer. Some of the facts relevant to liability may not be disclosed.

   In addition, proof of the *actus reus* may involve an evaluative question. For example, if Fred sustained injuries, having jumped out of a moving car to escape George's attack on him, the injuries will be attributed to George's attack if Fred's reaction was reasonably foreseeable – see Williams and Davis (1992). This is a question for the jury and you would be required to explain, by reference to authority, how the judge should direct the jury in respect of the issue and to make reference to those facts of the question that bear on the issue. But you are not required to put yourself in the place of the jury and come to a determination on the facts.

MENS REA /FAULT

1. Define the *mens rea*/fault requirement *precisely*. Again, use the exact words of the appropriate statute or other authority. Do *not* use your own words.

2. Address the issues raised by the question. Is there some element of the *mens rea* that requires explanation or definition? For example, you may be required to explain the meaning of 'intention' or 'recklessness'. Or a theft question may require you to explain the meaning of 'dishonesty' or 'intention to permanently deprive'. Explain how the judge should direct the jury in respect of these issues.

3. In the same way as for the *actus reus*, if the facts do not permit a conclusive answer acknowledge that in your answer.

Is it clear that D acted with the relevant intent? If there is doubt about D's intent say so and explain the alternative possible outcomes.

Deal with evaluative issues as discussed above (*actus reus*, point 3). These arise most commonly with objective fault requirements. For example, manslaughter by gross negligence requires the jury to consider whether the breach of duty by the defendant was so serious as to justify the imposition of criminal liability.

DEFENCES

1.   Read the question again carefully and consider whether D may have a defence.

By a defence is meant an excuse or a justification independent of the *actus reus* or *mens rea*. The most important defences are duress, necessity, loss of self-control, self-defence, diminished responsibility and insanity.

Remember that some defences apply to all crimes; others do not. Duress applies to all crimes except murder, attempted murder and treason. Diminished responsibility and loss of self-control apply only to murder.

Do not raise a defence if the facts do not imply that it ought to be discussed.

2.   State the source of the defence.

Duress, for example, is a common law defence whereas diminished responsibility is a statutory defence (s 2 of the Homicide Act 1957, as amended by the Coroners and Justice Act 2009).

Explain the effect of the defence. Duress is a complete defence whereas diminished responsibility is a partial defence reducing liability from murder to manslaughter.

3.   By reference to authorities, define the ingredients of the defence.

4.   Upon whom is the burden of proof?

Normally the burden of proof in respect of defences is on the prosecution. Insanity and diminished responsibility are exceptions – the burden of proof in respect of these defences is on the defendant.

5.   Identify the relevant issues and explain the elements of the defence by reference to the facts and issues.

6.   Apply as the facts permit.

Remember that most defences include an evaluative element. For example, a successful plea of self-defence requires that the force used to defend oneself was 'reasonable' and it is for the jury to evaluate the force used by the defendant. As before – see *actus reus* point 3 – you are required to explain, by reference to judicial statements or statutory provisions, how the judge should direct the jury in respect of the issue and to make reference to the facts of the question that bear on the matter but you are not required to put yourself in the place of the jury and come to a determination on the facts.

REPEAT IN RESPECT OF OTHER OFFENCES AND/OR DEFENCE

1. If the question raises issues of liability for other offences and/or the availability of other defences. If so, repeat the above processes.

2. When you believe you have finished your answer read the question one final time and then read your answer carefully checking that you have explained the relevant law as precisely as possible.

GENERAL POINTS

In general, when answering questions, the following approaches should be adopted.

1. When answering questions concerning offences against the person and the facts raise the possibility of liability for more than one offence it is normally wise to deal with the most serious offence first. So, if the facts permit, consider murder before manslaughter and causing grievous bodily harm with intent before maliciously inflicting grievous bodily harm.

    When tackling questions on offences contrary to the Theft Acts 1968 and 1978 and the Fraud Act 2006 it is often easier to structure your answer by following the narrative. That is, deal with offences as they arise according to the sequence of the events in the problem.

2. Do not start your discussion of a second crime or defence until you have completed your analysis of the first offence or defence.

3. If the facts raise the possibility of more than one defence, first explain and discuss the defence that has the best outcome and/or the best chance of success for the defendant and then consider the other relevant defences.

4. Remember there is an authority for all propositions of law. Cite them. You do not have to remember dates of case but see point 5 (below).

5. If there are conflicting authorities or the law is unclear, say so. Explain the nature of the conflict and explain the alternative outcomes depending on which of the authorities is followed. If one case was decided later than the other point that out. You might also explain why you believe that one approach is to be preferred.

6. In a question which raises issues of liability of accomplices (secondary parties), deal fully with the liability of the principal (perpetrator) first. Secondary liability is derivative of the liability of the perpetrator and should only be tackled when you have considered the principal's liability fully.

7. Always quote authorities for propositions of law. If you cannot remember the name of a case do not panic or spend valuable exam time trying to remember the name. It may come to you later. Simply write:

> *It has been decided that . . .* or
> *In a decided case it was held . . .* or for example
> *In a case where a Jehovah's witness refused a blood transfusion it was held . . .*

ESSAY QUESTIONS

Good structure is also important with essay questions. Again you should make a plan organising the material in a logical order. Your introduction should be followed by a discussion and a conclusion. Always answer the question set and not one which you would have preferred to answer. In particular if the question requires candidates to critically evaluate an aspect of criminal law it is necessary but not sufficient to give an account of the relevant law. You must consider its merits.

Many students lack confidence in their ability to critical analyse law but you can develop your critical faculties as you progress through your course by reflecting on the fundamental purposes and principles of criminal law.

As violations of criminal law result in the punishment of offenders a critical evaluation of criminal law rules almost always involves considering whether the rule in question might lead to unjust punishment or punishment without any rational purpose. Thus when evaluating a rule you should start by thinking about the standard justifications for punishment. Might application of the rule in question result in the punishment of those who do not deserve to be punished? This, in part, was the basis of the critique of the decision in *Caldwell* (1982) which is considered in question 3 of this book.

Another example of this approach to evaluation is illustrated by the answer to question 23 which looks at the rule that duress is not a defence to murder. Is it just to punish a person who has killed another to escape his own death or that of, say, a member of his family where a person of ordinary steadfastness would have done likewise? Is there any rational purpose in punishing a person in those circumstances? Would punishment deter the offender from repeating the behaviour? Would punishment deter others in a similar situation in future?

Although questions of the fairness and utility of punishment are sometimes complex and it is not always easy to come to a conclusive answer it is by considering the law in the light of the rationale of punishment that the most penetrating criticisms of criminal law rules are generally to be found.

Sometimes it is relevant to consider the practical effects of a rule of criminal law. Might criminalisation of the conduct in question do more harm than good? This is one of the concerns raised in the answer to question 1 which looks at the general issue of whether the fact that behaviour is immoral and/or causes harm to others is a sufficient condition of subjecting the behaviour to the criminal sanction.

Additionally one might consider whether a rule is expressed clearly and in a form which a jury might be expected to understand. Is the rule too vague? Is there a danger of it being applied inconsistently by juries? These considerations play a part in the answers to question 2 on the meaning of intention and part (a) of question 35 on dishonesty.

Finally, one might consider whether the rule in question is out of line with authority. Does it conflict with an established common law rule or statutory provision? The House of Lords in *R v G* (2003) in overruling the decision of the House of Lords in *Caldwell* (1982) made reference to the fact that the definition of reckless in the earlier case involved a misinterpretation of the Criminal Damage Act 1971. However, Lord Bingham acknowledged that this was not the most important reason for overruling *Caldwell*. Of greater significance was the fact that the decision was unjust.

Norman Baird
Academic director
QED Law Revision
http://www.qedlaw.co.uk

Common Pitfalls

The most common mistake made when using Questions & Answers books for revision is to memorise the model answers provided and try to reproduce them in exams. This approach is a sure-fire pitfall, likely to result in a poor overall mark because your answer will not be specific enough to the particular question on your exam paper, and there is also a danger that reproducing an answer in this way would be treated as plagiarism. You must instead be sure to read the question carefully, to identify the issues and problems it is asking you to address and to answer it directly in your exam. If you take our examiners' advice and use your Q&A to focus on your question-answering skills and understanding of the law applied, you will be ready for whatever your exam paper has to offer!

General Principles of Criminal Law

INTRODUCTION

This chapter contains questions concerning some of the fundamental principles of criminal law. Also included are questions regarding the objectives of punishment and the proper scope of the criminal law.

Inevitably, because of the subject matter, the majority of the questions in this chapter are of the essay type.

Checklist ✔

The following topics should be prepared in advance of tackling the questions:

- The competing theories of punishment. What objectives ought we to have in mind? 'Utilitarian' and 'desert' theories of punishment.

- The scope of the criminal law: what types of conduct ought to be subject to criminal sanctions? Should behaviour be subject to the criminal law merely because it is considered 'immoral', or should only 'harmful' conduct be criminalised? Other considerations that the legislature ought to bear in mind when deciding whether to make particular conduct unlawful.

- *Mens rea* terms – 'intention' and 'recklessness': the meaning of 'intention'; the meaning of 'recklessness'; the distinction between 'advertent' and 'inadvertent' recklessness.

- Liability for omissions: the circumstances in which criminal liability may be incurred for a failure to act; the duty principle; coincidence of *actus reus* and *mens rea*.

- Strict liability: what is meant by a crime of strict liability? How do the courts determine whether or not an offence requires *mens rea*? What are the justifications for imposing liability on a strict basis?

QUESTION 1 --

[For a practice to be subject to the criminal sanction] it is not enough in our submission that [it] is . . . regarded as immoral. Nor is it enough that it should cause harm. Both of these are minimal conditions for action by means of the criminal law, but they are not sufficient.

Clarkson, CMV and Keating, HM, *Criminal Law: Text and Materials*,

London: Sweet & Maxwell, 1990, p 25

▶ Discuss.

How to Answer this Question

The quotation expresses the commonly held view that immorality and harmfulness are necessary but not sufficient conditions of criminal liability; that the legislator ought to consider further matters when deciding whether to criminalise or legalise particular conduct. The starting point in answering this question is the well known 'debate' of the 1950s and 1960s between Lord Devlin and Professor Hart:

❖ the 'moral' theory: the Wolfenden Committee and Lord Devlin's response to the Report;

❖ criticisms of the 'moral' theory – its irrationalism;

❖ the 'harm' principle;

❖ the limitations of the 'harm' principle;

❖ considerations additional to the supposed immorality or harmfulness of the behaviour – the social effects of prohibition and enforcement;

❖ is immorality a 'necessary' condition?

Answer Structure

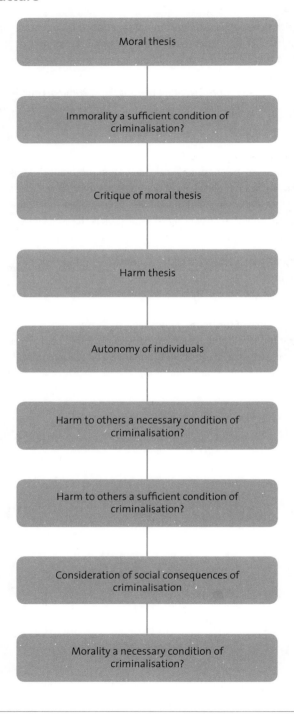

Moral thesis

Immorality a sufficient condition of criminalisation?

Critique of moral thesis

Harm thesis

Autonomy of individuals

Harm to others a necessary condition of criminalisation?

Harm to others a sufficient condition of criminalisation?

Consideration of social consequences of criminalisation

Morality a necessary condition of criminalisation?

ANSWER[1]

In 1959, Lord Devlin delivered the Maccabean Lecture in Jurisprudence of the British Academy under the title 'The enforcement of morals', in which he argued that the legislature is entitled to use the criminal law against behaviour which is generally condemned as immoral.[2]

The catalyst for Lord Devlin's thesis was the *Report of the Wolfenden Committee on Homosexual Offences and Prostitution*, 1957. The Committee had recommended that homosexual behaviour between consenting adults in private should no longer be a criminal offence. The Committee thought it was not the function of the law to intervene in the private lives of citizens or to enforce any particular morality except where it is necessary to protect the citizen from what is offensive or injurious and to provide protection against exploitation and corruption.

Lord Devlin disagreed. He contended that there are no limits to the power of the State to legislate against immoral behaviour: 'immorality', he believed, is a necessary and sufficient condition of criminalisation.

He based his argument upon the premise that social harmony is jeopardised if morality is not underwritten by the law. According to this view, tolerance of immorality threatens the social fabric, and therefore the legislature should criminalise behaviour where it is clear that there is a 'collective judgment' condemning the behaviour in question. Lord Devlin argued that morality forms a 'seamless web'. By this metaphor, he intended to convey the notion that 'society's morals' form a fragile structure and that if morality is not reinforced legally, then damage to the entire structure will follow.

According to Lord Devlin, immorality is what every 'right-minded' person considers to be immoral. If the behaviour in question provokes feelings of disgust and indignation in this 'individual', then it should be subject to the criminal sanction. Lord Devlin suggested that the judiciary are particularly well placed to express the appropriate standards by virtue of their familiarity with the 'reasonable man in the jury'.

There are a number of objections to Lord Devlin's thesis; the principal criticisms relate to its rejection of rationality. Instead of rational argument and empirical investigation of the effects of criminalisation or legalisation, Lord Devlin advocated that we place our reliance upon presumptions about the feelings of the right-minded individual and assumptions about the societal effects of liberalisation and tolerance.

---

1 Always read the question carefully and ensure that you answer it. Do not just write about the topic generally.
2 The first part of this answer considers whether immorality is a sufficient condition for behaviour to be subject to criminal sanctions.

Opponents of Devlin's thesis argue that although the feelings of the community are an important consideration, they cannot be the sole basis for deciding whether behaviour is to be subject to the criminal sanction, and if the revulsion of the ordinary person is a dangerous basis for criminalisation, then reliance on judicial estimates of that disgust is even more dangerous. Bentham warned us to be suspicious when officials claim that they are acting in the name of 'right-minded people'. In many cases, 'popular opinion' is used as a pretext to justify the prejudices of the legislators themselves (*Theory of Legislation*, 1876).

With reference to Lord Devlin's assertion that morality forms a seamless web, Professor Hart claimed in *Immorality and Treason* (1959) that there is no evidence that people abandon their moral views about murder, cruelty and dishonesty purely because a practice which they regard as immoral is not punished by law.[3]

He argued that the proper approach to determining whether the criminal law should intervene involves full consideration of the social consequences of the conduct in question. To this extent, he advocated the liberal approach, which stresses the importance of rational analysis in terms of the possible harmful consequences of the conduct. The principle of democracy may require the legislator to consider the values of the 'moral majority', but the liberal tradition urges that the autonomy of the individual be respected and that individuals have rights that may trump majority preferences. Professor Hart argued that a reasoned assessment of the harmful effects of the behaviour is a far better approach to the question of whether it should be outlawed than simple reliance on the feelings of disgust that the behaviour might cause us to feel.

The general approach of this tradition was expressed by John Stuart Mill in his essay, *On Liberty*. He maintained that the exercise of force over an individual is justified only if it is done to prevent harm to others. The fact that the behaviour might cause harm to the person who performs it is no justification for criminalisation.

Harm, however, is not to be understood as restricted to 'physical harm', but to include the violation of any recognised interest (Gross, H, *A Theory of Criminal Justice*, Oxford: OUP, 1979). Professor Hart contended that cruelty to animals should be outlawed, although there is no harm caused to other people. In addition, legal intervention may be appropriate to restrain young people from certain activities. This is justified not on the grounds that the behaviour may cause harm to the young person, but on the grounds that such a person is not sufficiently mature to appreciate the dangers of the behaviour in question.

---

3   This part of the answer considers the merits and limitations of 'the harm thesis' and whether the fact that behaviour causes harm to others is a necessary and sufficient condition of criminalisation.

It might be supposed that harm theorists would be opposed to legislation controlling narcotics or compelling the use of seat belts in motor vehicles, on the basis that legislation of this type involves a violation of the fundamental principle of individual autonomy. The harm theorist is opposed to legislation designed to protect the individual from himself.

In fact, legislation of this type is often supported by modern harm theorists. They point out that the prohibited behaviour is potentially harmful to others. In 'The role of law in drug control' (1971), Kaplan explains that there are different categories of harm, any one of which may be used to justify the criminalisation of behaviour that at first sight appears only to expose the actor to the risk of harm. The individual who drives a car without wearing a seat belt or the person who consumes drugs may expose others to a 'public ward harm'. That is, he may impose on others the cost of rectifying the damage he causes himself. He may be rendered incapable of discharging economic responsibilities he owes to others ('non-support harm'). Alternatively, a case may be made out that if the individual is allowed to indulge in certain behaviour, other susceptible individuals may copy or 'model' the behaviour and suffer harm as a consequence.

This reveals one of the limitations of the liberal 'harm' theory. When secondary harms are taken into account, the theory appears to lack precision. As Kaplan points out, if we acknowledge the broad concept of harm, there are few actions that one can perform that threaten harm only to oneself.

Moreover, the prohibition of particular harmful conduct may, in itself, result in harmful consequences. For example, the sale of certain commodities (heroin, alcohol, sugar, petrol, hamburgers, etc.) may directly or indirectly cause physical harm to consumers. However, prohibiting the sale of those commodities will cause economic harm to the business enterprises involved, and so we must weigh the harms resulting from tolerance against the harms of prohibition.

In *Principles of Morals and Legislation* (1781), Bentham recognised that in this process, careful consideration should be given to the general effects of prohibition. Even though certain behaviour may be regarded as immoral or harmful, it should not be prohibited if punishment would be inefficacious as a deterrent or the harm caused by prohibition would be greater than that which would be suffered if the behaviour was left unpunished.

For example, it is sometimes argued that as the demand for certain commodities and services (for example, prostitution, abortion, alcohol and other drugs) is relatively inelastic, there is little point in criminalisation of the behaviour concerned. Indeed, it is suggested that criminalisation may make matters worse. Prior to legalisation, backstreet abortions were carried out in conditions of great risk to the mother. Legalisation permits official control, allowing matters of public health to be addressed. Similarly, if prostitution were decriminalised, one condition of operating as a licensed or registered prostitute might be periodic health checks.

In addition, the criminalisation of certain types of conduct (for example, the possession of drugs) requires, for reasons of enforcement, intrusive forms of policing, involving, for example, powers of stop and search. There is the danger that these powers might be used in a discriminatory and oppressive manner against particular groups. The outlawing of homosexual behaviour meant that the police were often involved in dubious and degrading practices to catch offenders.

Thus, the fact that behaviour is harmful to others cannot be a sufficient condition of prohibition. The virtue of the harm theory is that, at least, it focuses attention on the empirical issues concerning the social effects of the conduct and the effects of legal intervention – issues which the moral principle patently ignores.

The quotation suggests that immorality is a necessary condition of criminalisation. Is this correct? What importance should be attached to the moral feelings of a section of the community?[4]

It is sometimes argued that support for the law is stronger where the prohibited conduct is perceived by a significant section of the population to be immoral. It is submitted, however, that immorality ought not to be regarded as a necessary condition of prohibition. Much of modern criminal legislation (for example, road traffic laws) is concerned with conduct which would not ordinarily be termed 'immoral', but one would be hard-pressed to deny the need for that legislation.

In any case, where behaviour is perceived to be immoral, it is normally supported by empirical claims expressed in terms of the harmful consequences, real or imagined, that will result if the behaviour is tolerated. For example, Lord Devlin believed that tolerance of homosexuality would result in harm – that is, damage to society at large. If this hypothesis were testable, and if there were empirical evidence in its support, it would provide a very good argument in favour of prohibiting homosexuality (Think Point (1)). On the other hand, the assertion that 'homosexuality should be prohibited because it is immoral' cannot be evaluated in the same way.

It is right that the debate should be focused on empirical claims. It is only by insisting upon arguments articulated in terms of the social consequences of tolerance, on the one hand, and prohibition, on the other, that a rational analysis of the fairness of legal intervention can be conducted.

---

4   Finally the question whether immorality is a necessary condition is considered.

The fact that a section of the community feels that certain behaviour is immoral cannot be either a necessary or a sufficient condition of prohibition. Although it may be prudent on some occasions for the legislator to acknowledge the 'feelings' of a section of the community – to ignore those irrational sentiments may result in the harmful consequence of social unrest – he should not rely upon the 'stomach of the man in the street'. Disgust or revulsion ought never to replace careful investigation of the social effects of prohibition.

Think Point

1　Emperor Justinian believed that homosexual behaviour was the cause of earthquakes.

QUESTION 2

Assess the modern approaches to the definition of 'intention' in English criminal law.

How to Answer this Question

The principal issues are:

- ❖ the hierarchy of fault elements;
- ❖ intention and recklessness contrasted;
- ❖ foresight and intention.

Principal authorities are as follows: *Hyam v DPP* (1975); *Moloney* (1985); *Hancock and Shankland* (1986); *Nedrick* (1986); *Woollin* (1998).

Answer Structure

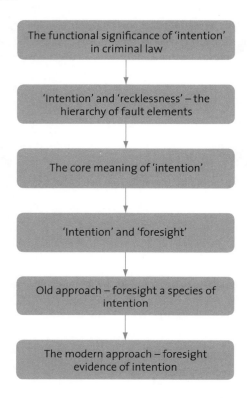

The functional significance of 'intention' in criminal law

↓

'Intention' and 'recklessness' – the hierarchy of fault elements

↓

The core meaning of 'intention'

↓

'Intention' and 'foresight'

↓

Old approach – foresight a species of intention

↓

The modern approach – foresight evidence of intention

ANSWER⁵

For a number of offences, the prosecution must prove beyond a reasonable doubt that the accused intended a particular consequence. To secure a conviction for murder, for example, it must be proved that the accused either intended to kill or intended to cause grievous bodily harm. Recklessness will not suffice. Similarly, intention, and intention alone, is the basis of liability for the offences of wounding or causing grievous bodily harm with intent, contrary to s 18 of the Offences Against the Person Act 1861 and for attempt contrary to s 1(1) of the Criminal Attempts Act 1981.

There is no statutory definition of intention. Its meaning is to be found in judicial decisions. Unfortunately, there has been a lack of consistency in the approach of the courts to the issue. Before reviewing these decisions, it is necessary to consider the

---

5   The question asks candidates to assess the modern approaches to intention. It is, therefore, not enough to explain how intention is defined. The answer must include an evaluation of the modern approaches.

functional significance of intention in criminal law and the principles which ought to be considered when constructing a definition of the concept.[6]

The fault elements most commonly encountered in the definition of offences – intention and recklessness – reflect different levels or degrees of blameworthiness. The concepts of intention and recklessness are distinct and stand in a hierarchical relationship one to the other. A person who kills, intending to kill, is, all other things being equal, more blameworthy than a person who kills being reckless as to causing death. This is reflected in the fact that the former is guilty of murder and subject to a *mandatory* term of life imprisonment (**Murder (Abolition of Death Penalty) Act 1965 s 1(1)**), whereas the latter, provided he did not intend to cause grievous bodily harm, is guilty of manslaughter which carries, at the discretion of the court, a life sentence (**Offences Against the Person Act 1861 s 5**).

Thus, the boundary between intention and recklessness (the essence of which is unjustified risk taking with respect to a defined consequence) should be clearly drawn to reflect a difference in degree of moral blameworthiness.

Furthermore, since it is the jury that has the task of determining whether the accused did or did not intend the consequence in question, the judicial instruction as to the meaning of intention should be clear and correspond as closely as possible to the ordinary meaning of the word. The greater the divergence of the legal definition from ordinary usage the greater the risk that the jury will not understand the judge's direction. In addition, it is often argued that the law should reflect ordinary principles concerning the attribution of moral responsibility.[7]

It is generally accepted that the central or core meaning of 'intention' is aim, objective or purpose. A person intends a consequence if he acts in order to bring it about. This approach to intention was adopted by the Court of Appeal in *Mohan* (1976), in which James LJ defined 'intention' as a decision to bring about a particular consequence, irrespective of whether the defendant desired that consequence.

The latter part of the definition indicates that a person can be said to intend a particular consequence, even though it is not desired, if it is a condition precedent to the desired consequence.

The definition in *Mohan* corresponds to the ordinary meaning of the word (Think Point (1)) but, on many occasions, the judiciary has accepted a wider definition. Prior to the

---

6   The concept of intention and its importance in criminal law is first explained.
7   In this part of the answer consideration is given to the question whether the definition of intention in criminal law should extend beyond its core meaning.

decision of the House of Lords in *Moloney* (1985), it was generally accepted that a person could be said to have intended a result if he foresaw that the result was virtually certain to result from his acts, even if the result was not his aim or purpose (Think Point (2)).

The point is commonly discussed by reference to the following hypothetical example:

> D places a bomb on a plane. The bomb is timed to explode when the plane is in mid-flight. His aim is to collect the insurance money on cargo he has placed on the flight. Although he hopes the passengers and crew will survive the explosion, D knows that it is practically certain that they will die.

Does D intend to kill in these circumstances, or is he 'merely' reckless with respect to killing the passengers and crew?

In 'Intention, recklessness and probable consequences' [1980] Crim LR 404, Duff put forward the view that a consequence is intended only where its non-occurrence would be regarded as a failure. Following this approach, D would not be regarded as having an intention to kill as he would not regard the survival of the passengers and crew as marking the failure of his plan.

On the other hand, it is often argued that although it is not D's purpose to kill the passengers, there is no moral distinction between his attitude and that of the purposeful killer, and for that reason D ought to be convicted of murder if death results when the plan is carried out. Intention, it is said, should be defined to include foresight of virtual certainty.

Until the 1980s, there had been some judicial recognition of an even broader definition. One of the leading cases was *Hyam v DPP* (1975), in which the House of Lords held that a person intends a result which he foresees as a (highly) probable result of his actions. This decision was, however, rarely followed as it was felt to blur the distinction between intention and recklessness: see *Belfon* (1976); *Bloomfield* (1978).[8]

In the 1980s, a series of cases adopted a different approach to the question of intention. In the first, *Moloney* (1985), the House of Lords held that, ordinarily, the judge need not define the word 'intention', except to explain that it is not the same thing as either 'desire' or 'foresight'. In 'rare' and 'exceptional' cases, however – those in which the primary purpose of the defendant was not to cause the defined harmful consequence – the judge may instruct the jury that if the defendant foresaw the consequence as a natural consequence of his act, then they may infer that he intended it.

---

8   The modern approaches to intention are considered and evaluated.

It is likely that Lord Bridge used 'natural consequence' believing that it conveyed the concept of a very high probability, but the guidelines did not make that clear. The problems caused by the guidance were raised in 1986 in the case of *Hancock and Shankland*. Two miners on strike had pushed a concrete block from a bridge onto a three-lane highway on which a miner was being taken to work by taxi. The concrete block hit the taxi and killed the driver. The defendants were charged with murder. They said that they merely intended to block the road and to frighten the nonstriking miner. Following the *Moloney* guidelines, the judge asked the jury to consider two questions: was death or serious injury a natural consequence of what was done?; and did the defendant foresee that consequence as a natural consequence? The jury convicted the defendants of murder.

The Court of Appeal held that the *Moloney* guidelines were misleading and quashed the conviction. There was an appeal to the House of Lords. In the only speech, Lord Scarman agreed that the *Moloney* guidelines were potentially misleading, as they omitted any reference to the probability of death or serious harm occurring. Lord Scarman pointed out that it should be explained to the jury that the greater the probability of a consequence, the more likely it is that the consequence was foreseen and that if the consequence was foreseen, the more likely it is that it was intended.

In the third case, *Nedrick* (1986), the Court of Appeal held that the jury were entitled to draw the inference of intention only where they were sure that the defendant foresaw the consequence in question as a virtual certainty. Indeed, Lord Lane thought that, in those circumstances, the 'inference may be irresistible' (Think Point (3)).

As a result of these decisions, it appeared that there was no longer a definition of intention. *Hyam* was effectively overruled. Foresight, even of a virtually certain consequence, was merely evidence of intention to be considered along with all other relevant evidence. Intention and foresight were not commensurable.

The decisions were heavily criticised for their failure to provide a definition of intention and for failing to explain how juries were to weigh the evidence of foresight against all the other evidence.

In *Woollin* (1998), the House of Lords reconsidered the earlier decisions. The appellant had lost his temper and thrown his baby son onto a hard surface. His son had sustained a fractured skull and died. The appellant was charged with murder. The Crown did not contend that the appellant desired to cause his son serious injury. The issue was whether the appellant nevertheless intended to cause serious harm. The appellant denied that he had any such intention. The recorder's summing-up was largely in accordance with the guidance given in *Nedrick*. However, he instructed the jury that if they were satisfied that the appellant realised that there was a substantial risk that he would cause serious injury to his son, then it would be open to them to find that he intended to cause injury to the child.

In the leading judgment, Lord Steyn observed, with the approval of all the Law Lords, that by using the phrase 'a substantial risk', the judge had blurred the line between intention and recklessness. The conviction of murder was quashed and a conviction for manslaughter substituted.

This part of the decision is, in itself, unremarkable but, in what appeared to be a revision of the previous approach, Lord Steyn observed that a consequence foreseen as virtually certain is an intended result. Doing acts with foresight that serious harm is a virtually certain result is a species of intention to cause serious harm.

Lord Steyn believed that this approach to intention was neither too narrow nor likely to confuse a jury. He also noted that it was similar to the definition proposed by the Law Commission in their Draft Criminal Code to the effect that a person acts intentionally with respect to a result if: (a) it was his purpose to cause it; or (b) he is aware that it would occur in the ordinary course of events if he were to succeed in his purpose of causing some other result (Think Point (4)).

In *Re A (Children) (Conjoined Twins: Medical Treatment) (No 1)* (2000), the Court of Appeal considered whether an operation to separate conjoined twins would be lawful where one of the effects of the operation would be the death of one of the twins. Ward LJ and Brooke LJ acknowledged that the decision in *Woollin* was authoritative on the issue of intention and concluded that a court would inevitably find that the surgeons intended to kill the twin, however little they desired that end, because they knew that her death would be the virtually certain consequence of their acts.

However, hopes that *Woollin* had settled the law concerning intention were dashed by the decision of the Court of Appeal in *Matthews and Alleyne* (2003). The court held that the trial judge had gone further than the law permitted when he directed the jury to find the necessary intent in murder proved if they were satisfied that the defendant appreciated that death or grievous bodily harm was virtually certain to result from his actions. Giving the judgment of the court, Rix LJ said that *Woollin* did not lay down a substantive rule of law, but approved the evidential rule in *Nedrick* subject to the substitution of 'find' for 'infer'. According to this view, the House of Lords in *Woollin* did not provide a definition of intention in terms of foresight of virtual certainty.

It is submitted that the Court of Appeal's interpretation of the decision is wrong. The decision to substitute the word 'find' for 'infer' was part of a change in approach to the issue of intention. Lord Steyn attached great importance to a passage in *Moloney* in which Lord Bridge stated that if a person foresees the probability of a consequence as little short of overwhelming, this will suffice to '*establish* the necessary intent' (Lord Steyn's emphasis).

Most commentators believed that *Woollin* marked a change in approach and welcomed the decision. It kept intention within narrow limits and the test was expressed in fairly simple language. Juries could be expected to understand it with little difficulty. Unfortunately, the Court of Appeal in *Matthews and Alleyne* reverted to the previous approach. Judges are required to direct juries that foresight that a consequence was virtually certain to result is merely evidence from which they may find that it was intended. Intention is again undefined.

Think Points

1   It also corresponds to the meaning of the word in the *Shorter Oxford English Dictionary*.

2   See, for example, the speech of Lord Hailsham in *Hyam v DPP* (1974).

3   In *Walker and Hayles* (1990), the Court of Appeal held that whilst a direction in terms of high probability was not a misdirection, it was preferable to direct the jury in terms of foresight of virtual certainty.

4   Law Commission, *Legislating the Criminal Code: Offences Against the Person and General Principles*, Law Com No 218, 1993.

Aim Higher ★

Essay questions often require candidates to assess an area of criminal law. You must also critically consider the relevant rules by reference to the underlying principles of criminal law. In answering this question an explanation of how intention is defined in criminal law is necessary but not sufficient.

QUESTION 3

'The interpretation of "reckless" in section 1 of the 1971 Act [by the majority in *Caldwell* (1982)] was ... a misinterpretation. If it were a misinterpretation that offended no principle and gave rise to no injustice there would be strong grounds for adhering to the misinterpretation and leaving Parliament to correct it if it chose. But

this misinterpretation is offensive to principle and is apt to cause injustice. That
being so, the need to correct the misinterpretation is compelling.'

Per Lord Bingham in *R v G and Another* (2003)

▶ Discuss.

How to Answer this Question

This quotation expresses the view that there is a significant moral distinction between
the advertent and the inadvertent wrongdoer and that the latter should not attract
criminal liability. The decision of the House of Lords in *R v G and Another* (2003)
overturned the earlier decision of the House of Lords in *Caldwell* (1982), in which it was
held that a person was reckless for failing to consider a risk that would have been obvious
to a reasonable person.

You should be familiar with:

❖ the justifications for the punishment of the advertently reckless wrongdoer;
   and
❖ the arguments for and against the punishment of the inadvertently reckless
   wrongdoer.

Answer Structure

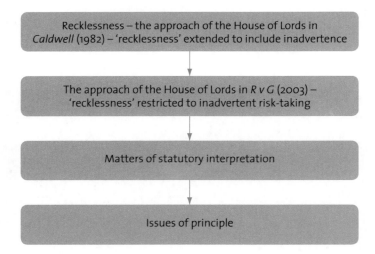

Recklessness – the approach of the House of Lords in
Caldwell (1982) – 'recklessness' extended to include inadvertence

The approach of the House of Lords in *R v G* (2003) –
'recklessness' restricted to inadvertent risk-taking

Matters of statutory interpretation

Issues of principle

ANSWER

INTRODUCTION

In *G and Another* (2003), the defendants were two boys aged 11 and 12 who had set fire to some newspapers in a bin behind a store. The fire spread and the store caught fire.

The boys were charged with reckless arson contrary to s 1(1) and 1(3) of the Criminal Damage Act 1971. They stated that they had expected the newspapers to burn themselves out and that it had not occurred to them that there was a risk that the fire might spread. The judge directed the jury in accordance with the decision of the House of Lords in *Caldwell* (1982) in which it was held that a person is reckless with respect to whether any property would be destroyed or damaged if: (a) he does an act which in fact creates an obvious risk that property would be destroyed or damaged; and (b) when he does the act, he either (i) has not given any thought to the possibility of there being such a risk, or (ii) has recognised that there was some risk involved and has nonetheless gone on to do it. The judge explained to the jury that the question of whether there was an obvious risk of property being damaged was to be assessed by reference to whether it would have been obvious to a reasonable man and not a person endowed with the age or other characteristics of the defendants.

The boys were convicted, and appealed to the Court of Appeal on the ground that the jury should have been instructed to take into account their age when considering whether the risk was obvious. The Court of Appeal dismissed the appeal. It acknowledged that there was great force in the criticisms of *Caldwell*, but held that it was bound by the decision. The test was intended to apply to all cases under s 1 of the 1971 Act and that no exception applied on the grounds of age, maturity or mental disability of the defendants.

THE DECISION OF THE HOUSE OF LORDS IN *CALDWELL*

The Criminal Damage Act 1971 replaced the Malicious Damage Act 1861. The older statute defined the fault element for a number of offences involving damage to property in terms of 'maliciousness' and it was settled law that this required proof that the defendant was aware of the risk of damage. Most of the 1861 Act was repealed by the Criminal Damage Act 1971, which replaced the term 'maliciousness' with 'recklessness'. However, in a series of decisions following its enactment, it was assumed by the Court of Appeal that it was not Parliament's intention to change the nature of the fault required; that the test of recklessness required the prosecution to prove that the accused consciously ran the risk in question. For example, in the case of *Stephenson* (1979), D lit a fire in the hollow of a haystack. The stack caught fire and was destroyed. D claimed that he had not foreseen the damage. Psychiatric evidence was given that D suffered from schizophrenia. This disorder could have deprived Stephenson of the normal capacity to weigh and foresee risks. The Court of Appeal held that the fact that the risk of damage would have been obvious to any normal person was not sufficient to give rise to criminal liability. The court held that the prosecution was obliged to prove that the defendant himself appreciated the existence of the risk. Recklessness was limited to advertent risk taking.[9]

In *Caldwell* (1982), however, the majority took the view that the old decisions on the meaning of maliciousness had no bearing on the meaning of recklessness and that to restrict recklessness to the conscious disregard of a recognised risk would impose an unnaturally narrow meaning on the word. In addition, Lord Diplock stated that as consciously taking a risk was not necessarily more blameworthy than failing to give any thought to the possibility of risk, to restrict recklessness to advertent risk taking was undesirable as a matter of policy. The *Caldwell* formula extended the concept of recklessness to include inadvertence.

The harshness of the *Caldwell* test was demonstrated in the case of *Elliott v C* (1983), which concerned a 14-year-old schoolgirl with learning difficulties who had been out all night and was cold, tired and hungry. She was charged with unlawfully destroying by fire a garden shed in which she was sheltering. She was acquitted by the magistrates who found as a fact that she was unaware that her behaviour carried with it a risk of damage to the shed and contents and would not have appreciated the danger even if she had stopped to think about it. The Divisional Court allowed the prosecutor's appeal (see also *R v Stephen Malcolm* (1984)), holding that where *Caldwell* recklessness sufficed, it was not only unnecessary for the prosecution to prove that the accused was aware of the risk in question, but it was also unnecessary to prove that the accused would have or could have been aware of the risk had he stopped to think about it.

THE DECISION OF THE HOUSE OF LORDS IN *R v G AND ANOTHER*

The defendants in *R v G and Another* appealed to the House of Lords, the Court of Appeal certifying the following point of law of general public importance:

> Can a defendant properly be convicted under s1 of the Criminal Damage Act 1971 on the basis that he was reckless as to whether property was destroyed or damaged when he gave no thought to the risk but, by reason of his age and/or personal characteristics the risk would not have been obvious to him, even if he had thought about it?

The House of Lords, allowing the appeal, answered the certified question in the negative. It was clear that Parliament's intention in respect of the 1971 Act was to replace the outdated term 'maliciously' in the 1861 Act with the term 'recklessly' but without altering the approach to the mental element required. The majority in *Caldwell* had concluded,

---

9   The evaluation of the decision of the House of Lords in Caldwell is only possible if its significance and impact are clearly explained.

incorrectly, that Parliament, when adopting the term 'recklessly', had intended to extend the mental element of property offences to include inadvertent risk taking. Recklessness required proof that the defendant was aware of a risk of damage to property belonging to another and that it was unreasonable for him to take that risk (Think Point (1)).

Furthermore, as the quotation above indicates, Lord Bingham believed that the rule in *Caldwell* was unjust. He stated that a person should not be regarded as reckless if he genuinely did not perceive a risk of damage. Such a person, he said, may fairly be accused of stupidity or lack of imagination, but neither of those failings should expose him to conviction and punishment for a serious offence such as arson. A majority of the Lords agreed with Lord Bingham that the decision was contrary to principle, Lord Steyn adding that 'in *Caldwell* the law took a wrong turn'. Lord Rodger, however, whilst agreeing that Parliament intended 'recklessness' to bear a subjective meaning in the 1971 Act, did not accept that it was always unjust to impose liability on the basis of inadvertence.[10]

THE ISSUES OF PRINCIPLE
The traditional justification for imposing criminal liability on the basis of 'advertent' recklessness is that a person who pursues a course of conduct aware of the risks of harm demonstrates that he is willing to take a chance with the person or property of another. The subjectively reckless individual has deliberately chosen to increase the risk of a defined harm occurring. Although a person who takes a risk in causing harm is regarded, in general, as less blameworthy than the person who sets out intentionally to cause harm, there is unanimity among commentators that the individual who willingly and without justification takes a risk with respect to another's protected interests deserves to be punished.

The commentators are divided, however, with respect to whether criminal liability should be extended to the inadvertent wrongdoer. Those who maintain that advertence is a necessary condition of liability argue that the standard justifications and objectives of punishment are implicitly based on a concept of 'subjective' fault. They contend that the retributive theory, for example, is based on the notion that punishment should be administered if, but only if, the accused deserves it, and that an accused deserves punishment only where he has chosen to gain an unfair advantage by breaking the primary rules of social life. A person who has failed to perceive a risk has not deliberately chosen to break the law and hence does not deserve to be punished.

The deterrent theory, it is said, also presupposes the existence of a 'guilty mind'. Punishment is threatened to discourage the potential wrongdoer from deliberately causing harm or taking risks with respect to the person or property of another. Similarly,

---

10 The question requires consideration of the issues of principle referred to by Lord Bingham. It is important to develop an understanding of the principles underlying criminal law as they are fundamental to the evaluation of any particular rule.

where an individual has deliberately chosen to risk causing harm, the theory of individual deterrence justifies punishing him to discourage him from taking similar risks in the future. The deterrent effect of the law cannot, however, operate on the mind of the inadvertent actor as one cannot be discouraged from taking risks of which one is unaware.

Duff, however, has argued that the person of full capacity who fails to consider an obvious risk may be as culpable as the person who consciously runs a risk. He suggests that the person who is unaware of an obvious risk may manifest not merely stupidity but an attitude and values which reflect a lack of concern for the interests of others (Duff, A, 'Recklessness' [1980] Crim LR 282). Provided the capacities of the defendant are taken into account, there is, it is contended, no injustice in punishing the inadvertent wrongdoer (Hart, HLA, 'Punishment and responsibility', 1968). If he could have done otherwise, if he failed to utilise his faculties to estimate and avoid risks inherent in his proposed conduct then, Fletcher argues, his actions may be described as voluntary (Fletcher, GP, 'The theory of criminal negligence: a comparative analysis' (1971) U Pa L Rev 401). From a utilitarian standpoint, the threat of punishment for inadvertence is said to promote adherence to a particular standard of care by encouraging reflection. A potential actor is encouraged to consider the possible consequences of his conduct and, if a person causes harm, having failed to consider an obvious risk, then punishment may serve the purpose of encouraging him to reflect on the potential consequences of his actions in the future.

As discussed above, the arguments in favour of redrafting the test in *Caldwell* to take into account the defendant's age or capacity or to require that the risk would have been obvious to the defendant if he had given thought to the matter were rejected in *Elliot v C* and *Stephen Malcolm*. In *R v G and Another*, Lord Bingham felt that such refinements were contrary to principle, would introduce unnecessary complexity and were not in accord with Parliament's intention.

Although there is disagreement as to whether it is always contrary to principle to punish the inadvertent risk taker, it is generally agreed that the extended definition of recklessness in *Caldwell* unjustly categorised as equivalent, levels of fault that are morally quite distinct. Criminal law recognises degrees of blameworthiness. Thus, even if it is accepted that the inadvertent wrongdoer is culpable and that there is some utility in punishing him, he ought to be formally distinguished in terms of liability from the conscious risk taker.

Professor Kenny argues that the advertent risk taker is not only more wicked than the inadvertent wrongdoer, he is also, in general, more dangerous and that, from a utilitarian standpoint, the threat of a more severe punishment is necessary to discourage a person from pursuing a course of conduct which he knows carries a risk of harm than is necessary for the less dangerous inadvertent actor (Kenny, A, *Free Will and Responsibility*, London: Routledge and Kegan Paul, 1978).

Brady agrees that there is a significant moral distinction between the person who consciously runs a risk and the individual who fails to consider a risk. The former is more culpable because he has 'manifested a trait' which demonstrates a greater degree of indifference to the interests of others. For this reason, we are justified in punishing him more severely (Brady, JB, 'Recklessness, negligence, indifference and awareness' (1980) 43 MLR 381). If criminal liability is to be imposed on the inadvertently reckless, a specific offence should be targeted at them and should reflect the lower degree of blameworthiness with an appropriately lower maximum penalty (Think Point (2)).

The extended meaning given to recklessness by Lord Diplock in *Caldwell* failed to acknowledge this important distinction. It not only resulted in the attribution of criminal responsibility to a defendant like the young girl in *Elliott v C*, but treated her and the deliberate risk taker as equally blameworthy. That was clearly contrary to principle (Think Point (3)).

Think Points

1   The House approved the definition of recklessness set out in cl 18(c) of the 1989 Draft Criminal Code (Law Com No 177):

A person acts recklessly within the meaning of section 1 of the Criminal Damage Act 1971 with respect to:

(i)   a circumstance when he is aware of a risk that it exists or will exist;

(ii)   a result when he is aware of a risk that it will occur;

and it is, in the circumstances known to him, unreasonable to take that risk.

2   In *Hoof* (1980), the Court of Appeal stated that where D is charged under subss 1(2) and (3) of the Criminal Damage Act 1971, there should be two counts:

(A)   arson with *intent* to endanger life; and

(B)   arson being *reckless* as to whether life would be endangered.

This is to ensure that, for the purposes of sentencing, the court is aware of the jury's verdict with respect to the degree of D's blameworthiness. However, as the law currently stood under *Caldwell*, no distinction could be drawn within category (b) between the advertently and inadvertently reckless. They were treated as legal equivalents although they are not moral equivalents: see also *Hardie* (1984).

3   The decision in *R v G and Another* has been applied by the Court of Appeal in *Cooper* (2004) and *Castle* (2004).

QUESTION 4

[T]here has for centuries been a presumption that Parliament did not intend to make criminals of persons who were in no way blameworthy in what they did. That means that whenever a section is silent as to *mens rea* there is a presumption that, in order to give effect to the will of Parliament, we must read in words appropriate to require *mens rea*.

In the absence of a clear indication in the Act that an offence is intended to be an [offence of strict liability], it is necessary to go outside the Act and examine all relevant circumstances in order to establish that this must have been the intention of Parliament.

Per Lord Reid in *Sweet v Parsley* (1970)

▶ Discuss.

How to Answer this Question

A fairly straightforward question. It requires a discussion of the approach of the courts to the task of interpreting statutory offences where it is not clear whether Parliament intended the offence to be one requiring proof of *mens rea*.

The following points need to be discussed:

❖   the presumption of *mens rea*;
❖   the meaning of strict liability; and
❖   intrinsic/extrinsic aids to interpretation.

Answer Structure

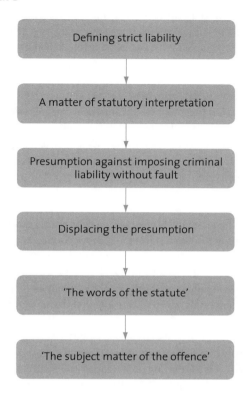

Defining strict liability

↓

A matter of statutory interpretation

↓

Presumption against imposing criminal liability without fault

↓

Displacing the presumption

↓

'The words of the statute'

↓

'The subject matter of the offence'

ANSWER

A crime of strict liability is one where there is no requirement of *mens rea* or negligence in respect of one or more of the elements of the *actus reus*. For example, in *Woodrow* (1846), the accused was convicted of the offence of 'having in his possession adulterated tobacco', despite his lack of knowledge that the tobacco was adulterated.

As the quotation indicates, most offences of strict liability are statutory and it is a question of interpretation whether a particular offence requires *mens rea* or not. Certain words or expressions (for example, 'knowingly', 'intentionally', 'recklessly', etc.) clearly indicate that proof of a particular form of *mens rea* is necessary. However, the absence of a *mens rea* term is not conclusive that the offence is one of strict liability. The presumption referred to by Lord Reid means that if a section is silent as to *mens rea*, the courts should imply *mens rea* unless Parliament has indicated a contrary intention either expressly or by implication. This is a corollary of the principle that where a penal provision is capable of two interpretations, the interpretation most favourable to the accused must be adopted (Think Point (1)).

In *B (A Minor) v DPP* (2000), Lord Hutton pointed out that the test is not whether it is a *reasonable* implication that the statute rules out *mens rea* as a constituent part of the crime – the test is whether it is a *necessary* implication. And in M (2009), Rix LJ said that only a 'compelling case for implying the exclusion of [mens rea] as a matter of necessity will suffice'.[11]

In one of the earliest cases to deal with the issue, *Sherras v de Rutzen* (1895), Wright J stated that, to give effect to the intention of Parliament, it is important, first of all, to consider the actual words used in the statute and, secondly, to consider the subject matter of the provision. This accords with the normal principle of interpretation that the court should look only to extrinsic factors when the intention of Parliament is not clear from the words of the statute.

THE WORDS OF THE STATUTE[12]

The court may look to the wording of the provision in its overall context. Words and terms used in other provisions of the same statute may provide a clue as to the intention of Parliament. For example, in *Pharmaceutical Society of Great Britain v Storkwain Ltd* (1986), the House of Lords decided that s 58(2)(a) of the Medicines Act 1968 imposed a condition of strict liability. They were influenced by the fact that, whereas s 58(2)(a) was silent with respect to fault, other provisions of the statute expressly required *mens rea*.

In *Cheshire County Council Trading Standards Department ex p Alan Helliwell & Sons (Bolton) Ltd* (1991), D was charged with an offence contrary to the Transit of Animals (Road and Rail) Order 1975 of permitting unfit animals to be carried so as to be likely to cause them unnecessary suffering (Art 11(1)). The court held that the offence was one of strict liability. It was partly influenced by the fact that another provision of the Order, concerning the transportation of pregnant animals, expressly imposed a requirement of knowledge. And in *Jackson* (2006) it was held that unlawful low flying contrary to s 51 of the Air Force Act 1955 was an offence of strict liability. It was unnecessary to prove that the pilot was aware that he was flying at a height less than that prescribed. The Judge Advocate of the General Court Martial, in a judgment which the Court of Appeal regarded as impeccable, pointed to the fact that other sections of the Act concerned with flying specifically imported elements of *mens rea*.

However, the fact that other sections of the statute expressly require *mens rea* is not, of itself, sufficient to justify a decision that a section which is silent as to *mens rea* creates an offence of strict liability. In *B (A Minor) v DPP*, the defendant was charged with inciting a girl under the age of 14 to commit an act of gross indecency with him contrary to s 1(1) of

---

11 It is important that the presumption is stated clearly.
12 A review of a number of important decisions illustrating how the words of the statute may or may not displace the presumption is essential.

the Indecency with Children Act 1960 (now repealed by s 140 and Sched 7 to the Sexual Offences Act 2003). The issue for the House of Lords was whether it was necessary for the prosecution to prove the absence of a genuine belief on the part of the defendant that the child was over the specified age of 14. The section was silent in respect of the issue. The Crown argued that the 1960 Act together with the Sexual Offences Act 1956 formed a code of sexual offences and that where Parliament intended belief as to age to be a defence, it had expressly so provided.

The House rejected the argument. Whilst accepting that the statutes formed a code, there was no clear or consistent pattern within the 1956 Act that provided compelling guidance in respect of the question whether an age-related defence applied to the offence under s 1.

In *R v K* (2001), the House considered a similar issue in respect of the offence of indecent assault contrary to s 14 of the 1956 Act (now repealed by s 140 and Sched 7 to the Sexual Offences Act 2003). The offence required proof that the defendant touched a woman indecently without her consent. Section 14(2) provided that a girl under the age of 16 could not in law give consent. The question for the House was whether a man who indecently touched a girl under the age of 16 but believed her to be over 16 and believed her to have consented to the contact was entitled to be acquitted. Again, the section was silent on this issue.

The Crown pointed out that subss (3) and (4) defined circumstances in which a defendant's belief, knowledge or suspicion exonerated a defendant from liability for what would otherwise be an indecent assault and contended that if it had been intended to excuse a defendant who believed a complainant to be 16 or over, this ground of exoneration would have been expressed in subs (2).

The House rejected the argument. Section 14 was not part of a single coherent legislative scheme; its provisions were derived from a variety of sources and thus no significance could be attached to the inclusion of grounds of exoneration in subss (3) and (4) and the omission of such a ground from subs (2). The 1956 Act was a consolidating statute and had perpetuated the anomalies of the previous legislation. Neither in s 14 nor elsewhere in the 1956 Act was there any express exclusion of the need to prove an absence of genuine belief on the part of a defendant as to the age of an under-age victim. Had it been intended to exclude that element of *mens rea*, it would have been very easy to do so by an appropriately worded provision in or following subs (2).

Nor was there anything in the language of the statute which justified, as a matter of necessary implication, the conclusion that Parliament must have intended to exclude this ingredient of *mens rea* from the offence of indecent assault. As far as the age-related offences of the statute were concerned, a compellingly clear implication displacing the presumption could only be established if the supplementation of the text by reading in words appropriate to require *mens rea* resulted in an internal inconsistency of the text. Section 14(2) could have provided that a genuine belief by the accused that the girl was over 16 was no defence but, equally, it could have provided that a genuine belief that the girl was under 16 was a defence; such a provision would not have been conceptually inconsistent with any part of s 14. Thus, there was nothing in s 14(1) which clearly indicated the displacement of the presumption.

THE SUBJECT MATTER OF THE OFFENCE

It is often stated that if the subject matter of the provision relates to 'acts which are not criminal in any real sense', the presumption against no fault liability may be displaced (per Wright J in *Sherras v de Rutzen*). The same principle was expressed in a positive form in *Gammon v Attorney General of Hong Kong* (1985), where Lord Scarman stated that the presumption in favour of the implication of a fault requirement is particularly strong where the offence is 'truly criminal' in character.[13]

In *Sweet v Parsley* (1970), the House of Lords implied a requirement of *mens rea* into the offence of 'being concerned in the management of premises used for the purpose of smoking cannabis' contrary to s 5(1)(b) of the Dangerous Drugs Act 1965. The House was influenced by the fact that the offence was regarded as serious, attracting 'social obloquy' (see also *Alphacell Ltd v Woodward* (1972)).

In *B (A Minor) v DPP*, the House was influenced by the fact that gross indecency was a serious offence carrying a maximum penalty of 10 years' imprisonment and to which the notification requirements under Pt I of the Sex Offenders Act 1997 applied. It was also felt that the presumption was reinforced by the fact that the offence was broad and would cover conduct ranging from predatory advances by an adult paedophile to consensual sexual contact, in private, between young teenagers. Lord Steyn observed that as the *actus reus* extended to incitement to an act of gross indecency, the subsection applied to verbal sexual overtures between teenagers if one of them was under the age of 14. For the law to criminalise such conduct of teenagers by offences of strict liability would be far-reaching and controversial.

In *M* the issue was whether the offence of bringing a prohibited article into prison, contrary to s 40C(1) of the Prison Act 1952, was an offence of strict liability. The Court of Appeal, was influenced by the fact that a more serious offence in the same statute – contrary to s 40B(1) – carried a potential 10 year penalty. The penalty indicated that the offence was 'truly criminal' and required proof of *mens rea*. As the s 40C(1) offence used identical language it followed that it too required proof of *mens rea*.

---

13   A review of the decisions in which the courts have considered a number of extrinsic factors to assist them in deciding whether the presumption is displaced should be considered.

By contrast, in *Gammon v Attorney General of Hong Kong*, the Privy Council were prepared to impose strict liability in the case of an offence punishable with a fine of $250,000 and imprisonment for three years. In *Hussain* (1981), the Court of Appeal held that s 1 of the Firearms Act 1968, which prohibits the unlawful possession of a firearm, should be interpreted strictly, even though it carried a maximum penalty of three years' imprisonment. And in *Jackson* (2006) it was stated that the fact that the offence carried a maximum sentence of two years' imprisonment did not prevent liability being imposed on a strict basis.

A factor that may influence the court in favour of imposing strict liability is where the provision is concerned with an issue of public safety. In *Howells* (1977), which concerned s 58 of the Firearms Act, the Court of Appeal stated that the danger to the community resulting from the possession of lethal firearms was so obviously great that an absolute prohibition against their possession must have been the intention of Parliament. In *Jackson* the fact that low flying created a serious hazard and risk of serious danger to person and property was cited as an additional reason for dispensing with a requirement of *mens rea*.

Indeed, most offences of strict liability are contained in legislation concerned with the sale of food and drugs, the operation of licensed premises, industrial activity (for example, pollution) and other hazardous activities in which individuals may voluntarily engage, like driving a car.

The courts often express a willingness to impose strict liability out of a protectionist concern for the welfare of 'ordinary' citizens exposed to the hazardous activities of others, particularly where the dangerous activity is performed predominantly by corporate undertakings (see, for example, *Gammon v Attorney General of Hong Kong*).

In *Alphacell Ltd v Woodward*, for example, it was said that the imposition of strict liability might encourage businesses to comply with important social welfare regulations. In *Sweet v Parsley*, Lord Diplock stated that where the subject matter of a statute is the regulation of an activity involving potential danger to public health or safety, the court may impose liability on a strict basis to enforce the obligation to take whatever measures may be necessary and without reference to considerations of cost or business practicability.

In response to the argument that it is 'unfair' to use the weight of the criminal law in this way and that principles of justice prohibit the imposition of criminal liability where the defendant has not chosen to break the law, the proponents of strict liability point out that those principles are not appropriate when we are dealing with questions of corporate liability. A corporate enterprise, when deciding whether to engage in the activities in question, is in a position to consider and weigh the potential costs of any unintentional infringement of the law.

In any event, the presumption of *mens rea* remains unless it can be shown that the objects of the legislation will be better promoted by strict liability (see *Gammon v Attorney General of Hong Kong*, above, and also *Lim Chin Aik v R* (1963)). Thus, for example, one of the factors influencing the Divisional Court in the *Cheshire County Council* case was the difficulty of proving *mens rea* of one of the controlling officers of the respondent company. By dispensing with a requirement of *mens rea*, liability could be imposed on the company, thereby encouraging the officers to take positive steps to prevent an offence being committed in the future.

CONCLUSION

There is no single test that the courts will apply in deciding whether the presumption is displaced in respect of a particular offence. The courts are influenced by a number of intrinsic and extrinsic factors (Think Point (1)). Although there is a great deal of inconsistency, the modern cases concerning strict liability have tended to look principally to the subject matter of the offence when in doubt as to Parliament's intentions. Although there have been a number of cases where the presumption of no liability without fault has been reaffirmed, it would appear that it is most likely to be rebutted where the subject matter of the offence relates to a serious social danger or a matter of social concern and adherence to the law is perceived to be more likely to be achieved by the imposition of strict liability.

Think Point

1 In *R v Muhamad* (2002), the Court of Appeal rejected the submission that in order to be compatible with Art 7 of the European Convention on Human Rights, a provision had to be read so as to import a requirement of *mens rea*. States are free to enact offences of strict liability. The case concerned an offence contrary to s 362(1)(a) of the Insolvency Act 1986. The court held that the offence was one of strict liability. The statute created 'a clear and coherent regime'. The majority of the offences included an express requirement of a mental element. The fact that s 362 was one of the few provisions which did not specify a mental element was 'a clear pointer to Parliament's intention'. Further support was found from the fact that offences for which no mental element was specified attracted considerably lower sentences and, furthermore, the legislation dealt with an issue of social concern. See also *R (Grundy & Co Excavations Ltd and Parry) v Halton Division Magistrates' Court* (2003). In *R v G* (2008) UKHL 37 the House of Lords held that Art 6.2 did not restrict the power of a State to enact and enforce a crime of strict liability. It held that the article was concerned with the procedural fairness of a trial and not with the substantive law.

QUESTION 5

PART (A)

In what circumstances does the criminal law impose a duty to assist other individuals?

PART (B)

Gorge was employed as a lifeguard at a beach. He had just returned from lunch when he noticed that one of the swimmers, Flop, appeared to be distressed and was screaming and shouting. Gorge was about to take steps to rescue her when Flop stopped screaming. She had become too tired. Gorge thought she had stopped screaming as she was no longer in danger. He returned to the life station. Flop drowned.

▶ Discuss Gorge's criminal liability.

Would your answer differ if Gorge had returned from lunch in a state of drunkenness and concluded that Flop was screaming with enjoyment?

How to Answer this Question

You should discuss:

❖ liability for omissions;
❖ duty to act;
❖ duty of care in negligence; and
❖ manslaughter – basic intent and drunkenness.

Principal authorities are as follows: *Miller* (1983); *Stone and Dobinson* (1977); *Adomako* (1994); *DPP v Majewski* (1977).

Answer Structure

(a)

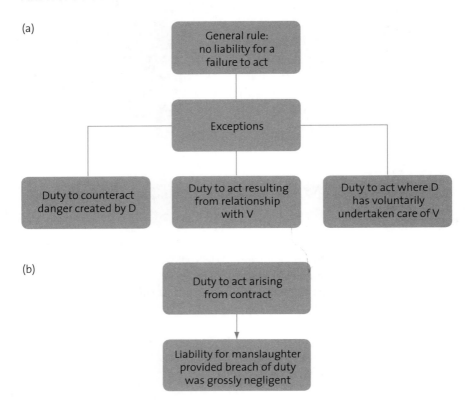

(b)

ANSWER

PART (A)

Criminal law is, in general, concerned with prohibiting certain forms of behaviour. Offences are normally defined in active terms and not in terms of a failure to do something. Liability for a failure to act will only arise in those rare situations where a legal duty to act is recognised.[14]

The law in this area has developed considerably in recent years, but there are still some uncertainties. First, the House of Lords in *Miller* (1983) held that a person who accidentally creates a potentially harmful situation is under a duty, upon becoming aware of the risk

14 Start by stating the general rule concerning omissions and then outline the bases upon which a duty to act may be founded.

of harm, to take steps to minimise the effects of his act. Lord Diplock said that if a defendant failed to take measures to counteract a danger that he himself has created, then his failure can be regarded as amounting to the commission of the *actus reus* of an appropriate offence. One is under a duty (Lord Diplock preferred the word 'responsibility') to take steps that lie within one's power to rectify the danger created. A person who neglects to discharge the duty is guilty of an offence, provided the failure to act was accompanied by the appropriate *mens rea*.

The case concerned arson but it is clear that Lord Diplock intended the principle to apply to all result crimes and, in *Lawford* (1994), the Supreme Court of South Australia held that if D was responsible for V being rendered unconscious and, as a consequence, placed in a dangerous situation, a duty to take positive steps to render assistance would arise and D would be guilty of murder by omission if, with malice aforethought, he failed to act and, as a result, V died. In *DPP v Santana-Bermudez* (2003), D, an intravenous drug user, falsely assured V, a police officer who was about to search him, that he had no needles in his pocket. The police officer cut her finger on a syringe in his pocket. On a prosecutor's appeal to the Divisional Court, Maurice Kay J assumed that the *Miller* principle was of general application and stated that where someone (by act or word or a combination of the two) creates a danger and thereby exposes another to a reasonably foreseeable risk of injury which materialises, there is an evidential basis for the *actus reus* of an assault occasioning actual bodily harm. And in *Evans* (2009) D was convicted of manslaughter by gross negligence on the basis of her failure to take reasonable steps for the safety of the deceased, V, once D appreciated that the heroin she procured for V was having a potentially fatal impact.

Secondly, duties may be imposed on individuals as a result of their relationship with the victim. The Children and Young Persons Act 1933, for example, imposes duties on parents. By virtue of s 1, it is an offence for a parent to wilfully neglect a child in a manner likely to cause unnecessary suffering or injury to health. This offence carries a maximum sentence of 10 years' imprisonment (s 45 of the Criminal Justice Act 1988).

In addition to this statutory duty, the common law recognises a parental duty to act which may give rise to liability for an offence against the person. Thus, for example, although there is no general duty to take steps to save the life of another, a parent would be under a duty to take reasonable steps to save the life of his or her child. A failure to discharge such a duty may result in liability for either murder or manslaughter, depending on the defendant's *mens rea*.

Gibbons and Proctor (1918) provides a rare case of murder by omission. The defendants killed the child of the father by withholding food. As the parties' failure to look after the child was accompanied by 'malice aforethought', they were guilty of murder. Most commonly, in cases of 'neglect' of this sort, it will be difficult to prove an intent adequate for murder and the person will normally be guilty of manslaughter 'by gross negligence'.

It is not clear to what other familial relationships the common law duty extends. It is not clear, for example, whether a duty is owed by one spouse to another or whether an adult child owes a duty to his or her parent. There are a couple of nineteenth-century decisions which denied the existence of a duty towards adult sons and daughters (*Smith* (1826) and *Shepherd* (1862)), suggesting that the parental duty is terminated when the child becomes 'independent'.[15]

In addition to familial relationships, it has been held that a duty may be imposed on one who has voluntarily undertaken the care of another. In *Stone and Dobinson* (1977), Stone's sister, Fanny, whilst living with the defendants, had become unable to care for herself. She became extremely ill and died. It was held, as a matter of fact, that the defendants had undertaken to care for her. Such an undertaking gave rise to a legal duty to care for her. As they had committed a 'reckless' breach of that duty – by failing to get medical assistance – they were both guilty of manslaughter (Think Point (1)).

In *Pittwood* (1902), it was held that a duty may arise from contract. In that case, a railway gatekeeper failed to comply with his contractual duty to close a gate at a level crossing. As a consequence, a person crossing the tracks was killed. Wright J held that the defendant could not rely on the doctrine of privity of contract to deny the existence of a duty to users of the crossing. The obligation arose from the fact that others were dependent on the proper performance of the contract. Likewise, a duty may arise by virtue of the 'office' that a person holds (see *Curtis* (1885) and *West London Coroner ex p Gray* (1987)).

Whether other situations or relationships might give rise to a legally recognised duty to provide assistance is a question of law (*Evans* (2009)). In *Khan* (1998), the appeal against the manslaughter conviction of a supplier of heroin who had failed to summon medical assistance when his customer suffered an overdose was allowed as the trial judge had failed to direct the jury as to whether the facts were capable of giving rise to a duty to summon assistance.

PART (B)

Provided that Flop's life could have been saved if Gorge had taken reasonable steps to rescue her, then her death may be attributed to Gorge's failure to act. As explained above, a duty to act may arise from a contractual obligation (*Pittwood*).[16]

Whether he is guilty of an offence of unlawful homicide depends on his intent at the relevant time. There is no suggestion that he intended to kill or cause gbh – the necessary intent for murder – but he may be guilty of manslaughter.[17]

. . . .

15   Point out where the law is unclear.

16   It is acceptable and saves time to make reference to an earlier discussion of a relevant rule.

17   The fact that D had a duty to act is not enough to give rise to criminal liability. It must be proved that D's failure to discharge the duty was accompanied by the relevant *mens rea*/fault.

In *Adomako* (1994), the House of Lords held that in cases of manslaughter by gross negligence involving a breach of duty, the ordinary principles of the law of negligence apply. Where the death of the victim is attributable to a breach of duty to take care, it is for the jury to determine whether the breach was such a serious departure from the proper standard of care as to amount to gross negligence and, therefore, to give rise to criminal liability. Thus, in this case, the central question for the jury is whether, having regard to the risk of death from his failure to go to Flop's aid, Gorge's conduct was, in all the circumstances, so bad as to amount, in their judgment, to a criminal omission (see also *Misra and Another* (2004)).

ALTERNATIVE FACTS

Provided that Gorge's failure to act was the imputable cause of Flop's death, he is guilty of manslaughter. A person charged with an offence of basic intent, like manslaughter, cannot rely on voluntary intoxication as a defence if his act was causative of the death of the victim (*DPP v Majewski* (1977); *Lipman* (1970)).

Think Point

1   Stone was the deceased's brother, but it is not clear from the judgment whether the family relationship alone would have given rise to a duty to act. In *Sogunro* (1997), the defendant was convicted of manslaughter by gross neglect (sic) for failing to provide for his fiancée. She died of starvation after he kept her without food and drink.

Common Pitfalls

In answering part (b) of this question it is insufficient to consider whether Gorge owed a duty to Flop. A failure to act in breach of a duty owed establishes the *actus reus* for an offence of manslaughter. It is then necessary to address the fault element for manslaughter by gross negligence.

QUESTION 6

PART (A)

Julian and Dick decided to have a picnic in Farmer Giles' field. Julian decided to build a fire next to a haystack. When Dick asked him whether it would be safe, Julian explained that the wind was blowing from a direction that would keep the flames away from the haystack. Julian made the fire and began to prepare the food. After a few minutes, the wind changed direction, blowing the flames towards the haystack. Part of the haystack started to smoulder. Dick suggested that they should use the contents of their bottle of wine to douse the fire. Julian disagreed and told Dick to help him quickly pick up their belongings and move to a neighbouring field. This they did. The haystack was destroyed.

PART (B)
Anne was taking a walk by a lake. She noticed a young boy in the lake. He was having difficulty swimming and called for help. Anne swam out to him and dragged him back to the edge of the lake. His breathing had stopped. Anne did not give mouth to mouth resuscitation as she was afraid of catching a disease. She ran to a nearby public telephone and called an ambulance. When the ambulance arrived, the boy was already dead.

▶ Discuss the criminal liability of the parties.

How to Answer this Question
A relatively straightforward question in which both parts relate to the question of liability for omissions. The first part raises the issue in the context of criminal damage where D fails to take steps to counteract a dangerous situation for which he was 'responsible'. The problem can be seen as one relating to the issue of coincidence of *actus reus* and *mens rea*. The second part concerns liability for omissions in the context of unlawful homicide.

The principal issues are:

❖ the rule in *Miller* (1983); and
❖ the voluntary assumption of a duty to act for the benefit of another.

Answer Structure Part A

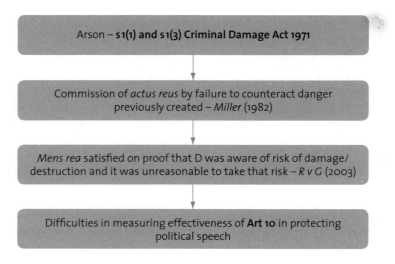

Arson – s1(1) and s1(3) Criminal Damage Act 1971

Commission of *actus reus* by failure to counteract danger previously created – *Miller* (1982)

Mens rea satisfied on proof that D was aware of risk of damage/destruction and it was unreasonable to take that risk – *R v G* (2003)

Difficulties in measuring effectiveness of **Art 10** in protecting political speech

Answer Structure Part B

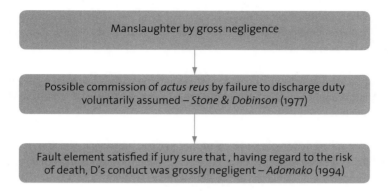

ANSWER

- -

PART (A)

Julian may be liable for the offence of criminal damage contrary to s 1(1) of the Criminal Damage Act 1971. This provides that a person who, without lawful excuse, destroys or damages any property belonging to another, intending to destroy or damage any such property or being reckless as to whether any such property would be destroyed or damaged, shall be guilty of an offence. By virtue of s 1(3), where, as in this case, the unlawful destruction or damage of property is by fire, the offence is charged as arson. By s 4, arson is punishable with a term of imprisonment for life.

It appears that Julian was not guilty of the offence when the haystack first caught fire. Although he committed the *actus reus*, he was not reckless at that stage, as he apparently believed there was no risk of damage. In *R v G and Another* (2003), the House of Lords held that a person acts recklessly within the meaning of s 1(1) of the Criminal Damage Act 1971 when he is aware of a risk of damage and it is, in the circumstances known to him, unreasonable to take the risk. Julian did not believe there was a risk of damage; he thought the construction of the fire near the haystack was safe.[18]

However, he may be guilty of arson for his later failure to take steps to extinguish the fire. In *Miller* (1983), the House of Lords held that the *actus reus* of criminal damage may continue over some considerable period of time. If D does an act which he believes initially to be harmless but later becomes aware that his act has set in train events that

. . . .

18   It is necessary to consider the problem in stages.

present a risk that property belonging to another will be damaged, then he is under a duty to try to prevent or reduce the damage by taking such steps as are reasonable and without danger or difficulty to himself. D's state of mind throughout the entire period from immediately before the property caught fire to the completion of the damage is relevant to the issue of liability.

The question of whether Julian failed to take reasonable steps is one for the jury. If they believe that he ought, say, to have used the wine to try to extinguish the fire, then he is guilty of arson.

Dick has committed no offence. He is clearly not liable as a principal offender nor can he be regarded as an accomplice to the offence perpetrated by Julian. Although he assisted Julian to remove their belongings and to get away from the scene, Dick neither assisted nor encouraged Julian to commit criminal damage.[19]

PART (B)

MANSLAUGHTER

In English law, there is generally no liability for omissions. Thus, it is often said that D incurs no criminal liability if he stands and watches a stranger drown even where he could have acted to save the stranger without risk to himself. The death of the stranger in these circumstances is not regarded in law as a consequence of D's inaction. A failure to act which, as a matter of fact, causes the death of another will give rise to liability only where the defendant was under a duty to act.

In *Stone and Dobinson* (1977), the Court of Appeal held that a duty may arise where D has voluntarily undertaken to care for another incapable of looking after him/herself and the Court agreed with the trial judge that the proper approach is to leave the question of whether there has been a voluntary assumption of a duty to the jury.

The evidence in that case showed that the deceased, Fanny, had lodged with Stone and Dobinson for three years, that the defendants had looked after her for many weeks and had been aware of her deteriorating condition for a similar period, during which they had taken ineffectual steps to help her.

In Anne's case, although the period of involvement was much shorter, it is submitted that there is sufficient evidence of an assumption of duty to warrant consideration by the jury.[20]

---

19 Secondary liability is always considered after the principal's liability.

20 The question whether a duty was voluntarily assumed is for the jury to decide in the light of all the relevant evidence and, therefore, candidates are not required to come to a conclusive answer as to whether a duty was assumed in this case.

The duty to act is, however, not an absolute duty. A conviction for manslaughter will not follow unless the prosecution proves that there was a breach of duty which was so bad as to amount to gross negligence. In *Adomako* (1994), the House of Lords held that whether or not the defendant's conduct was grossly negligent is a question to be decided by the jury, who should consider whether, having regard to the risk of death involved, the conduct of the defendant was so bad in all the circumstances as to amount in their judgment to a criminal act or omission. In *Stone and Dobinson* it was said that the appellants could have discharged their duty by summoning outside help. On this basis, the jury might conclude that Anne was not in serious breach of her duty to provide assistance.[21]

In addition, it must be proved that the boy's death was causally related to the breach of duty. If the boy would have died even had Anne discharged her duty then there can be no liability for manslaughter.

Aiming higher

For the best marks to part (a) it is important to explain that the *Miller* (1983) principle addresses the requirement that the *mens rea* coincides with the *actus reus* and provides that the failure to take reasonable steps to counteract the continuing effects of earlier innocent conduct goes to establishing the *actus reus* of a relevant offence – in this case, arson. It is also necessary to consider the *mens rea* requirements of the offence of arson. Similarly for part (b) it is not only necessary to consider whether Anne owed a duty to the boy but whether she committed a serious breach of duty which caused his death.

Common Pitfalls

In questions involving omissions candidates often fail to consider the mens rea or fault element of the offence under consideration. It is not enough to consider whether (or demonstrate that) D was under a duty to act. It is also necessary to explain that criminal liability will depend upon proof of the particular mens rea or fault required for the offence in question.

---

21 Again, the question whether a breach of duty is sufficiently serious to justify the imposition of criminal liability is one for the judgment of the jury and, therefore a conclusive answer to the problem is not required.

QUESTION 7

'All punishment in itself is evil. It ought only to be admitted in so far as it promises to exclude some greater evil'.

> Bentham, J, 'An introduction to the principles and morals and legislation', in Bentham and Mill, *The Utilitarians*, 1961

'It is only as deserved or undeserved that a sentence can be just or unjust.'

> Lewis, CS, 'The humanitarian theory of punishment'
> (1953) VI Res Judicatae 224

▶ Assess critically both of the above statements. With which of the above statements do you agree?

How to Answer this Question

Occasionally, examiners in criminal law include a question concerning the aims, objectives and justifications of punishment. The question above requires a critical assessment of the utilitarian thesis (Bentham) and the retributive thesis (Lewis). You are also asked to express a preference for one.

Answer Structure

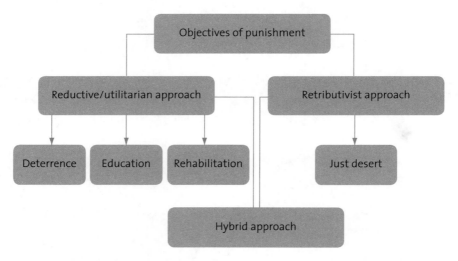

This diagram demonstrates the dual approach needed to answer this question.

ANSWER

The first quotation expresses the reductive or utilitarian view that punishment is justified to the extent that it is administered with the objective of reducing the overall level of 'evil' or 'harm' in society. The argument runs that punishment normally takes the form of penalties, for example, deprivation of liberty, financial penalties, etc., which would in themselves constitute 'evils' were they not justified by reference to the objective of an overall reduction in the balance of social 'evil'. From this standpoint, the legitimacy of punishment stems from the attempt to reduce further crime and the imposition of punishment is justified if the reduction in criminal behaviour is greater than the pain inflicted on the individual offender.[22]

Thus, it is legitimate to punish a wrongdoer in order to deter him from repeating the offence. Most sentencers probably have this objective in mind when they impose punishment on convicted criminals. In addition, the sentencer might attempt to influence the behaviour of potential wrongdoers. This is known as the general deterrence objective.

Deterrence theories are based on the idea that we are rational creatures motivated by self-interest and that we weigh up the consequences of our actions before acting. It is hoped that when faced with the choice of breaking or observing the law, the threat of punishment will persuade us to choose the latter course.

Empirical research based on reconviction rates is often pessimistic regarding the effectiveness of punishment as an individual deterrent. It is more difficult to measure the effectiveness of punishment as a general deterrent. How can one know the number of occasions when potential wrongdoers decided against breaking the law because they feared detection and punishment?

It is often argued that the deterrent effects of punishment are likely to be weaker for impulsive or opportunist crimes than for crimes that involve planning and deliberation. In addition, where detection rates are low, the potential criminal might feel that his interests are best served by breaking the law.

Reductivists contend that punishment also serves an educative purpose. It is suggested that members of any society learn to avoid behaviour that they know attracts penalties. Punishment, it is said, expresses general disapproval of the behaviour, reinforces certain standards and (as human beings are presumed to be motivated to avoid pain and to gain social approval) results in learned inhibitions against violating those standards.

It is sometimes argued that the educative effects of punishment are of even greater value than deterrent effects because obedience resulting from the absorption of values will not be adversely affected by the perception that the chances of detection are low.

There are enormous difficulties, however, in assessing empirically the educative effects of punishment. How could one reliably determine whether law-abiding behaviour was a

22 The principles and objectives of the reductive approach to punishment should be explained and evaluated.

result of having internalised a particular set of social values rather than, say, a conscious fear of detection and punishment? For many people, the consequences of conviction may be so unpleasant that even a relatively low risk of detection would discourage them from breaking the law. Indeed, the inverse relationship between the likelihood of detection, on the one hand, and willingness to break the law, on the other, implies that, for many members of the community at least, educative effects are weak.

Rehabilitation as an objective of punishment is also reductive. It is based upon the premise that criminal behaviour is maladjusted. The development of the behavioural sciences such as psychology and sociology in the nineteenth century challenged the view that criminality would respond positively to deprivation. Indeed, as the causes of human behaviour were examined, anti-social behaviour was perceived as a response to privations and adopted only where the drive to behave in a pro-social way had been inhibited for some reason or another. The individual may have chosen his criminal career because there were, or there appeared to be, no other opportunities available. The criminal may simply not realise that his interests would be better served by adopting a law-abiding course of conduct. He may require retraining so that he can satisfy his economic and social needs in socially approved ways. It may be necessary for him to learn the effect of his criminal acts on his victims.

The rehabilitative ideal stimulated reform of punishment and, in particular, reform of the prisons. Research concerning the effectiveness of rehabilitation, however, has not always been encouraging.

In addition to criticisms regarding the effectiveness of deterrent and rehabilitative sentencing, there are a number of 'principled' objections to reductive justifications.[23]

The major objection is that the reductive approach would justify the imposition of a disproportionately severe sentence in certain cases. An individual offender might receive a greater punishment than he 'deserve' because, for example, there was a perceived epidemic of the type of crime he committed. Similarly, the rehabilitative ideal might justify the imposition of a severe penalty even for a trivial infraction if that was felt necessary to 'cure' him of his criminal attitudes.

This 'retributivist' objection, expressed in the second of the quotations above, is based partly on the Kantian view that respect for individual autonomy requires that a person should never be treated solely as a means whereby certain social ends are achieved. Thus, we ought to punish a criminal because he deserves it and the punishment should be proportionate to the seriousness of the offence. Advocates of this approach point out

---

23 The limitations of the reductive approach are considered. This serves as an introduction to the retributivist approach expressed in the second of the two quotations.

that it ensures uniformity in sentencing practice and does not result in the criminal being used unfairly to achieve some further social purpose.

However, what does it mean to say that an offender 'deserves' to be punished?

Desert theory is often based upon the notion that the offender has gained an 'unfair advantage' by breaking the law. The equilibrium with other law-abiding members of society must be restored by punishment. Alternatively, it is argued that the offender has broken the 'social contract' which binds him and his fellow citizens to observing the law.

Critics of this approach ask: 'in what sense can a theory of real obligations be based upon the fiction of a social contract?' In addition, the concept of 'desert' is said to be too vague a basis for sentencing.

Professor Hart, among others, has argued that although 'just desert' should be the guiding principle when determining whether a given individual should be punished and calculating the appropriate level of punishment that an individual should suffer, it cannot provide the justification for the institution of punishment as a whole. The 'general justifying aim' of punishment is to reduce or at least contain the level of criminality in society.

According to this 'hybrid' theory, 'desert' is a necessary but not a sufficient condition of punishment in any individual case; the principle of 'just desert' operates as a limitation on the utilitarian objectives discussed above. It means, for example, that no punishment may be imposed on a person, even for laudable utilitarian purposes, unless he has voluntarily committed a clear breach of the criminal law. So, for example, although the punishment of a friend or relative of an offender might be an effective deterrent, both individually and generally, it cannot be justified as the friend and the relative have not broken the law. Punishment is not justified if punishment is not deserved.

Supporters of this perspective point out that there is no inherent incompatibility between punishment administered with the objective of reducing the level of crime in society yet limited, out of respect for individual autonomy, to those deserving it. Indeed, it is argued that individual autonomy – which includes the freedom to plan one's life according to one's own preferences – can only flourish in a legally ordered society and, thus, respect for the moral distinctness of persons informs both the general justifying aim and the principles governing the distribution of punishment.

Other theorists argue that the hybrid theory rests on vague metaphysical assertions. There is, it is argued, no need to turn to abstract notions of 'desert' to explain why victimisation is unacceptable: limiting rules on the application of punishment to those who have broken the law is a feature of reductivism. The argument runs as follows. The deterrent effect of the law depends partly at least on the legal institutions being respected. Victimisation of an innocent person would be counterproductive as it would weaken that respect. In addition, by punishing only those who are guilty, the general population are reminded of what conduct amounts to an offence and should, therefore, be avoided. Furthermore, if it were known that an innocent person might be punished instead of the guilty person, the deterrent effect of the law would be weakened.

The point has been made, however, that it is conceivable that unjust victimisation could be an effective deterrent if, for example, the general public were fooled into believing that the convicted person was guilty and, therefore, it follows that reductivist objectives cannot be a sufficient justification of punishment.

In conclusion, the dominant theory of punishment reflects both of the views expressed in the quotations above. Punishment is justified if two conditions are satisfied – it is deserved and it is aimed at reducing criminal conduct in the future.

Fatal and Non-Fatal Offences Against the Person

2

INTRODUCTION

The questions in this chapter concern offences against the person, ranging from common assault at one end of the spectrum to murder at the other. Offences of this type are graded partly in terms of the harm caused but also by reference to the *mens rea* of the accused. The harm caused will define the offences that ought to be considered. Thus, if D kills V, then liability for murder, manslaughter and/or causing death by dangerous driving, if appropriate, should be considered. Similarly, if as a result of D's actions V has suffered serious bodily harm, then liability for the offences under ss 18, 20 and 23 of the Offences Against the Person Act 1861 should be examined. In addition, offences contrary to the Sexual Offences Act 2003 are considered.

Checklist ✔

The questions in this chapter concern, principally, the following offences:

- Homicide: murder and manslaughter.
- Non-fatal offences against the person: common assault; battery; offences contrary to the **Offences Against the Person Act 1861** including wounding with intent contrary to **s 18**; malicious wounding contrary to **s 20**; assault occasioning actual bodily harm contrary to **s 47**; and offences of poisoning contrary to **sections 23** and **24** of the **1861 Act**.
- Sexual offences: offences contrary to the **Sexual Offences Act 2003**.
- In addition, the following defences are dealt with in this chapter: loss of self-control; diminished responsibility; and consent.
- It is important that you have mastered some of the issues dealt with in detail in the previous chapter, in particular the definitions of 'intention' and 'recklessness'. As 'mixed problems' are popular with some examiners, some of the questions also raise issues of liability for property offences.

QUESTION 8

Bob, a builder, has an extremely violent temper. He was driving to a building site one day and was late. He turned in to a road which was being dug up by the electricity board. He stopped at the set of traffic lights. They remained at red for more than three minutes. Full of rage, he picked up a hammer lying in the back of his van and threw it at Sabatini, a workman who was working near the lights, shouting 'fix those lights'. Sabatini ducked and the hammer missed him. It hit a passer by, Wendy, on the head, causing her a serious injury. Wendy who was 26 weeks pregnant immediately went into premature labour and gave birth. The baby was too weak to survive and died within hours. Wendy was taken to hospital and put on a life support machine. After a few days, the doctors decided, as she was brain stem dead and there was no hope of recovery, to switch off the machine. Medical evidence shows that the shock of the blow to the head had caused Wendy to go into labour prematurely.

▮ Discuss Bob's criminal liability.

How to Answer this Question

The principal issues are:

- ❖   Murder
- ❖   Manslaughter
- ❖   Transferred malice.

Answer Structure   Normal murder + Baby.

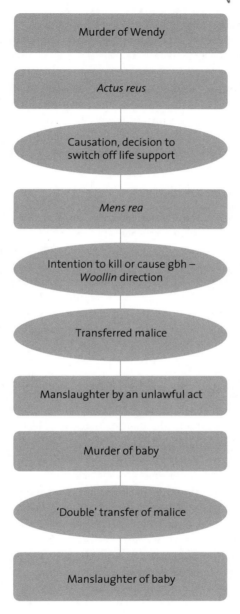

Murder of Wendy

Actus reus

Causation, decision to switch off life support

Mens rea

Intention to kill or cause gbh – *Woollin* direction

Transferred malice

Manslaughter by an unlawful act

Murder of baby

'Double' transfer of malice

Manslaughter of baby

ANSWER

MURDER OF WENDY

The *actus reus* of murder requires proof that D's actions were a factual and legal cause of V's death. That is clearly the case here. In *Malcherek; Steel* (1981) it was held that where medical treatment given by competent and careful medical practitioners includes putting a victim of an attack on a life support machine, the bona fide decision by the medical practitioners to disconnect the machine does not relieve the assailant from responsibility for the death, if, at the time of death, the original injury was a continuing or operating cause of the death.

The *mens rea* for murder requires proof that D intended to kill or cause grievous bodily harm (*Moloney* (1985)).

This is a question of fact for the jury and, except in rare cases where further elaboration may be necessary, the judge should leave it to the jury's good sense to decide whether the accused acted with necessary intent (*Moloney*). The 'rare cases' include those where the defendant's direct intent or purpose was not to kill or cause gbh but he performed an act which was manifestly dangerous and as a result someone died (*Nedrick* (1986)). In that situation the jury should be directed that they are entitled to find the necessary intention if they are sure that death or serious bodily harm was a virtual certainty and that the defendant appreciated that such was the case (*Woollin* (1998)).[1]

The fact that Bob threw the hammer at Sabatini and not at Wendy does not affect his liability. The 'doctrine' of transferred malice applies where D misses his intended victim and causes injury to another. In such cases D is liable for the injuries suffered by the actual victim to the same extent as he would have been had he hit his intended victim (*Latimer* (1886)).

Although Bob may have lost his self-control he is unable to raise the partial defence of loss of control provided by s 54 of the Coroners and Justice Act 2009. Bob did not fear serious violence within s 55(3) and there was nothing 'done or said' amounting to a qualifying trigger within section s 55(4) of the Act. Where s 55(4) is relied upon there must be some evidence that the killing was a result of an uncontrolled reaction to specific words or conduct amounting to a qualifying trigger; a loss of self-control caused by sheer bad temper or circumstances like a slow down of traffic would not be enough to raise the defence.

---

1   The facts do not disclose Bob's intent so the answer should explain the requirements of both murder and manslaughter.

MANSLAUGHTER

Baby .

If Bob lacked the *mens rea* for murder then his liability for manslaughter should be considered. Manslaughter is committed, constructively, where D commits an unlawful and dangerous act which causes the death of another (*Goodfellow* (1986); *Newbury* (1977)).

The offence of assault contrary to common law will suffice as an unlawful act for the purposes of manslaughter (*Lamb* (1967)). This offence is committed if, D intentionally or recklessly, causes V to apprehend unlawful and immediate personal violence (*Venna* (1976)) and it is clear from the facts that Bob committed an assault when he threw the hammer at Sabatini.[2]

The question whether the unlawful act was dangerous is one for the jury who should be directed to consider whether all sober and reasonably people would inevitably have recognised that it subjected another to the risk of some harm, albeit not serious harm (*Church* (1966)). It is submitted that a reasonable jury, properly directed, would conclude that the act of throwing a hammer at a person carried a risk of harm and thus that the requirement of 'dangerousness' is satisfied.

The requirement that death was caused as a result of the unlawful act and the principle of transferred malice was discussed above.

MURDER OF THE BABY

In *Attorney General's reference (No. 3 of 1994)* (1997) the House of Lords considered whether, provided an intention to kill or cause gbh is established, murder is committed where unlawful injury is deliberately inflicted on a pregnant woman, the child is subsequently born alive, enjoys an existence independent of the mother, but thereafter dies and the injuries inflicted while *in utero* were a legal cause of the death.

The Crown presented two arguments. The first was that the foetus could be regarded as part of the mother so that an intention to cause grievous bodily harm to the mother is equivalent to the same intent directed towards the foetus. The second, relied upon the doctrine of transferred malice (discussed above) – that the malice towards the mother could be transferred to the newly born baby.[3]

The House pointed out that it was well established in English law that the killing of a foetus is not murder. It is only when a child has an existence independent of its

2   In any problem always identify the specific offence which constitutes the unlawful act for the purposes of constructive manslaughter. This is an important stage in the analysis of liability.

3   A clear explanation of the reasoning underlying landmark decisions – particularly those which are controversial – will be given credit.

mother that it is regarded as a human being protected by the law against unlawful homicide.

It rejected the first of the Crown's arguments on the ground that the mother and foetus are two distinct organisms living symbiotically, not a single organism with two aspects.

The second argument was rejected on the ground that it required a double 'transfer' of intent: first from the mother to the foetus and then from the foetus to the child. Lord Mustill felt that there was no justification for extending the principle of transferred malice to a case where the defendant acted without an intent to injure either the foetus or the child which it will become.

MANSLAUGHTER OF THE BABY
Curiously the House held that D could be convicted of the manslaughter of the baby on the basis that all that it is needed for constructive manslaughter, once causation is established, is an act creating a risk of harm *to anyone*; it is unnecessary to prove that D knew that his act was likely to injure the person who died as a result of it and equally it is unnecessary to prove that D was aware the woman was pregnant.

Speaking in general terms, the House held that manslaughter can be established against someone who does any wrongful act leading to death, in circumstances where it was foreseeable that it might injure anyone at all.

Thus, it is sufficient that, at the time of throwing the hammer, Bob committted an act amounting to assault against another person, that the death of the child was caused by that act and that all sober and reasonable people would recognise the risk that some harm (to anyone) would result.

Turning to the issue of causation, the House held that the fact that the death of the child is caused solely as a consequence of injury to the mother rather than as a consequence of direct injury to the foetus does not negative liability for manslaughter. The unlawful and dangerous act of Bob 'changed the maternal environment of the foetus' with the result that after the child was born he died when he would otherwise have lived. The requirements of causation and death were satisfied, and the ingredients of 'unlawful act' manslaughter are present.

QUESTION 9
Basil managed a restaurant belonging to Sybil. One night the waiter and the chef failed to turn up. Rather than close the restaurant Basil decided to take the orders and to cook the meals. While preparing a gourmet meal, he accidentally knocked the dial controlling the temperature of the deep fat fryer. After a few minutes the fat in the fryer started to

smoke. Basil noticed the smoke coming from the fryer. He switched off the smoke alarm so that it would not disturb him or his customers. Basil then went to pour a customer a glass of wine. While doing so, smoke started to pour into the dining room. Unable to ignore the pleas of the terrified customers, Basil finished pouring the wine and went back into the kitchen. Noticing that flames from the fryer had set fire to a cupboard, he sauntered back to the dining room to get a fire extinguisher. Pretending to aim it into the kitchen, he sprayed foam over Audrey, a customer who earlier had asked for her steak 'well done'. Her face and dress were soaked. The foam caused her eyes to 'burn' and her skin to become irritated. Another customer, Clive, was crawling on the floor to escape the smoke fumes. Clive was a very poor tipper. Hoping to cause him a serious injury, Basil dropped the extinguisher on Clive's head, fracturing his skull and knocking him out. Feeling a little remorse for what he had done, Basil dragged Clive out of the restaurant so that he could receive medical help but, unfortunately, Clive's head hit the pavement a couple of times and the blows killed him.

Basil considered informing the occupants of the flat above the restaurant about the fire but decided not to as they would probably just complain. In fact the flat upstairs was empty as the occupants were no longer able to bear living near Basil.

The fire brigade arrived and put out the flames. Basil invited them into what remained of the restaurant for some Lapsang Souchong and toast.

▶ Discuss Basil's criminal liability.

How to Answer this Question

In addition to a discussion of liability for the common law offences of murder and manslaughter and offences contrary to the Offences Against the Person Act 1861 of causing grievous bodily harm with intent – s 18 – and maliciously administering a noxious thing with intent to injure, aggrieve or annnoy – s 24 – this question raises issues in respect of criminal damage, aggravated criminal damage and arson – s 1(1), s 1(2) and s 1(3) of the Criminal Damage Act 1971.

got fire : arson - criminal dmg act s1

Applying the Law

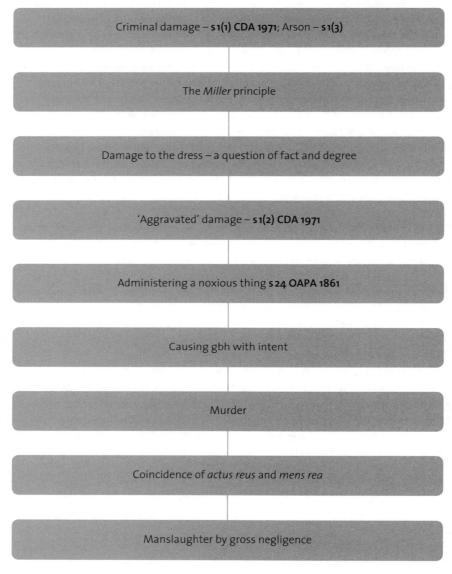

Criminal damage – **s 1(1) CDA 1971**; Arson – **s 1(3)**

The *Miller* principle

Damage to the dress – a question of fact and degree

'Aggravated' damage – **s 1(2) CDA 1971**

Administering a noxious thing **s 24 OAPA 1861**

Causing gbh with intent

Murder

Coincidence of *actus reus* and *mens rea*

Manslaughter by gross negligence

This diagram highlights the principles you need to include in your answer.

ANSWER

CRIMINAL DAMAGE

Although Basil accidentally knocked the dial on the fryer which started the fire, his failure to take reasonable steps to prevent it spreading gives rise to liability for arson – an offence committed when D, by fire, intentionally or recklessly destroys or damages property belonging to another (s1(1) and s1(3) of the **Criminal Damage Act 1971**).[4]

In *Miller* (1983) the House of Lords held that the whole period from immediately before the moment of ignition to the completion of the damage to the property by the fire is relevant to the question of guilt. Lord Diplock, who delivered the leading judgment, said that this period may be considerable, and during it the conduct of the accused that is causative of the result may consist not only of his doing physical acts which cause the fire to start or spread but also of his failing to take measures that lie within his power to counteract the danger that he has himself created. If, at the time of any particular act or omission by the accused that is causally related to the damage, the state of mind that actuates his conduct includes an intention to damage property belonging to another or being reckless as to whether such property would be damaged then he is guilty of an offence contrary to s1(3) of the Act.

And in *G and another* (2003) the House of Lords held that a person is reckless as to property being damaged if he is aware of a risk that it would be damaged and it was, in the circumstances known to him, unreasonable to take that risk.

Although it is a question of fact for the jury it seems clear that Basil did not take measures that lay within his power to extinguish the fire which he had accidentally started. Thus, as he was aware of the risk of fire spreading and damaging Sybil's property and it was unreasonable for him to take the risk that the property would be damaged or destroyed he is guilty of arson.

He may also be guilty of an offence of criminal damage in respect of Audrey's dress. Whether property is damaged is a matter of fact and degree to be determined by the jury (*Roe v Kingerlee* (1986)). In *Samuels v Stubbs* (1972) the Court held that the jury must be guided by the circumstances of each case, the nature of the article and the mode by which it was affected. In *Hardman v Chief Constable of Avon* (1986) the Court held that damage need not be permanent and in *Roe v Kingerlee* (1986) the Divisional Court held that mud spread on the walls of a police cell costing merely £7 to remove could amount to damage. However, in *A (a juvenile) v R* (1978) it was held that spitting on a policeman's coat was not criminal damage as the spittle could be easily removed by wiping it with a

---

4 Note that when applying the **Miller** principle it is important not to overlook the *mens rea* element of the offence under consideration.

cloth. If Audrey's dress is soaked and soiled to the extent that it requires the expense of cleaning then it may, in law, amount to damage within the 1971 Act and it is a question of fact for the jury whether in fact it does.

AGGRAVATED DAMAGE

The offence of aggravated criminal damage is committed where D intentionally or recklessly damages property either intending or being reckless as to the life of another being endangered (s 1(2) of the Criminal Damage Act 1971). Again, where the destruction or damage is caused by fire an offence is charged as arson – s 1(3).

It is not necessary to prove that life was actually endangered or indeed that there was even a risk of life being endangered. It is sufficient that D believes that life might be endangered by his unlawful act or omission. Thus, as Basil believed the flat to be occupied he will be guilty of this provided he believed that there was a risk that the lives of the presumed occupants would be endangered (*Sangha* (1988)).[5]

ADMINISTERING A NOXIOUS THING

It is offence contrary to s 24 of the Offences Against the Person Act 1861 to unlawfully administer to or cause to be . . . taken . . . a noxious thing, with intent to injure, aggrieve or annoy such person.

Basil may be guilty of the s 24 offence in respect of the foam sprayed onto Audrey's face and swallowed by her. In *Gillard* (1988) D had sprayed CS gas into V's face. It was held that there may be an 'adminstration' without physical contact between D and V and, although 'taking' implied ingestion 'administration' did not. Neill J, delivering the judgment of the Court of Appeal, also noted that although such conduct might in law also amount to a battery to charge it as such would not be appropriate.

A substance is a 'noxious thing' if it is 'injurious, hurtful, harmful or unwholesome' (*Marcus* (1981)). Clearly the foam, having caused irritation and burning falls within this definition.

The *mens rea* of the s 24 offence requires proof of an intention to administer the noxious thing and an intention to injury, aggrieve or annoy. This requirement is satisfied on the facts.

CAUSING GBH WITH INTENT

It is an offence contrary to s 18 of the Offences Against the Person Act 1861 unlawfully to cause any grievous bodily harm to any person with intent to do grievous bodily harm. It is

---

5   Take care when analysing 'aggravated damage'. One of the most common errors made by candidates is to assume that there is a requirement that life was in fact endangered by the destruction or damage of property.

clear that Basil is guilty of this offence in respect of the initial injuries suffered by Clive. Although it is a question of fact for the jury, a fractured skull would generally be regarded as serious harm and is categorised as such in the Charging Standard published by the Crown Prosecution Service (see also *Smith* (1961); *Saunders* (1985)) and, as the facts state, he acted with the necessary *mens rea* – an intention to do grievous bodily harm (*Re Knights Appeal* (1968); *Bryson* (1975)).

MURDER

Murder is committed where a person, intending to kill or cause gbh, unlawfully kills another human being (*Moloney* (1985)).

In the instant problem although Basil struck Clive with the extinguisher with the *mens rea* for murder, death was caused by the blows to Clive's head some moments later and that conduct was not accompanied by an intention to kill or cause gbh.[6]

The general principle in criminal law is that *actus reus* and *mens rea* must coincide in time. In *Church* (1965), however, it was held that where the unlawful application of force accompanied by *mens rea* and the eventual act causing death were parts of the same sequence of events or 'transaction' the act which caused death and the necessary mental state did not have to coincide in point of time (see also *Thabo Meli* (1954)).

In *Le Brun* (1991) Lord Lane, delivering the judgment of the Court of Appeal, added that the rule in Church applied where the appellant's subsequent actions which caused death, after the initial unlawful blow, were designed to conceal his commission of the original unlawful assault. In such cases the original unlawful blow was simply the opening event in a series which was to culminate in death: 'the first link in the chain of causation'. Where, however, the second act is intended as an act of assistance the chain of causation is broken.

Thus, in this case, Basil is not guilty of murder. His earlier *mens rea* cannot be superimposed on the subsequent act of dragging Clive out of the restaurant as that was done so that he could receive medical assistance.

He may, however, be guilty of the manslaughter of Clive, by gross negligence. When Basil took steps to remove the injured Clive from the restaurant he owed a duty of care not unreasonably to expose him to the risk of further harm. If the jury is sure that, bearing in mind the risk of death, the conduct of Basil in dragging Clive out of the restaurant amounted to a serious breach of the duty of care, justifying the imposition of criminal liability, then a conviction for manslaughter will follow (*Adomako* (1994)).

---

6   Demonstrating that there was an apparent lack of coincidence between *actus reus* and *mens rea* is a necessary step in discussing the application of **Church**, **Thabo Meli** and **Le Brun** to the facts of a problem.

QUESTION 10

What is meant by an 'unlawful act', for the purposes of constructive manslaughter?

How to Answer this Question

The principal issues are:

* ❖ the definition of an unlawful act;
* ❖ the question of whether the prosecution are required to prove that D acted with the *mens rea* for the unlawful act; and
* ❖ the meaning of 'dangerousness'.

Answer Structure

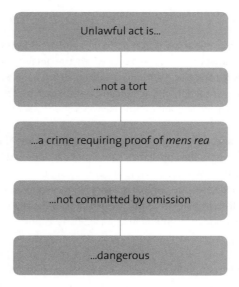

Unlawful act is...

...not a tort

...a crime requiring proof of *mens rea*

...not committed by omission

...dangerous

ANSWER

The essence of constructive crime is that liability for one offence is based upon the commission of another less serious offence. It was once the law that a person was guilty, constructively, of murder if he killed in the course of a felony, and guilty of manslaughter if he killed in the course of a misdemeanour. Although the felony murder rule was abolished by the Homicide Act 1957 and the distinction between felonies and misdemeanours was abolished by the Criminal Law Act 1967, this species of manslaughter remains. Liability for the death of the victim is constructed upon an 'unlawful act' for which the defendant would have been liable even if death had not resulted, and which is causally related to the death.[7]

It is not every unlawful act, however, that will suffice for constructive manslaughter. A tort is insufficient (*Franklin* (1883)). Furthermore, it was settled by the House of Lords in *Andrews v DPP* (1937) that an offence whose basis is negligence is not an unlawful act for the purposes of constructive manslaughter. *A fortiori*, an offence of strict liability ought not to suffice. However, in the case of *Andrews* (2003), the Court of Appeal treated the strict liability offence under s 67 of the Medicines Act 1968 of unlawfully administering a prescription-only medicine (insulin) as a sufficient unlawful act. In *Lowe* (1973), the Court of Appeal held that the commission of the offence under s 1(1) of the Children and Young Persons Act 1933 – of wilful neglect of a child – did not make the parent liable for constructive manslaughter. Lord Phillimore stated that a criminal omission would not generally give rise to liability for constructive manslaughter, although it may justify a verdict of manslaughter by gross negligence.

Most commonly, the unlawful act will be an assault or some other offence against the person (see, for example, *Larkin* (1943)), but it need not be. An offence of criminal damage may, in appropriate circumstances, suffice (*Goodfellow* (1986)) and, in *Watson* (1989), the Court of Appeal held that liability might be constructed upon a burglary contrary to s 9(1)(a) of the Theft Act 1968.

Whether or not it is necessary for the prosecution to prove that D acted with the *mens rea* for the unlawful act is, surprisingly, a moot point. In *Lamb* (1967), the defendant pointed a revolver at his friend. He neither intended to injure nor alarm his friend, nor was the friend alarmed. Lamb and his friend thought it was safe to pull the trigger. They did not realise that the gun was primed. Lamb pulled the trigger and the friend was shot dead. The trial judge took the view that the pointing of the revolver and the pulling of the trigger was something which could, in itself, be unlawful, even if there was no attempt to alarm or intent to injure. This was rejected by the Court of Appeal. The defendant lacked the *mens rea* for a criminal assault or battery and consequently had not committed an unlawful act 'in the criminal sense of the word' (per Sachs LJ). Constructive manslaughter could not be established without proving that element of intent without which there could be no assault.

Similarly, in *Jennings* (1990), the Court of Appeal held that possession of a knife in a public place was not an unlawful act unless the prosecution could prove that the defendant possessed it with intent to cause injury – that is, the intent necessary for the offence of possession of an offensive weapon contrary to s 1(1) of the Prevention of Crime Act 1953.

---

7   Focus on the question. This question does not require an analysis of all the ingredients of manslaughter – just the meaning of 'unlawful act'.

These cases support the principle that there can be no 'unlawful act' unless the defendant has committed the *actus reus* of an identified offence with the requisite *mens rea* for that offence.

However, the decision of the House of Lords in *Newbury* (1977) casts doubt on this principle. Two 15-year-old boys pushed part of a paving stone from the parapet of a railway bridge onto the path of an oncoming train. The stone went through the glass window of the driving cab and struck and killed the guard. The boys were convicted.[8] On appeal, the House of Lords upheld the conviction.

The unlawful act may have been an offence of criminal damage, but the House of Lords was not clear on this issue. Lord Salmon, with whose speech the other Law Lords concurred, stated that as manslaughter was a crime of 'basic intent', the only *mens rea* that needed to be proved was 'an intention to do the acts which constitute the crime'. Lord Edmund-Davies said that, for manslaughter, it was sufficient to prove the 'intentional' commission of the unlawful act. In the later case of *Goodfellow*, the Court of Appeal held that, for constructive manslaughter, the act must be intentional and unlawful. (See also *Attorney General's Reference (No 3 of 1994)*. Lord Hope, with whose speech the other Law Lords agreed, said that 'all that need be proved is that [the defendant] intentionally did what he did'.)

These statements are ambiguous. They could mean (and the general tenor of the speeches in *Newbury* supports this interpretation) that all that is required for constructive manslaughter is that the accused's actions are performed deliberately; that is, voluntarily. Although Lamb lacked the *mens rea* for an assault, his actions were performed deliberately, in the sense that he pulled the trigger of the gun consciously. The gun did not go off 'by accident'. He was not an automaton. This, perhaps, is the reason that Lord Salmon in *Newbury* thought that Lamb was 'lucky' to have his conviction quashed on appeal.

The other possible (but less natural) interpretation of the opinion of the House in *Newbury* is that the statement that the unlawful act must be performed intentionally was not meant to be understood as a complete account of the mental element of manslaughter and that, since an act is unlawful for the purposes of the criminal law only if performed with the appropriate *mens rea*, manslaughter is not committed constructively unless D acted with that *mens rea*.

Lord Salmon stated that there was no basis upon which counsel for the defendant could dispute that his act was unlawful. Without specifying the unlawful act, it is difficult to assess this statement.

....

8   Where a decision is unclear acknowledge that and explain the nature of the ambiguity.

Another difficult decision is that of the Court of Appeal in *Cato* (1976). D caused the death of his friend, V, having injected him with heroin. V had consented to the administration of heroin. The Court of Appeal stated that the offence under s 23 of the Offences Against the Person Act 1861 would suffice as an unlawful act. The court added, however, that even if it had not been possible to rely on the s 23 offence, there would have been the unlawful act of 'injecting the friend with heroin which the accused had unlawfully taken into his possession'. This is puzzling. There is neither a statutory nor a common law offence of 'injecting heroin'. *Cato* suggests that the unlawful act need not be an offence!

The approach of the House of Lords in *Newbury* and that of the Court of Appeal in *Cato* is harsh. The decisions imply that a person may be convicted of the serious offence of manslaughter without proof of all the elements of the unlawful act. It is submitted that the approach of the Court of Appeal in *Jennings* is preferable. The decision of the Court of Appeal in *O'Driscoll* (1977) also supports the view that there is no liability for constructive manslaughter unless all the ingredients of liability for a specified offence are satisfied.[9]

Finally, the unlawful act must be 'dangerous' and a legal cause of death. In *Church* (1966), Lord Edmund-Davies, delivering the judgment of the Court of Appeal, explained the meaning of 'dangerous'. He said that an unlawful act is dangerous if all sober and reasonable people would inevitably recognise that the unlawful act subjected the victim to the risk of some harm, albeit not serious harm (Think Point (1)). This was endorsed by the House of Lords in *Newbury* (above). In addition, the House approved the decision of the Court of Appeal in *Lipman* (1970), to the effect that the test for 'dangerousness' is framed in objective terms. For constructive manslaughter, it is quite unnecessary for the prosecution to prove that the defendant knew that his conduct carried the risk of harm. However, as the earlier discussion reveals, it would seem that the House did not appreciate that the requirement that the act be dangerous is additional to, and not a replacement for, the requirement that the unlawful act is performed with full *mens rea*.

In *Carey, Coyle, Foster* (2006), the defendants had verbally abused and physically attacked a group of young friends who were taking a walk. One of the defendants had assaulted the deceased by pulling back her head and punching her in the face. The girl died as a result of a heart attack which she suffered after running home following the attack. There was medical evidence that she might not have died had she not exerted herself to the extent that she did. The defendants were convicted of manslaughter and affray contrary to s 3 of the Public Order Act 1986 and appealed.

Allowing the appeal, the Court of Appeal held that even if the affray had caused the deceased to suffer shock leading to the heart attack, the affray lacked the quality of

---

9   It is always a good idea to give an account of the relevant and then expand upon its meaning and application.

dangerousness in the relevant sense. This is because it would not have been recognised by a sober and reasonable bystander that an apparently healthy 15-year-old (or indeed anyone else present) was at risk of suffering shock as a result of this affray. The only relevant dangerous act perpetrated on the victim was the punch. The punch, however, did not cause her death. The law requires for a conviction of constructive manslaughter that the defendant committed an unlawful act which was dangerous in the sense that sober and reasonable people would have recognised that it subjected the victim to the risk of physical harm and which was also a legal cause of the death (see also *Dhaliwal* (2006)).

> ## Think Point
>
> 1   In *Dawson* (1985) the Court of Appeal held that the 'harm' referred to in the test is limited to physical harm. Emotional disturbance is not sufficient.

QUESTION 11

Jason decided to go out for the evening and drove to a local public house. At the pub, he met Julie. As there were not many people there, Jason suggested that they go to a club in a neighbouring town. Whilst driving to the club, Jason made advances towards Julie. When Julie rejected those advances, Jason told her that he had beaten up girls who had refused him in the past. Julie jumped out of the moving car and suffered serious injuries. She was taken to hospital where she was informed that she needed a blood transfusion. As she feared contracting AIDS, she refused the transfusion and died.

▶ Discuss Jason's criminal liability.

How to Answer this Question

This problem is a standard question concerning murder and manslaughter. It raises issues of causation and is 'open' with respect to the *mens rea* of Jason. In these circumstances, as murder and manslaughter share a common *actus reus* and differ according to their *mens rea* requirements, it is sensible to consider the issues of causation before dealing with those concerning the *mens rea*.

The principal issues to be discussed include:

❖   principles of causation in cases where the victim of an assault takes evasive action and where the victim refuses medical treatment; and
❖   the *mens rea* requirements for murder and manslaughter.

Answer Structure

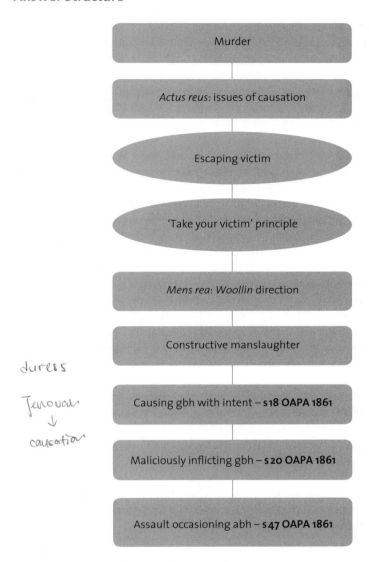

duress

Jenoval
↓
causation

Murder

Actus reus: issues of causation

Escaping victim

'Take your victim' principle

Mens rea: *Woollin* direction

Constructive manslaughter

Causing gbh with intent – **s18 OAPA 1861**

Maliciously inflicting gbh – **s20 OAPA 1861**

Assault occasioning abh – **s47 OAPA 1861**

ANSWER

MURDER AND MANSLAUGHTER

The first issue to consider in answering this question is whether Julie's death is attributable to Jason's actions – that is, whether he has caused the death of Julie.

It is necessary to deal with the issue of causation in two stages: first, to examine whether Jason's actions were the cause of Julie's injuries; and secondly, assuming that they were, to establish whether the injuries were the cause of Julie's death. If Jason's actions were the legal cause of Julie's injuries and the injuries were the legal cause of death, then, logically, we may attribute Julie's death to Jason.[10]

It is for the judge to direct the jury with reference to the relevant principles of law relating to causation, and then to leave it to the jury to decide, in the light of those principles, whether or not the necessary causal link has been established (*Pagett* (1983)).

In *Williams and Davis* (1992), the Court of Appeal held that where, as in the present case, a person leaps from a moving car to avoid some threatened attack, the jury should be directed to consider whether the evasive action was within the 'range of responses' that might reasonably be expected from a person in that situation. If the response of the deceased was disproportionate to the threat, then it should be regarded as a voluntary act, breaking the 'chain of causation'. It was said that, in applying this test, the jury should consider appropriate characteristics of the victim. Presumably, these characteristics include the age and sex of the victim. In *Corbett* (1996), the victim was a mentally handicapped man who was extremely drunk at the time he was attacked by D. He ran away and was fatally struck by a passing car. The Court of Appeal approved the trial judge's direction that the jury had to consider whether what the victim had done was something that might reasonably be expected as a reaction of somebody in that state. In addition, the jury should bear in mind that the victim might, in the agony of the moment, act without careful reflection.

In *Marjoram* (2000), the Court of Appeal rejected the appellant's submission that the question of whether the evasive action of V was reasonably foreseeable should be determined by reference to the foresight of a reasonable person of the same age and sex as the defendant. The test was objective and thus the personal characteristics of the assailant were irrelevant.

Assuming that Julie's evasive reaction was reasonably foreseeable and proportionate to the threat and, therefore, that the injuries sustained were attributable to Jason, the next issue to consider is whether the injuries were the cause of death.[11]

In *Blaue* (1975), a Jehovah's Witness, having been stabbed by D, refused a blood transfusion on religious grounds. The Court of Appeal held that the cause of death was

---

10 Break the problem down and tackle the issues logically.

11 It is not necessary for you to decide whether the response of V was reasonably foreseeable. Indeed, it is not possible for you to do so. You should restrict yourself to giving a full explanation of how the jury should be directed on the issue.

the original stab wound. Lawton LJ, extending the principle that 'one must take one's victim as one finds them' – that is, that a defendant may not point to a particular vulnerability or peculiarity of the victim as breaking the chain of causation between his act and the death of the victim – stated that if D attacks another, he may not argue that the religious beliefs of the victim, which prevented treatment, were in the circumstances unreasonable; the refusal to have treatment does not break the chain of causation.

In *Blaue*, it was the victim's religious convictions which prevented her from having a blood transfusion. It is not clear whether the principle is of wider application and, in particular, whether it covers a situation like that of the present problem, where the victim refuses treatment because of a fear of contracting a disease.

If the principle in *Blaue* does apply to the present problem, then the injuries are the cause of death and, assuming, as we have above, that those injuries are attributable to Jason, the death is also attributable to him.[12]

(If the court were to distinguish *Blaue* and to hold that the death of Julie was attributable to Jason only if the refusal of the blood transfusion was reasonably foreseeable (and the jury were to conclude that it was not reasonably foreseeable), then Jason could not be convicted of an offence of homicide. His liability would extend only to the initial injuries sustained as a result of Julie's evasive action in jumping from the car. For an analysis of his liability in those circumstances, see the discussion of 'aggravated assaults' (below).)

The next issue to consider is Jason's *mens rea*, for it is his intent at the time of the intimidatory behaviour which will determine whether he is to be convicted of murder or manslaughter.

The *mens rea* for murder is satisfied on proof that he either intended to kill or cause grievous bodily harm (*Moloney* (1985)).

If his aim or purpose was to cause death or grievous bodily harm, then he intended death or grievous bodily harm. If it was not his aim or purpose, but he was aware that either death or grievous bodily harm was virtually certain to result from intimidating Julie, then the jury may find that he intended death or grievous bodily harm (*Hancock and Shankland* (1986); *Nedrick* (1986); *Woollin* (1998); *Matthews and Alleyne* (2003)).

If, as the facts imply, he did not intend to kill or cause grievous bodily harm, his liability for manslaughter should be considered. For constructive manslaughter, the prosecution

---

12   Where the facts of a question are distinguishable from those of a previous decision explain the distinction and consider alternative outcomes.

must prove that the defendant intentionally committed an unlawful and dangerous act that resulted in death (*Goodfellow* (1986)).[13]

In this case, it would appear that when he intimidated Julie, Jason committed an unlawful act, that is, an assault. An assault is any act by which the defendant intentionally or recklessly causes the victim to apprehend immediate and unlawful personal violence (*Venna* (1976)). Although recklessness will suffice, the facts of the problem indicate that Jason intentionally assaulted Julie.

An unlawful act is 'dangerous' if all sober and reasonable people would inevitably recognise that some harm, albeit not serious harm, was likely to result from the unlawful act (*Church* (1966)). Thus, if the jury are sure that, objectively, it was likely that Julie would jump from the car and sustain an injury, then the requirement of dangerousness is satisfied. It is unnecessary to prove that the defendant was aware that his unlawful act was dangerous (see, for example, *Lipman* (1970); *Williams and Davis* (1992); *Newbury* (1977)).

The issue of causation was discussed in detail above.

As we have seen, Jason's liability is dependent upon a number of in disclosed questions of fact. Thus, it is not possible to provide a conclusive answer to this problem. The facts do, however, imply liability for manslaughter, in which case Jason would face a maximum sentence of imprisonment for life (s 5 of the Offences Against the Person Act 1861).

AGGRAVATED ASSAULTS

If the injuries sustained by Julie were attributable to Jason but her death was not (see the discussion of *Blaue*, above), then Jason's liability would be limited to one of the non-fatal offences against the person.

As the question states that Julie suffered 'serious injuries', it is proposed to consider, first, those offences involving grievous bodily harm; that is, causing grievous bodily harm with intent contrary to s 18 of the Offences Against the Person Act 1861 and maliciously inflicting grievous bodily harm contrary to s 20 of the same Act (see *Saunders* (1985)).[14]

To establish liability under s 18, the more serious offence, the prosecution would have to prove that Jason intended to cause serious harm (Think Point (1)). Recklessness will not

13   Where the facts do not expressly state or necessarily imply that D lacked the *mens rea* for an offence then explain the alternative possible outcomes. It is not for you to resolve questions of fact.

14   The offences against the person are hierarchically ordered and so, where the facts of a question do not disclose the degree or nature of injuries sustained or the intent with which D acted, first consider liability for the most serious offence. Always work down the 'ladder' of offences explaining the conditions of liability for each in turn.

suffice (*Belfon* (1976)). Intention probably bears the same meaning for this offence as it does for murder (*Bryson* (1985); *Purcell* (1986); *Woollin* (1998)).

If intention to cause grievous bodily harm cannot be proved, then liability under s 20 should be considered.

Although a number of decisions imply that 'inflicts' is a narrower concept than 'causes' (for example, *Wilson* (1984)), Lord Ackner in *Savage; Parmenter* (1991) stated that grievous bodily harm is inflicted where D frightens V into taking reasonably foreseeable evasive action and V suffers injury as a result (and see *Lewis* (1970)) (Think Point (2)).

The *mens rea* requirement for s 20 is recklessness with respect to some harm. Thus, the prosecution would be required to prove in this case that when he intimidated her, Jason was aware that Julie might suffer some harm, albeit not serious harm (*Savage; Parmenter* (1991); *Rushworth* (1992)).

The maximum punishment for the offence under s 20 is five years' imprisonment and, under s 18, life imprisonment.

If it is not possible to prove that Jason acted with the *mens rea* for either of these offences, his liability for the offence under s 47 – assault occasioning actual bodily harm – ought to be considered. For this offence, it is sufficient to prove that D assaulted V as a result of which V suffered some harm. It is not necessary to prove that D intended or was reckless as to the occasioning of harm (see *Savage; Parmenter*, above). The ingredients of assault and the relevant principles of causation are discussed above.

Think Points

1 In *Dakou* (2002), Sachs J cited with approval a passage from the judgment of Diplock LJ in *Mowatt* (1967) which appears to suggest that an intention to cause serious harm or an intention to wound will suffice for an offence under s 18. This is not correct. Only an intention to cause serious injury will suffice.

2 In *Ireland; Burstow* (1997), the House of Lords held that there is no significant difference in meaning between 'causing grievous bodily harm' in s 18 and 'inflicting grievous bodily harm' in s 20. It is unnecessary in either case to prove a direct or indirect application of force (see also *Mandair* (1995)). It is not clear whether this part of the decision in *Ireland; Burstow* is restricted to cases involving the infliction of psychiatric harm, although this seems unlikely. In any case, as explained above, serious injury was inflicted indirectly by force in the instant problem.

QUESTION 12

Arthur suffered from autism and had a very low IQ. His neighbour, Dave, liked to play practical jokes on him. One evening, shortly before Arthur was due to return home from work, Dave painted the handle to Arthur's main door and sat in his garden so that he could observe Arthur when he touched the handle. When Arthur went to open the door his hand was covered in paint. He saw Dave grinning and realised immediately what had happened. Losing his self-control, and intending to cause serious injury, Arthur picked up a spade with which he hit Dave on the head. Dave died instantly.

▶ Discuss Arthur's criminal liability.

How to Answer this Question

This question raises the defences of loss of self-control and diminished responsibility. Both are partial defences to murder reducing liability to murder so it is important to start the answer with a consideration of Arthur's liability for murder.

Answer Structure

[handwritten: IOW EQ | charge on loss control / diminishing / partial def / murder → mans.]

Murder
Actus reus
Mens rea
Manslaughter loss of control – s 54(1) CJA 2009
Diminished responsibility – s 2 HA 1957 as substituted by s 52 CJA 2009

This flowchart shows the main principles you need to discuss in your answer.

ANSWER

MURDER

A person who, intending to kill or cause grievous bodily harm, unlawfully kills another human being, is guilty of murder (*Vickers* (1957); *Moloney* (1985)). The facts disclose that Arthur killed Dave with the required intent and will be convicted of murder unless he can take advantage of either the defence of 'loss of self-control' – defined in s 54(1) of the Coroners and Justice Act 2009 or 'diminished responsibility' – s 2(1) of the Homicide Act 1957 as substituted by s 52 of the Coroners and Justice Act 2009 – both of which reduce liability to murder.[15]

LOSS OF SELF-CONTROL – s 54(1) OF THE CORONERS AND JUSTICE ACT 2009

Section 54(7) provides that, if the defence of loss of self-control is successfully pleaded, a person who would otherwise be guilty of murder will be convicted of manslaughter.

---

15   Always analyse the positive ingredients of liability before discussing any defences which may be available to D.

The defendant bears an evidential burden in respect of the defence – s 54(6). Only where, in the opinion of the judge, a jury properly directed could reasonably conclude the defence might apply should it be left for their consideration. Provided this threshold requirement is met, the probative burden is on the prosecution s 54(5) who must prove beyond reasonable doubt that D's fatal acts or omissions did not result from a loss of self-control – s 54(1)(a) and/or the loss of self-control was not a result of a 'qualifying trigger' as defined in s 55 and/or a person of D's sex and age, with a normal degree of tolerance and self-restraint and in the circumstances of D, would not have reacted in the same or in a similar way to D – s 54(1)(c).

The facts of the question indicate that Arthur suffered a loss of self-control as required by s 54(1)(a). Provided what Dave did constituted 'circumstances of an extremely grave character' and caused Arthur to have a 'justifiable sense of being seriously wronged' it would qualify as a trigger under s 55(4). Ultimately these are questions for the jury and presumably they should be approached objectively.

The question whether a person with a normal degree of tolerance and self-restraint might, in the circumstances, have reacted in a similar way to Arthur is again an objective question ultimately for the jury. Arthur's autism might be taken into account if it affected his ability to respond verbally to Dave's 'joke' as might his low IQ. But evidence that his intellectual limitations and his disability caused him to be exceptionally volatile would not be admissible in support of a plea of loss of control as s 54(3) excludes from consideration circumstances 'which bear upon D's general level of tolerance and self-restraint'.[16]

DIMINISHED RESPONSIBILITY – s 2(1) OF THE HOMICIDE ACT 1957 AS SUBSTITUTED BY s 52 OF THE CORONERS AND JUSTICE ACT 2009

For a successful plea, Arthur must prove on the balance of probabilities (s 2(2); *Dunbar* [1958]) that, at the time of the fatal act, he was suffering from an abnormality of mental functioning which arose from a recognised medical condition, which substantially impaired his ability to (a) to understand the nature of his conduct or (b) to form a rational judgment or (c) to exercise self-control – subsection (1A) and provides an explanation for his acts and omissions in doing or being a party to the killing.

The facts disclose that Arthur suffered from autism and a low IQ. Both these conditions might amount to conditions which substantially impaired his ability. There are various forms of autism recognised as mental disorders by the *World Health Organisation ICD-10* and, depending on the overall level of Arthur's intellectual ability, his low intelligence

---

16 As the jury is required to evaluate what was said or done by Dave and to evaluate whether an ordinary person might have behaved in a similar way to Arthur means that it is not possible to come to a conclusive answer as to the availability of the defence of loss of control.

may amount to mental retardation which is also recognised as a mental condition by the *World Health Organisation*. It is for the jury to decide on the basis of the medical evidence and other relevant circumstances whether the autism and/or degree of retardation suffered by Arthur amounted to an abnormality of mental functioning (*Dix* (1981); *Byrne* (1960); *Walker* (2009)).

The facts indicate that Arthur lacked self-control at the time of the killing but it must be proved that his ability to exercise self-control was impaired *by* his mental abnormality. This again is a question for the jury to decide on the basis of the medical evidence and other relevant circumstances.

The requirement that the impairment was 'substantial' involves consideration of the degree of impairment and it is for the jury and not for the medical experts to decide. Under the old law the jury was required to decide the issue in a 'broad commonsense way' (*Byrne* (1960); *Hill* (2008); *Khan (Dawood)* (2010)) and it was held that the impairment must be more than 'trivial' or 'minimal' but need not be 'total' (*Lloyd* (1967); *R v R* (2010)). A similar approach is likely to be followed in respect of the new legislation. Although a medical expert might give evidence on the nature of Arthur's disorder and its likely effects on his ability to exercise self-control it will be for the jury to decide whether there was a 'substantial impairment'

Finally it must be proved that abnormality of mental functioning provides an explanation for Arthur's act of killing Dave. This entails showing that there was a 'significant' causal connection between the abnormality and the killing – s 2(1B). The abnormality need not, however, be the sole cause.

If Arthur's plea of diminished responsibility is successful his liability will be reduced from murder to manslaughter – s 2(3) of the Homicide Act 1957 (Think Point (1)).[17]

Think Point

1   In *Ali; Jordan* (2001), the Court of Appeal held that the requirement that the defendant bears the burden of proof in respect of diminished responsibility does not contravene Art 6 of the European Convention for the Protection of Human Rights and Fundamental Freedoms.

---

17   As a number of the relevant facts about Arthur's condition are not disclosed by the facts and as the question whether than impairment is 'substantial' is an evaluative one for the jury it is not possible to come to a conclusive answer as to the availability of the defence of diminished responsibility. Note the way in which the answer is expressed.

QUESTION 13

(a) Gemma, a prostitute, agreed to have anal intercourse with Punch for a fee of £50. Punch had no intention of paying and, after intercourse had taken place, left without paying.

(b) Ben was at the Longitude Rock festival. He did not have a tent. Late at night he started to feel cold and so he silently sneaked into one of the tents set up in the festival grounds. When he entered the tent he saw Laura asleep. He lay down next to her and started to stroke her breasts. Laura woke up and screamed. Ben apologised and left.

How to Answer this Question

This question raises issues of liability in respect of a number of offences contrary to the Sexual Offences Act 2003.

Answer Structure

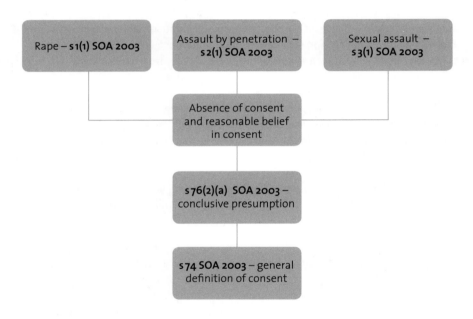

ANSWER

(A) SEXUAL OFFENCES

This question raises issues of liability in respect of a number of overlapping offences contrary to the Sexual Offences Act 2003.

Section 1(1) of the Sexual Offences Act 2003 provides that a person (A) is guilty of rape if (a) he intentionally penetrates the vagina, anus or mouth of another person (B) with his penis, (b) B does not consent to the penetration, and (c) A does not reasonably believe that B consents.

Second, assault by penetration contrary to s 2(1) of the Act requires proof that A intentionally penetrated the vagina or anus of another person (B) with a part of his body or anything else, B did not consent to the penetration, A did not reasonably believe that B consented and the penetration was sexual.

Third, sexual assault contrary to s 3(1) is committed where A intentionally touches another person (B), B does not consent to the touching and A does not reasonably believe that B consents and the touching is sexual.

For the purpose of the offences contrary to s 2(1) and s 3(1), s 78 (a) provides that a penetration or touching is sexual if a reasonable person would consider that, *because of its nature*, it is sexual. Clearly, the act performed by Punch was sexual.[18]

Liability for each of the offences centres on the question of whether Gemma consented to the sexual intercourse and whether Punch reasonably believed that she consented. Did the deception as to payment practised by Punch vitiate Gemma's apparent consent to the act of sexual intercourse?

Section 76 of the Act provides circumstances in which consent is conclusively presumed to be invalid and that the defendant had no reasonable belief in consent. These include where the defendant deceives the complainant as to the nature or purpose of the penetration – s 76(2)(a). Might it be argued that Gemma has been deceived as to one of the purposes of the sexual act – to be paid?[19]

In *Jheeta* (2007) the Court of Appeal gave a narrow interpretation to 'purpose' stating that s 76(2)(a) applies only in those 'comparatively rare cases' where the defendant deliberately deceives the complainant about the nature or purpose of the sexual act itself. Simon J, delivering the judgment of the court, commented that *Linekar* (1995), a case decided under the Sexual Offences Act 1956 and whose facts were similar to those of the instant problem, would not fall within the ambit of s 76. The prostitute was deceived about the defendant's intentions, but not about either the nature or the purpose of the act. The conclusive presumption does not apply in such situations.

Where the statutory presumptions do not apply, the issue of consent falls to be decided under the general definition in s 74 which provides that, for the purposes of the Act, 'a person consents if he agrees by choice and has the freedom and capacity to make that

18 In a question where liability for a number of sexual offences rests on the question of consent which is common to them all it is efficient to deal with the ingredients of each offence before tackling the issue of consent.

19 When dealing with consent start by considering **s 76** because if the conditions apply, consent and absence of reasonable belief in consent are conclusively presumed.

choice'. It would appear from the facts that Gemma had the capacity to make the choice. The issue is whether she freely chose to have sexual intercourse. It is submitted that she did. Fraud in respect of a promise to pay for sexual intercourse would not have vitiated the consent under the common law and the 2003 Act does not appear to change that. In *R v B* (2006) EWCA 2945 it was held that where one party to sexual activity has a sexually transmissible disease which is not disclosed to the other party any consent that may have been given to that activity by the other party is not thereby vitiated. This implies that the fact that the complainant would not have consented had she known the truth does not, of itself, vitiate consent.

FRAUD ETC
Punch may, however, be guilty of an offence of fraud contrary to s1 of the Fraud Act 2006 by false representation in breach of s2.[20]

He made a false representation that he would pay, intending to make a gain for himself by keeping the money that he promised to pay Gemma. The offence requires proof of dishonesty. If Punch raises evidence that he was not dishonest then the issue is one for the jury who should be directed that a person is not dishonest if what he did was, in the jury's opinion, not dishonest according to the ordinary standards of reasonable people or he mistakenly believed that it was not dishonest according to those standards (*Feely* (1973); *Ghosh* (1982)).

He may also be guilty of an offence of obtaining services dishonestly contrary to s11 of the Fraud Act 2006. This offence is committed where D, dishonestly obtains, for himself or another, a service knowing that payment is required and intending to avoid payment. Services are not defined but there is nothing in the Act to suggest that they do not extend to sexual services provided by a prostitute. There is no requirement that the services are lawful or that payment is legally enforceable.

Punch is, however, not guilty of an offence contrary to s3(1) of the Theft Act 1978. Although he made off without having paid as expected, s3(3) provides that an offence is not committed under the section if the payment avoided relates to the doing of a service which is contrary to law or where payment is not legally enforceable.

(B) SEXUAL ASSAULT
Ben is guilty of sexual assault contrary to s3(1) of the Sexual Offences Act 2003. He intentionally touched Laura and the touching was sexual. Section 75(1) sets out a number of circumstances in which both consent and a reasonable belief in consent are presumed to be lacking. These include where the complainant was asleep or otherwise unconscious at the time of the relevant Act – s75(2)(d). Although the presumption is rebutted if sufficient

---

20 Note that fraud is an offence contrary to **s1** of the **Fraud Act** 'in breach of' **s2** or **s3** or **s4**.

evidence is adduced that the complainant did in fact consent or that D had a reasonable belief that the complainant consented there is nothing in the facts of this problem to suggest that such evidence might exist.

TRESPASS WITH INTENT TO COMMIT A SEXUAL OFFENCE

Section 63 of the Sexual Offences Act 2003 provides that D commits an offence if

(a)   he is a trespasser on any premises;
(b)   he intends to commit a relevant sexual offence on the premises;
(c)   and he knows that or is reckless as to whether he is a trespasser.

Ben is guilty of the offence contrary to s 63. Premises are defined in s 63(1) to include a tent. Clearly Ben knew that he was on the premises without consent or authority and thus was a trespasser, and s 62(2) provides that sexual assault is a 'relevant sexual offence'.

QUESTION 14

PART (A)

Molar visited his dentist, Spitoon, for a dental examination. Spitoon discovered that one of Molar's teeth needed filling. Molar, who did not realise that Spitoon had been suspended from practice by the General Dental Council (GDC), agreed to the surgery and it was performed there and then. Later that afternoon, Kite, a newcomer to the area, visited the surgery needing an emergency extraction. John, the receptionist, had always wanted to be a dentist. He had watched Spitoon at work, had read the best dentistry books and was confident of his ability. So he pretended to be Spitoon and performed the treatment. (Spitoon was drunk and asleep in one of the treatment rooms.) In both cases, the treatment was perfect.

▶ Discuss the criminal liability of Spitoon and John for offences contrary to the Offences Against the Person Act 1861.

PART (B)

Mark and Jodie were engaged to be married when Jodie decided she no longer wished to see Mark. He was extremely angry and, over the course of the next few months, he made a number of telephone calls to her during which he did not speak. As a result of these calls, Jodie suffered a psychological breakdown.

▶ Discuss Mark's criminal liability.

How to Answer this Question

Both parts of this question raise issues concerning a number of the non-fatal offences against the person. In addition, the first part involves the defence of consent. The second part deals with liability where psychiatric harm, without physical harm, results from the defendant's unlawful conduct. Note that it is not possible to provide a definitive answer to the second part, as a number of relevant facts are not disclosed.

The principal authorities are: *Ireland; Burstow* (1997); *Clarence* (1888); *Richardson* (1998); *Tabassum* (2000); *Chan Fook* (1994); *Savage; Parmenter* (1991).

Applying the Law

(a)

(b)

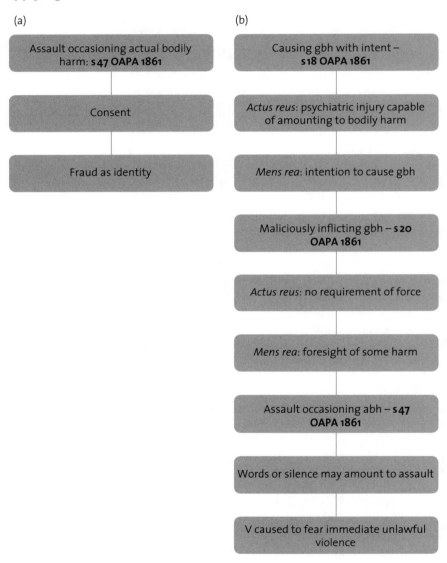

This mind map illustrates the main legislation and practical factors to consider in your answer.

ANSWER

PART (A)

It is proposed to consider liability of both parties for the offence of assault occasioning actual bodily harm under s 47 of the Offences Against the Person Act 1861. The basic ingredients of liability for this offence are that the defendant intentionally or recklessly performed an assault or a battery which resulted in some injury (*Ireland; Burstow* (1997)).

There are a number of circumstances where consent may render lawful, the infliction of bodily harm. One of those is where the victim gives his consent to surgery (*Attorney General's Reference (No 6 of 1980)* (1981)).

The issue, in the cases of Spitoon and John concerns the effect of fraud on the validity of consent.[21]

In *Clarence* (1888), it was held that fraud does not necessarily negative consent. Only where the fraud goes to the nature of the act performed or the identity of the person performing it is any apparent consent vitiated. This principle was considered in *Richardson* (1998). The Court of Appeal had to decide whether the consent given to the defendant, a dentist, to perform treatment had been nullified by the defendant's implied and false representation that he was qualified. The dentist had been suspended from practice by the GDC. The Court of Appeal held that the consent had not been negatived. The complainants were fully aware of the appellant's identity. They knew who he was. The Crown's submission that the identity of the person should be extended to cover the qualifications or attributes of the dentist on the basis that the patients consented to treatment by a qualified dentist and not a suspended one was rejected.

In *Tabassum* (2000), the appellant, having led three women to believe that he was medically qualified and was carrying out research into breast cancer, examined the women's breasts. Each of the women said that they had only consented because they thought the appellant had either medical qualifications or relevant training.

At his trial on charges of indecent assault, he submitted that the case should be stayed on the basis that the prosecution could not prove the absence of consent and therefore no assaults had taken place. The judge ruled against that submission; the nature and quality of the act performed was different from that consented to. His appeal against conviction was dismissed. As the appellant had no medical qualifications, he could not

---

21   The liability of both parties in this problem raises issues in respect of consent and so the general effect of consent is considered before applying to each individual case.

have been touching the complainants' breasts for a proper medical purpose. The complainants had consented to a medical act and not a sexual act and thus although there was consent as to the nature of the act, there was no consent as to its quality.

The Court of Appeal distinguished *Richardson* as that case proceeded solely by reference to the issue of identity. The Crown had not argued that the act performed by Richardson differed in nature and quality from the act consented to. It is submitted that it is unlikely that such an argument would have been successful. The appellant had consented to dental treatment and that is what Richardson performed. There was consent as to the nature and quality of the act. Thus, Spitoon is not guilty of an offence contrary to s 47 (Think Point (1)).

John, on the other hand, did practise a fraud as to his identity. He represented, by his conduct, that he was the dentist in practice and, as a result of this fraud, Kite was induced to give consent to the treatment. John is guilty of an offence contrary to s 47.

PART (B)

In *Ireland; Burstow*, the House of Lords, approving the decision of the Court of Appeal in *Chan Fook* (1994), decided that a recognised psychiatric illness, whether of a neurotic, psychoneurotic or psychotic nature, may amount to bodily harm. Simple states of fear or 'problems in coping with everyday life' are not, however, included. Nor are psychological injuries not amounting to an identifiable clinical condition (*Dhaliwal* (2006)).

Whether or not psychiatric illness amounts to 'actual' or 'grievous' bodily harm depends, of course, upon the seriousness of the illness in question and is ultimately a question for the jury.

As the extent of Jodie's psychological breakdown is not disclosed, it is proposed to consider liability for a number of offences, including 'unlawfully causing grievous bodily harm with intent', 'maliciously inflicting grievous bodily harm', and 'assault occasioning actual bodily harm' contrary to ss 18, 20 and 47 of the Offences Against the Person Act 1861, respectively.[22]

LIABILITY UNDER s 18

Provided the psychiatric injury sustained was serious, the only practical difficulty in prosecuting under this section will be proving that the defendant intended to cause grievous bodily harm. Nothing less will suffice (*Belfon* (1976)).

It is generally assumed by commentators that the approach to intention adopted by the House of Lords in *Woollin* (1998), in respect of murder, applies also to this offence. And

---

22 In problems such as this, where the extent of injuries are not disclosed, explain the conditions of liability for each of the relevant offences.

thus, if Mark's aim or purpose was to cause grievous bodily harm, he intended grievous bodily harm. If it was not Mark's aim or purpose, but he was aware that grievous bodily harm was virtually certain to result from his repeated calls, then the jury are entitled, but not obliged, to find that he intended Jodie grievous bodily harm (*Hancock and Shankland* (1986); *Nedrick* (1986); *Woollin* (1998); *Matthews v Alleyne* (2003)). The maximum penalty for an offence contrary to s 18 is life imprisonment.

If the jury is not sure that Mark intended to cause grievous bodily harm, then his liability for an offence contrary to s 20 of the 1861 Act should be considered.[23]

LIABILITY UNDER s 20

Counsel for Burstow argued that the House of Lords in *Wilson* (1984) decided that a direct or indirect application of force was necessary for the s 20 offence. Lord Steyn agreed that there were passages which supported the appellants' argument, but he believed overall that the judgments on this point were 'neutral'. In addition, Lords Steyn and Hope considered the 'troublesome authority' of *Clarence*. This decision appeared to hold that a battery – a direct application of violence – was a necessary element of the s 20 offence. Both of their Lordships considered the decision to be of little weight as it was decided before the concept of psychiatric injury had been recognised. The decision was dated. As a matter of current usage, 'inflict' could embrace the idea of one person causing psychiatric injury to another without any need for an assault or other application of force (see also *Mandair* (1995)).

As far as the *mens rea* for this offence is concerned, it is sufficient to prove that the defendant intended or foresaw the risk of some harm, not necessarily serious harm (*Mowatt* (1967), referred to with approval in *Savage; Parmenter*).

The maximum penalty for maliciously inflicting grievous bodily harm is a term of imprisonment not exceeding five years.

If the psychiatric injury suffered by Jodie is not serious or the jury is not sure that he acted with the intent required for s 20, Mark's liability for an offence of assault occasioning actual bodily harm contrary to s 47 should be considered.[24]

LIABILITY UNDER s 47

An assault is committed where D intentionally or recklessly causes V to apprehend an imminent application of violence (*Savage; Parmenter* (1991)). Might there be an apprehension of immediate and unlawful violence in a case such as the present, where there was a lack of physical proximity between the defendant and the victim and when the act complained of consisted of telephone calls?

23 Note how the transition is made from analysis of liability under **s 18** to liability under **s 20**.
24 Note here how the transition is made from analysis of liability under **s 20** to liability under **s 47**.

The House of Lords in *Ireland*, overruling *Meade and Belt* (1823), decided that an assault can be committed by words alone or indeed silence, and that silent telephone calls may amount to an assault. However, there is no assault unless the victim is caused to fear *immediate* personal violence or the possibility thereof and it was acknowledged in *Ireland* that this might prove problematic in cases such as the present one (see also *Constanza* (1997), decided before *Ireland*) (Think Point (2)).

As far as the *mens rea* of the offence under s 47 is concerned, the prosecution must prove that the accused either intended the victim to apprehend violence or foresaw the risk that the victim might apprehend violence (*Savage; Parmenter*). The maximum penalty for this offence is five years' imprisonment (Think Point (3)).

Think Points

1   It is an offence contrary to s 38 of the Dentists Act 1984 to practise or hold oneself out to practise dentistry when not qualified. The maximum penalty on summary conviction is a fine not exceeding level 5 on the standard scale.

2   The House acknowledged that immediacy of the violence was not an issue in Ireland, as he had pleaded guilty to assault, but Lord Steyn accepted that:

> 'the concept of an assault involving immediate personal violence as an ingredient of the s 47 offence is a considerable complicating factor in bringing prosecutions in respect of silent telephone callers and stalkers. That the least serious of the ladder of offences is difficult to apply in such cases is unfortunate.'

See also *Cox* (1998).

3   Other offences. Section 43(1) of the Telecommunications Act 1984 makes it an offence persistently to make use of a public telecommunications system for the purpose of causing annoyance, inconvenience or needless anxiety to another. The maximum penalty is six months' imprisonment.

Sections 1 and 2 of the Protection from Harassment Act 1997 make it an offence to pursue a course of conduct which amounts to harassment of another and which the accused knows or ought to know amounts to harassment. In *Kelly v DPP* (2002), the Divisional Court held that three threatening and abusive calls in five minutes constituted a 'course of conduct'.

A person guilty of this offence is liable, on summary conviction, to a term of imprisonment not exceeding six months or a fine not exceeding level 5 on the standard scale (s 2(2)).

Section 4(1) of the same statute creates a more serious offence, where a person, D, whose course of conduct causes another to fear, on at least two occasions, that violence will be used against him and where D knows or ought to know that his course of conduct will cause the other so to fear on each of the occasions. The maximum penalty for this offence is a term of imprisonment not exceeding five years (s 4(4)) – a penalty which Lord Steyn in *Ireland* thought was inadequate to deal with the persistent offender who causes serious injury to his victim.

Aim Higher

In questions raising liability for non-fatal offences against the person examiners often do not disclose the extent of injuries sustained by the victim. Similarly the intent with which the defendant acted may not be disclosed. This is done deliberately. You should explain the alternative outcomes by reference to the requirements of each of the possible offences. Consider the most serious offence consistent with the disclosed facts and work your way down the ladder of offences to the least serious, explaining the requirements of each.

Common Pitfalls ✗

Poor explanation of the requirements of each of the relevant offences is the most common failing in answers to questions of this type. Explain the requirements precisely.

QUESTION 15

(i) Julian met Annie for the first time at a concert. They found each other attractive and so agreed to meet the following evening. Julian changed his mind and asked his twin brother Sandy to meet Annie. Sandy met Annie. She assumed he was Julian. They had sexual intercourse that evening and agreed to meet the following evening. On this occasion Julian met Annie and they had sexual intercourse.

▶ Discuss the criminal liability of the parties.

(ii) At a party, Abigail was drinking a lot of alcohol and, during the course of the evening, she eventually became too drunk to stand unaided and fell over. Laurence who had met her for the first time at the party helped her upstairs to bed. After several minutes, as she did not protest, he had sexual intercourse with her. Abigail claims that she did not consent to sexual intercourse.

▶ Discuss Laurence's criminal liability.

How to Answer this Question

This question raises issues of liability in respect of a number of offences contrary to the Sexual Offences Act 2003.

Answer Structure

(a)

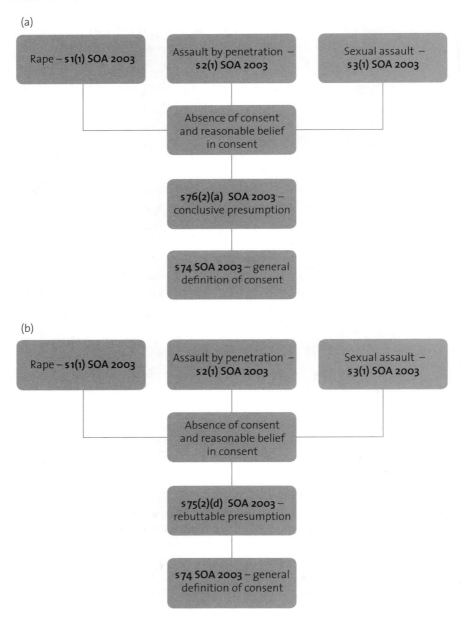

(b)

ANSWER

(I) NON-CONSENSUAL SEXUAL OFFENCES

It is proposed to consider the liability of Julian and Sandy for offences of rape, assault by penetration and sexual assault.

Section 1(1) of the Sexual Offences Act 2003 provides that a person (A) is guilty of rape if (a) he intentionally penetrates the vagina, anus or mouth of another person (B) with his penis, (b) B does not consent to the penetration, and (c) A does not reasonably believe that B consents.

Assault by penetration contrary to s 2(1) of the Act requires proof that A intentionally penetrated the vagina or anus of another person (B) with a part of his body or anything else, B did not consent to the penetration, A did not reasonably believe that B consented and the penetration was sexual.

And sexual assault contrary to s 3(1) is committed where A intentionally touches another person (B), B does not consent to the touching and A does not reasonably believe that B consents and the touching is sexual.

For the purpose of the offences contrary to s 2(1) and s 3(1), s 78 (a) provides that a penetration or touching is sexual if a reasonable person would consider that, *because of its nature*, it is sexual. Clearly, the acts performed by Sandy and Julian were sexual.

SANDY

Section 76(2)(b) provides that it is to be conclusively presumed that the complainant did not consent to the relevant act and that the defendant did not believe that the complainant consented to the relevant act if the defendant intentionally induced the complainant to consent to the relevant act by impersonating a person known personally to the complainant.

It is, however, unclear whether this provision applies to the facts of the instant problem. Is Julian 'known personally' to Annie? It is arguable that the presumption only applies where the parties are relatively well acquainted.[25]

In addition, there must be a causal link between the impersonation and the obtaining of consent. Only if it can be said that Annie would not have had sexual intercourse with Sandy had she known the truth might the presumption in s 76(2)(b) apply.

---

25 Where the law is unclear suggest at least one possible approach. Note the use of the expression 'it is arguable'.

If s 76(2)(b) does not apply the question of consent is answered by reference to the general definition in s 74 which provides that, for the purposes of the Act, 'a person consents if he agrees by choice and has the freedom and capacity to make that choice'.

It would appear from the facts that Annie had the capacity to make the choice. The issue is whether she freely chose to have sexual intercourse and engage in other sexual acts. It is submitted that she did. Fraud or a mistaken belief in the identity of D would not have vitiated the consent under the common law and, except where the conditions in s 76(2)(b) apply, the 2003 Act does not appear to change that.

JULIAN

Although it is arguable that, as a result of their intimate relations, Sandy was now someone who was known personally to Annie, Julian did not impersonate him and thus the presumption in s 76(2) does not apply. Again, the issue of consent is decided by reference to s 74 and, as before, it is submitted that Annie consented to the act of sexual intercourse (and other sexual acts) with Julian.

(II) NON-CONSENSUAL SEXUAL OFFENCES

Laurence may be guilty of offences contrary to s 1(1), s 2(1) and s 3(1) of the 2003 Act. Clearly he has committed the conduct element of each of the offences.

The issues are, firstly, whether Abigail, despite her intoxicated state, consented to the act of sexual intercourse and secondly whether Laurence lacked a reasonable belief that she consented.

The presumptions as to consent and lack of a reasonable belief in consent in s 76 have no application to the facts of the question, but the rebuttable presumption in s 75(2)(d) might. This provides that, if the prosecution can prove, firstly, that Abigail was unconscious at the time Laurence had sexual intercourse with her and that, secondly he knew that she was unconscious, then it will be presumed both that consent and a reasonable belief in consent were lacking.[26]

If the presumption is raised it is for the accused to raise evidence that the complainant did nonetheless consent or that the accused had a reasonable belief that, despite being aware that she was unconscious, she consented. Where sufficient evidence is raised by the defendant the prosecution are required to prove beyond reasonable doubt that the complainant did not in fact consent and that the defendant did not believe, on reasonable grounds, that the complainant consented. The presumption may be displaced, for example, where A wakes his sexual partner with a sexual touch.

---

26 The facts of the problem are sketchy and so it is not possible to answer the question conclusively. Consider the various possibilities and explain their outcomes.

The facts of the problem do not disclose any evidence upon which Laurence could advance an argument that he reasonably believed that Abigail would have consented to him having sexual intercourse while she was unconscious. Laurence and Abigail had only just met. Nor could he argue that he reasonably believed that Abigail would have consented to him having sexual intercourse with her while she was conscious and thus it was reasonable for him to believe she would have consented while unconscious (*Cicarelli* (2011)).

If it cannot be proved that Abigail was unconscious at the time of the relevant act the presumption in s 75(2)(d) does not apply and the issue of consent is decided by reference to s 74 which provides that, for the purposes of the Act, 'a person consents if he agrees by choice and has the freedom and capacity to make that choice'.

Neither 'freedom' nor 'capacity' are defined in the Act and are complex issues that present difficulties of application in cases such as the present.

In *Bree* (2007) prior to having sexual intercourse, the parties had been drinking alcohol. The complainant contended that she had drunk so much her ability to resist had been hampered by its effects.

The defendant's case was that the complainant had been consenting and was conscious throughout; and that he had reasonably believed that she was consenting. He was convicted of rape and appealed against his conviction.

The Court of Appeal held that the question whether there was a lack of consent and lack of a reasonable belief in consent in cases where the complainant had consumed a quantity of alcohol depended on the specific facts of each case. It could not be answered by reference to a prescribed level of alcohol consumption; the effects of alcohol vary from one individual to the next.

However, although application to particular facts may prove difficult, the basic principles in such cases are straightforward. Firstly, if, as a result of drink the complainant had temporarily lost her capacity to choose whether to have intercourse on the relevant occasion, she did not consent. And the jury should be reminded that capacity may be lost before a state of unconsciousness is experienced.

Thus, if the alcohol prevented Abigail from knowing what was happening she lacked capacity and did not consent. The fact that she did not protest or communicate her lack of consent is not fatal to a conviction.

However, if Abigail had voluntarily consumed even substantial quantities of alcohol, but nevertheless remained capable of choosing whether or not to have intercourse and, despite being drunk, had indeed consented to do so, it would not amount to rape. The fact that she would not have engaged in sexual intercourse had she been sober would not negative consent nor would the fact that she regretted having had sexual intercourse.

If Abigail did not consent, Laurence's criminal liability depends on whether or not he mistakenly believed, on reasonable grounds, that she was consenting. This involves a subjective question: 'did D believe that the complainant was consenting?' and, if so, an objective question: 'was the belief, in the circumstances, reasonable?'

The facts of the question do not disclose Laurence's intent at the time. If he mistakenly believed Abigail was consenting then the question of whether it was a reasonable belief should be determined 'having regard to all the circumstances including any steps taken [by Laurence] to ascertain whether [Abigail] consented' (s1(2) SOA 2003).

The Home Affairs Committee, in its report on the Sexual Offences Bill (Fifth Report, Session 2002–03, HC 6390) expressed the view that the test allowed the jury to take into account characteristics of the defendant and, Beverley Hughes, the Minister for Citizenship and Immigration stated that it would be for the judge or jury to take into account any characteristics or circumstances that they wished to (House of Commons Standing Committee 9th September 2003). However, intoxication of the defendant may not be taken into account when assessing the reasonableness of a mistake as to consent (*Heard* (2007)).

QUESTION 16

(a)   Acid, who was aware that he was HIV positive, had unprotected consensual sexual intercourse with his girlfriend Alkali. As a result, Alkali contracted the virus. Discuss Acid's liability.
(b)   Lisa asked Gerald to prepare a syringe of heroin and to inject her with it. Gerald did so. Lisa died instantly. Discuss Gerald's criminal liability.

Would your answer differ if Gerald had, as instructed by her, prepared the syringe of heroin for Lisa who then injected herself with it?

How to Answer this Question

PART (A)
This part of the question raises issues concerning liability for the offences of 'maliciously inflicting grievous bodily harm' and 'causing grievous bodily harm with intent' contrary to ss20 and 18 of the Offences Against the Person Act 1861, respectively, where D communicates a sexual disease to V and considers the question whether V's consent to the risk of contracting the infection negatives liability. The principal authority is *Dica* (2004).

Liability for the offence of rape contrary to s1 of the Sexual Offences Act 2003 and the statutory definition of consent applying to that offence are also considered.

PART (B)

This part concerns liability for manslaughter and the offence contrary to s 23 of the Offences Against the Person Act 1861 where D, with V's consent, injects V with heroin and V dies and, secondly, where D prepares a syringe with heroin and V dies following self-injection. The principal authorities are *Dalby* (1982); *Dias* (2001); *Finlay* (2003) and *Kennedy No. 2* (2005).

Answer Structure

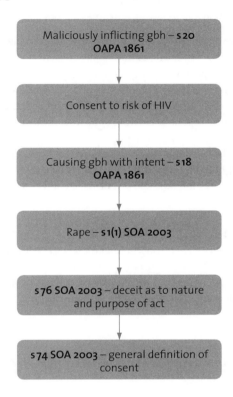

Maliciously inflicting gbh – **s 20 OAPA 1861**

Consent to risk of HIV

Causing gbh with intent – **s 18 OAPA 1861**

Rape – **s 1(1) SOA 2003**

s 76 SOA 2003 – deceit as to nature and purpose of act

s 74 SOA 2003 – general definition of consent

ANSWER

PART (A)

MALICIOUSLY INFLICTING GRIEVOUS BODILY HARM

Section 20 of the Offences Against the Person Act 1861 provides that it is an offence 'unlawfully and maliciously to wound or inflict any grievous bodily harm upon any person'.[27]

27 Exceptionally, possible liability for an offence contrary to **s 20** is considered before liability under **s 18**. This is because, in this type of case, analysis of liability under **s 20** raises more complex issues.

Grievous bodily harm can be inflicted on a person by infecting them with a serious disease such as the human immunodeficiency virus (HIV), and there is no requirement that the infection immediately follows the act which communicated it (*Chan Fook* (1994); *Dica* (2004)). In addition, there is no need for direct or indirect personal violence and so the fact that Alkali consented to the physical contact does not preclude liability for the offence under s 20. However, Alkali may have been aware that Acid was HIV positive. Following the decision of the Court of Appeal in *Dica* (2004), and depending on the facts undisclosed in the question, the following outcomes are possible:

(a) If Alkali was aware of the risk of infection because, for example, Acid had informed her that he had contracted the disease, then her consent to the risk would negative criminal liability in respect of the s 20 offence.

(b) If Alkali was not aware of the risk of infection and Acid was aware of her lack of knowledge, then he will be guilty of the s 20 offence, provided, as seems likely, the prosecution can prove that he was aware of the risk of causing Alkali some harm (*Mowatt* (1967); *Savage; Parmenter* (1991); *Konzani* (2005)).

(c) If Acid mistakenly believed that Alkali was aware that he was infected then, it is submitted, he ought to be excused. If D mistakenly believes that V is consenting to the risk, then he neither intends nor is reckless as to inflicting harm unlawfully (see *Kimber* (1983)).

CAUSING GRIEVOUS BODILY HARM WITH INTENT

If Acid deliberately infected Alkali with intent to cause serious bodily harm, then he is guilty of an offence contrary to s 18 of the 1861 Act, even if Alkali was aware of the risk of infection. Although there are exceptions (none of which apply here), the general rule is that V's consent to the intentional infliction of serious bodily harm does not excuse (*Brown* (1994); *Dica*).

RAPE

Section 1 of the Sexual Offences Act 2003 provides that D is guilty of rape if:

(a) he intentionally penetrates the vagina, anus or mouth of V with his penis;

(b) V does not consent to the penetration; and

(c) D does not reasonably believe that V consents.

Under s 76, there is a conclusive presumption of no consent if D has intentionally deceived the complainant as to the 'nature and purpose' of the act. However, it has been held that cases such as the present one do not fall within s 76. The Court of Appeal in *Dica* expressed its approval of dicta in *Tabassum* (2000), in which it was said that if V has consensual sexual intercourse unaware of a risk of infection, then she nonetheless consents to the nature and the quality of the act.[28]

----

28 There is no need to make reference to the rebuttable presumptions in **s 75(1)** as there is no evidence of any of the circumstances referred to in **s 75(2)**.

Where the statutory presumptions do not apply, consent is assessed by reference to s 74 which provides that, for the purposes of the Act, 'a person consents if he agrees by choice and has the freedom and capacity to make that choice'. It is arguable that a deception that D was not infected deprives V of real choice and that consent is negatived if the victim would not have agreed to the act if he or she had known all the facts. However, in *R v B* (2006) EWCA 2945 it was held that D's failure to disclose his HIV status was not relevant to whether the woman had consented to the intercourse. Latham LJ, delivering the judgment of the court, stated that, as a matter of law, the fact that D may not have disclosed his HIV status was not a matter which could in any way be relevant to the issue of consent under s 74 in relation to the sexual activity.

Therefore, Acid is not guilty of rape. Neither is he guilty of assault by penetration contrary to s 2(1) of the Act or sexual assault contrary to s 3(1) as both of these offences also require that the complainant did not consent to the penetration or the touching.

PART (B)

CONSTRUCTIVE MANSLAUGHTER
D is guilty of constructive manslaughter if he intentionally commits an unlawful and dangerous act which causes the death of V (*Goodfellow* (1986)). An unlawful act is dangerous if all sober and reasonable people would inevitably recognise that the unlawful act subjected the victim to the risk of some harm, albeit not serious harm (*Church* (1966)).

In *Cato* (1976), it was held that if D injects V with a dangerous substance, he will be guilty of this form of manslaughter if V dies as a result, even if the drug was selected and prepared by V and injected with his consent. The unlawful act is the offence of unlawfully and maliciously administering or causing to be adminstered a noxious thing so as to endanger life contrary to s 23 of the Offences Against the Person Act 1861.[29]

Heroin is 'a noxious thing' because it is 'liable to injure in common use'. There is no need to prove that D intended or was reckless as to endangering life. Indeed, it was held that where the noxious substance was administered directly as by injection there is no need to prove that D foresaw any harm (cf *Cunningham* (1957)) and V's consent is, on public policy grounds, no defence where actual bodily harm is intended or caused (*Attorney General's Reference (No 6 of 1980)* (1981); *Brown* (1994)).

MANSLAUGHTER BY GROSS NEGLIGENCE
Gerald may also be guilty of manslaughter by gross negligence. It is clear that a duty of care is owed in the given circumstances. A person is under a duty not to expose another

---

29 Always identify the unlawful act upon which liability for constructive liability is based.

to a risk of harm and, for the purposes of the criminal law, the duty to take reasonable care is recognised despite the fact that the deceased was party to a criminal activity (*Wacker* (2003)).

The jury would be required to evaluate the conduct of Gerald and to determine whether, in the light of the risk of death, it demonstrated such a high degree of negligence that it ought to be categorised as criminal; whether, in other words, there was, objectively, a sufficiently serious risk of death as to justify the imposition of criminal liability (*Adomako* (1994)). This will involve a consideration of all the facts including the quantity and quality of the drug and, arguably, whether Lisa was an experienced user.

ALTERNATIVE FACTS

What is the position, as in the alternative facts, where D prepares the syringe for V who self-injects and dies as a result of the effects of the drug?

In *R v Kennedy* [2008] 1 A.C. 269 the House of Lords considered when it might be appropriate to find someone guilty of manslaughter where that person has been involved in the supply of a class A controlled drug, which is then freely and voluntarily self-administered by the person to whom it was supplied, and the administration of the drug then causes his death.

The facts of the case were straightforward and similar to those of the instant problem. The defendant prepared and gave the deceased a syringe containing heroin. The deceased injected himself. The heroin affected his breathing and he died as a result.

The Court of Appeal dismissed Kennedy's appeal against conviction for manslaughter on the basis that, as he had actively assisted and encouraged the deceased, he was liable as a secondary party to V's unlawful self-injection.

The ruling attracted widespread criticism on the basis that there can be no secondary liability without a principal offender and self-injection of heroin is not an offence.

In *Dias* (2001), a case involving similar facts to those in Kennedy, the Court of Appeal agreed that the analysis in Kennedy was flawed but added that there might be situations where the supplier of the drug is guilty of manslaughter as a *principal*.

And in *Finlay* (2003) the Court of Appeal held that the supplier might be guilty of manslaughter on the basis that he had committed the s 23 offence of *causing a noxious thing to be administered* rather than the straightforward offence of administration of a noxious thing.[30]

---

30 The various approaches of the Court of Appeal are summarised before explaining the decision of the House in ***Kennedy (No. 2)***.

The decision in Kennedy was referred to the Court of Appeal for reconsideration by the Criminal Cases Review Commission – *Kennedy (No. 2)* (2005). Lord Woolf, delivering the judgment of the Court, reviewed the first appeal, and the decisions in *Dias* and *Finlay*. His Lordship agreed that the decision in the first appeal by Kennedy was flawed. The supplier of the drug could not be regarded as an accessory. But the appeal was nonetheless dismissed.

Dismissing the approach taken in *Finlay* as 'unnecessarily sophisticated' the Court, attempting to sidestep the issues of causation, held that Kennedy and the deceased were carrying out a 'combined operation' for which they were jointly responsible. The self-injection by V did not break the chain of causation between the act of D and V's death as the parties were acting in concert.

The House of Lords allowed Kennedy's appeal.

The House reviewed the earlier decisions and held, firstly, that *Finlay* was wrongly decided. There is a well established principle of English law that a free and voluntary act of a person with full capacity is not regarded as having been caused by another and thus where V self-injects, it is not appropriate to regard the supplier of the drug as having caused the drug to be administered.

The prosecution were therefore restricted to arguing that the drug was administered by Kennedy. Again the logical conclusion of the fact that the deceased's decision to self-inject was free and voluntary was that the heroin was not administered by the defendant. D may have encouraged or assisted the deceased to inject himself but he did not administer the drug.

Finally the House rejected the analysis of the Court of Appeal in Kennedy's second appeal. This was not a case of a 'combined operation' for which Kennedy and the deceased were jointly responsible. The deceased had a choice, knowing the facts, whether to inject himself of not. The heroin was, therefore, self-administered, not jointly administered.

Where a person freely and deliberately injects himself neither that act nor its consequences is attributable to the supplier. This is in accordance with the general principle that the free deliberate and informed acts of an individual initiate a fresh chain of causal responsibility.

Thus, Gerald is not guilty of the manslaughter of Lisa. Although the House restricted itself to a consideration of liability for constructive manslaughter it is clear that there can also be no liability for manslaughter by gross negligence. The death of Lisa is not attributable to the acts of Gerald.

General Defences

INTRODUCTION

There are a number of defences of general application in criminal law. Most of them are dealt with in this chapter. Defences which apply only to particular offences – for example, loss of control and diminished responsibility – appear in the chapter in which the relevant offence is considered.

Questions concerning the general defences are necessarily set in the context of a particular crime. You should deal with the positive ingredients of liability before discussing the availability of appropriate defences.

Although 'automatism' and 'mistake' are not truly defences, but rather a lack of the positive requirements of 'voluntariness', on the one hand, and *mens rea*, on the other, they are dealt with in this chapter because of their relationship to other defences.

Note that the point made regarding 'open' questions in the introduction to the previous chapter applies with equal force to problem-type questions under this heading. The facts of the problem do not always disclose the state of mind of the defendant. In addition, in the case of many of the defences discussed, a successful plea depends upon an objective evaluation of the conduct of D (for example, force used in self-defence must be reasonable). Evaluative questions of this type are generally for the jury. Thus, it may not be possible to come to a conclusive answer in respect of the availability of a defence.

Checklist ✔

The following issues are covered in this chapter:

- automatism: the distinction between 'sane' and 'insane' automatism; the *M'Naghten Rules* (1843); the meaning of a 'disease of the mind';
- mistake: the various types of mistakes and their effect upon liability, including mistakes induced by drunkenness and mistakes of law;
- compulsion: necessity and duress; the ingredients of the recognised defences; the limitations on the availability of defences of compulsion; duress and murder;

- the effect of drunken mistakes upon liability: the distinction between crimes of 'specific' and 'basic' intent;

- the *Dadson* (1850) principle: the availability of defences where D is unaware of the justifying or excusing conditions; and

- the distinction between justifications and excuses.

QUESTION 17

How have the courts limited the availability of the defence of automatism?

How to Answer this Question

This question requires a discussion of the legal treatment of involuntary conduct. The principal issues are:

- ❖ the general principle regarding automatism;
- ❖ automatism caused by a 'disease of the mind';
- ❖ automatism caused by the voluntary consumption of alcohol or 'dangerous' drugs; and
- ❖ other cases of self-induced automatism.

The principal authorities are: *Brady* (1963); *Quick* (1973); *DPP v Majewski* (1977); *Bailey* (1983); *Sullivan* (1984); *Hennessy* (1989); *Burgess* (1991).

Answer Structure

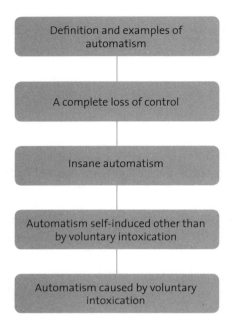

Definition and examples of automatism

A complete loss of control

Insane automatism

Automatism self-induced other than by voluntary intoxication

Automatism caused by voluntary intoxication

ANSWER

A state of automatism is one where the acts of a person are beyond their physical control. Typical examples are sleepwalking, acts done in a hypnotic trance, reflex actions and convulsions. Such states normally excuse a defendant for the consequences of his actions on the basis that no responsibility can fairly attach to unwilled actions. However, the 'defence' is limited in application and does not always result in a complete acquittal (Think Point (1)).[1]

LOSS OF CONTROL

Firstly, in *Attorney General's Reference (No 2 of 1992)* (1993), the Court of Appeal held that automatism is only available where there was a complete destruction of voluntary control. The defendant, a lorry driver, was charged with causing death by reckless driving. He raised a defence of automatism and produced expert evidence that the repetitive visual stimuli experienced as he drove along the straight, flat, featureless motorways had induced a trance-like state.

The judge allowed the defence to go before the jury and he was acquitted. The prosecution appealed, successfully. The Court of Appeal held that as there had not been a

---

1   This question is fairly specific. It is not sufficient to write generally about automatism.

total destruction of voluntary control the judge ought not to have allowed the defence of automatism to go to the jury. The defendant had been driving with awareness, albeit diminished and had managed to steer the vehicle for about half a mile.

The Draft Code (Law Com No. 177 Cl.33) would allow the defence where a person was deprived of effective control, but this Code has not as yet become law.

INSANE AUTOMATISM

Secondly where the automatism results from a 'disease of the mind' the defendant is entitled only to a qualified acquittal – 'not guilty by reason of insanity'.

The defence of insanity is defined in the *M'Naghten Rules* (1843). It must be proved that, at the time he committed the act, the accused was labouring under such a defect of reason, due to a disease of the mind, as either not to know the nature and quality of his act or, if he did know that, he did not know that what he was doing was wrong. Since a defendant in a state of automatism is clearly labouring under a defect of reason such that he does not know the nature and quality of his act, the central issue in cases of automatism is whether that state results from a disease of the mind and thus amounts to insane automatism or is from some other cause, in which case it is sane automatism.[2]

The question whether a condition amounts to a 'disease of the mind' amounting to insanity is a question of law and it has been held that any condition which impairs the functioning of the mind may amount to a 'disease'. It does not matter whether the cause of the impairment is organic, as in epilepsy, or functional, as in schizophrenia. Nor does it matter whether the impairment is permanent, or transient and intermittent, provided that it was operative at the time of the alleged offence (*Sullivan* (1984)).

The central policy underlying the insanity defence is to allow control of those who, although not responsible for their conduct, are suffering from a condition which means they present a continuing danger – that is, a condition which is likely to recur (see *Bratty v Attorney General for Northern Ireland* (1963); *Sullivan* (1984)). As Lord Denning said in *Bratty*:

> any mental disorder which has manifested itself in violence and is prone to recur is a disease of the mind. **At any rate it is the sort of disease for which a person should be detained in hospital rather than be given an unqualified acquittal**.

And thus in *Sullivan* it was held that epilepsy amounted to insanity. Lord Diplock explained that, despite the natural reluctance to attach the label of insanity to epilepsy, the purpose of the legislation relating to the defence of insanity is to protect society

---

2   Note that the central issue in many cases involving automatism is whether the condition results from a disease of the mind.

against a recurrence of dangerous conduct and the fact that the suspension of control is temporary is not relevant.

If, however, the immediate cause of the malfunctioning is an 'external factor', such as a blow to the head, or alcohol or drugs, the condition does not constitute a disease (*Quick* (1973); *Sullivan* (1984)). In most situations the distinction between internal and external causes works effectively and respects the underlying policy of the law relating to insanity as internal causes are more likely to recur than external causes. However, it can result in anomalies. For example, whereas hyperglycaemia, caused when a diabetic fails to take insulin, is regarded as internally caused (by the diabetes itself) and, therefore, a 'disease of the mind', hypoglycaemia, resulting from a failure to take food after taking insulin or taking too much insulin, is regarded as externally caused and amounts to sane automatism (*Hennessy* (1989); *Bingham* (1991)).

Where a defendant is found not guilty by reason of insanity, the judge must make one of a number of various orders, which include a hospital order with or without restrictions on discharge (s 5 of the Criminal Procedure (Insanity) Act 1964, as substituted by Sched 1 to the Criminal Procedure (Insanity and Unfitness to Plead) Act 1991).

SELF INDUCED AUTOMATISM

As we have seen, automatism caused by the transient effects of alcohol or drugs is externally caused and therefore not attributable to a 'disease of the mind' (see *Quick*). However, where it results from voluntary consumption it is not a defence to all crimes. The rule is that where the accused lacks the *mens rea* for an offence due to the effects of alcohol or other (non-prescribed) drugs, voluntarily consumed, then the absence of *mens rea* is an 'excuse' only for so called crimes of 'specific intent', such as murder, but not for crimes of 'basic intent', such as manslaughter (*DPP v Majewski* (1977); *Lipman* (1970)) (Think Point (2)).[3]

In addition to murder, the following have been acknowledged as crimes of specific intent: wounding or causing grievous bodily harm with intent contrary to s 18 of the Offences Against the Person Act 1861 (*Pordage* (1975)); theft contrary to s 1 of the Theft Act 1968 (*Ruse v Read* (1949)); handling stolen goods (*Durante* (1972)); and attempts (*Mohan* (1976)).

Offences of basic intent include, in addition to manslaughter: malicious wounding or inflicting grievous bodily harm contrary to s 20 of the Offences Against the Person Act 1861 (*Sullivan* (1981)); assault occasioning actual bodily harm (*Bolton v Crawley* (1972)); and rape (*Fotheringham* (1988)) (Think Point (3)).

In *Bailey* (1983), the Court of Appeal held that self-induced automatism other than that due to intoxication from alcohol or drugs will provide a defence even to crimes of basic

3   Take care when expressing the '***Majewski*** rule'. It is an inculpatory rule applying where D, because of voluntary intoxication, lacks the *mens rea* for a crime of basic intent.

intent except where the defendant was 'reckless' – in a general subjective sense – as to the risk of becoming an automaton.

That is, if the accused knew that by doing or failing to do something (for example, in the case of a diabetic taking too much insulin or not eating after having taken insulin) there was a risk that he might become aggressive, unpredictable or dangerous with the result that he might cause some harm to others and that he persisted in the action or took no remedial action when he knew it was required then it would be open to the jury to find that he was reckless and convict of an appropriate crime of basic intent (for example, malicious wounding, inflicting grievous bodily harm or assault occasioning actual bodily harm).

In these circumstances, despite the fact that he lacked the *mens rea*, the defendant may be convicted of an appropriate offence of basic intent (Think Point (4)).

This rule was also applied in *Hardie* (1984), where the defendant took a quantity of valium, a sedative drug. The valium was not prescribed to the defendant and the judge treated the case as an ordinary one of voluntary intoxication, ruling that, as it was self-induced, it was no defence to a crime of basic intent. The Court of Appeal quashed the conviction. The court held, distinguishing *Majewski*, that the rule regarding voluntary intoxication does not apply where the drug is not generally recognised as dangerous. That is, if the drug does not normally cause unpredictable behaviour, automatism resulting from its consumption may provide an excuse to all crimes, even those of basic intent. Only if the defendant was reckless in the *Bailey* sense can he be convicted of an offence (of basic intent).

CONCLUSION

Although automatism will often afford a 'defence' entitling the defendant to a complete acquittal, the causes of the condition must be examined. If there is prior fault on the part of the defendant either because he is voluntarily intoxicated or has 'recklessly' failed to take steps to prevent himself falling into a state of automatism then his condition will not excuse a basic intent crime. If he is not responsible for the automatism, but it is the result of an internal condition that is likely to result in recurrent 'malfunctioning', the defendant will be classified as legally insane and entitled only to a qualified acquittal.

Think Points

1   Although automatism has been referred to as a 'defence', the legally accurate analysis is that since 'voluntariness' is a basic ingredient of criminal liability and the onus is on the prosecution to prove beyond reasonable doubt that the conduct of the accused was willed, it will not be able to do so where the defendant's acts were involuntary. In *Roach* (2001), D's appeal against conviction for an offence of wounding with intent was allowed as the judge had not made it clear to the jury that the burden of proof lay upon the prosecution.

2 The general tenor of the speeches in *DPP v Majewski* (1977) supports the notion that the rule is a substantive one – that is, that where a defendant is charged with an offence of basic intent and he raises evidence that, due to drink or drugs, he was not in control of his actions at the relevant time, he can be convicted on proof that he committed the *actus reus*. Liability is, in effect, strict. In *Woods* (1982), however, a case involving the 'old' offence of rape, it was held that the jury should be instructed to decide whether the defendant had the requisite *mens rea*, but to ignore all evidence of self-induced intoxication. See also *Aitken* (1992), where it was said that for the purposes of s 20 of the Offences Against the Person Act 1861, D acts maliciously if he foresees the risk of injury or would have foreseen injury but for the drink consumed.

3 Although the basis for the distinction was never entirely clear it was generally accepted that crimes of 'specific intent' were those which required proof of intention as to one or more of the elements of the *actus reus*. Crimes satisfied on proof of recklessness, (gross) negligence and crimes of strict liability were crimes of 'basic intent'. In *Heard* (2008), however, the Court of Appeal said that a specific intent is a 'purposive', 'ulterior' or 'bolted on' intent going beyond the elements in the *actus reus* (eg the intention to steal, cause grievous bodily harm or cause criminal damage required for conviction of burglary under s 9(1)(a)). The case concerned sexual assault contrary to s 3 of the Sexual Offences Act 2003. The requirement of an 'intentional' touching was not a specific intent, as it related to an element of the *actus reus* (that is, the touching).

   If the Court of Appeal is correct then the classification of murder as a crime of specific intent has been misguided as there is no need to prove an intention going 'beyond' the *actus reus* of killing a human being. As it is well established that murder is a crime of specific intent (see *Majewski*) it is unlikely that the basis of distinction in *Heard* will be followed generally.

4 In *Marison* (1996), the defendant, a diabetic, had a hypoglycaemic episode whilst driving. As he was aware that there was a risk he might become an automaton, he was guilty of causing death by dangerous driving before an attack caused him to lose control of the vehicle (see also *Kay v Butterworth* (1947)).

Common Pitfalls

Note that the question asks you to explain how the courts have limited the availability of the defence of automatism. It is not sufficient to simply give an account of the defence.

QUESTION 18

Samson is a diabetic. He is required to take insulin regularly to control his condition. On one occasion, he took insulin as prescribed but, not having eaten, he became semi-conscious whilst driving his car. He lost control of the car and it collided with Jeanette, a pedestrian. Jeanette was taken to hospital suffering from multiple fractures. Two weeks later, whilst still in hospital, Jeanette contracted a serious infection which proved fatal.

▶ Discuss Samson's criminal liability.   *involuntary intoxication*

Would your answer differ if Samson's loss of control had been caused by a failure to take his insulin?

How to Answer this Question

This question involves consideration of liability for a number of offences against the person and the application of the rules concerning involuntary conduct. The same issues of automatism are raised with respect to each of the offences. Repetition may be avoided by reference to principles previously explained.

The principal issues are:

❖   the question of causation and intervening medical treatment;
❖   automatism – the loss of control;
❖   'reckless' automatism; and
❖   automatism caused by a 'disease of the mind'; the distinction between 'internal' and 'external' causes.

The principal authorities are: *Smith* (1959); *Kemp* (1957); *Cheshire* (1991); *Quick* (1973); *Brady* (1963); *M'Naghten* (1843); *Sullivan* (1984); *Hennessy* (1989).

Answer Structure

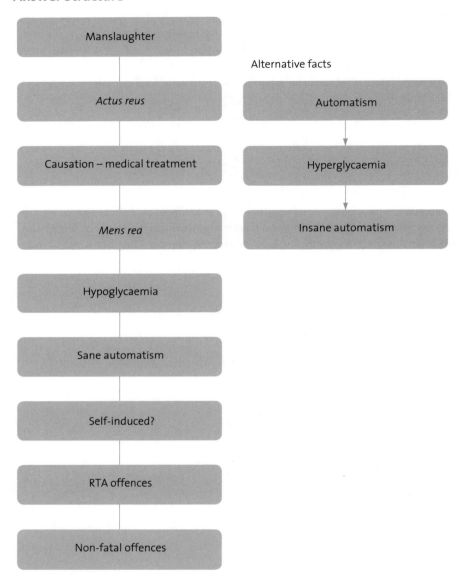

ANSWER

MANSLAUGHTER

It is proposed initially to consider Samson's liability for manslaughter.

As far as the *actus reus* of this offence is concerned, the only issue requiring consideration is whether Jeanette's death was caused by Samson's actions.[4]

Clearly, his conduct was a factual cause of death: that is, but for Samson losing control of the car, she would not have suffered the injuries which led to her hospitalisation and subsequent death. The onus is on the prosecution to prove that Samson's actions were a legal cause of death. The facts of the problem do not disclose the cause of the infection and, in particular, it is not clear whether it was contracted as a direct result of the injuries or their treatment or from some other cause.[5]

In *Cheshire* (1991), the Court of Appeal held that even if negligent treatment of the victim was the immediate cause of the death, the responsibility of the defendant will not be excluded if the treatment was itself a direct consequence of the defendant's acts and the contribution of the defendant's acts were still significant at the time of death. Only if the medical treatment was a 'potent' cause of death and 'independent' of the defendant's actions would it relieve him of responsibility (and see *Mellor* (1996)).

In *Gowans* (2003), it was held that if the attack necessitated treatment which had rendered the victim vulnerable to the infection, then the death would be attributable to the acts of the defendant. If, however, the hospitalised victim of an attack contracted a fatal infection 'purely by chance' – for example, by breathing in airborne germs – the attack would merely amount to the setting in which another cause operated. In those circumstances, the death of the victim would not be attributed to the acts of the assailant.

Assuming, for the purposes of further analysis, that Samson's acts are a legal cause of death, his criminal liability will be determined by reference to his *mens rea*.[6]

It would appear that Samson went into a hypoglycaemic episode – a deficiency of blood sugar resulting in an impairment of consciousness. In these circumstances, he may raise the 'defence' of automatism, which, if successfully pleaded, results in a complete acquittal. Samson will be required to produce medical evidence to support his claim that, at the relevant time, he was an automaton (*Hill v Baxter* (1958)). Provided he does so, the probative burden lies with the prosecution. In other words, if the prosecution wish to contest his claim, they must satisfy the jury that Samson did not lack conscious control of his actions (*Bratty v Attorney General for Northern Ireland* (1963)). The facts of the problem state that Samson was semi-conscious. It is not clear from the authorities as to whether this amounts to automatism.

----

4 Issues of causation bear on the *actus reus* and ordinarily should be tackled before issues relating to the *mens rea* or defences.

5 Acknowledge those factual uncertainties which are relevant to the resolution of the problem.

6 Where the facts are uncertain it is permissible to progress the answer by clearly expressing any assumptions as to the facts upon which further analysis is based.

There are authorities which support the view that even where the defendant suffers only a partial loss of consciousness and has some control over his actions, the defence will be available, provided he lacks effective control (see *Kemp* (1957); *Charlson* (1955); *Quick* (1973)). On the other hand, in *Attorney General's Reference (No 2 of 1992)* (1993), the Court of Appeal held that a total destruction of voluntary control was required (see also *Broome v Perkins* (1987)).[7]

It is not clear whether Samson's partial loss of consciousness was accompanied by a partial or total loss of control. Control does not always accompany awareness and it is submitted that if the loss of control suffered by Samson was of such a degree that he could not be said to be responsible for his 'actions', then the defence of automatism should be available to him.

If Samson was in a state of automatism, then, as it was externally caused, it will amount to sane automatism, entitling him to a complete acquittal unless it was 'self-induced' (*Quick*). That is, Samson is not guilty of an offence unless the prosecution prove that, prior to becoming an automaton, he was aware that by not eating food after taking insulin there was a risk that he might lose conscious control of his actions and deliberately ran that risk. If that is the case, then he will be guilty of an appropriate offence of 'basic intent', in this case, manslaughter (*Bailey* (1983); *Hardie* (1984)). (It was decided in *Lipman* (1970) that manslaughter is a crime of basic intent. Murder, on the other hand, is a crime of 'specific intent' – see *Sheehan* (1975).)

The maximum punishment for manslaughter is imprisonment for life (s 5 of the Offences Against the Person Act 1861).

NON-FATAL OFFENCES AGAINST THE PERSON

If the injuries were not a legal cause of death then, clearly, Samson could not be convicted of manslaughter. In those circumstances, his liability would be limited to the injuries suffered by Jeanette.[8]

Provided the injuries caused were serious and that the automation was 'self-induced', as explained above, then Samson may be convicted of the offence under s 20 of the Offences Against the Person Act 1861 (see *Brady*). (It was held in *Bratty v Attorney General for Northern Ireland* that malicious wounding is a crime of 'basic intent' and that the offence under s 18, wounding with intent, is a crime of 'specific intent'.)

---

7   Acknowledge legal uncertainties and 'submit' a view as to the better approach.
8   Having progressed the answer on the basis of one particular assumption as to the facts now consider the legal outcome on the basis of any alternative assumption(s) which are also compatible with the stated facts.

The maximum punishment for the offence of malicious wounding is a term of imprisonment not exceeding five years.

DANGEROUS DRIVING AND CAUSING DEATH BY DANGEROUS DRIVING

Samson may be guilty of the offence of dangerous driving contrary to s 2 of the Road Traffic Act 1988, as substituted by s 1 of the Road Traffic Act 1991; if his actions are a legal cause of the death of Jeanette, he may be guilty of causing death by dangerous driving contrary to s 1 of the 1988 Act, as substituted by s 1 of the Road Traffic Act 1991.

Again, even were he an automaton, Samson may be convicted of these offences if the prosecution prove that the automatism was self-induced, as they are offences of basic intent.

The offence under s 2 carries a maximum punishment of two years' imprisonment and that under s 1 is punishable with up to five years' imprisonment.

ALTERNATIVE FACTS – INSANITY

The ingredients of the defence of insanity were laid down in the *M'Naghten Rules*. These state that insanity consists of a defect of reason due to disease of the mind, such that the defendant either did not know the nature and quality of his act or, alternatively, did not know that what he was doing was wrong.

In *Hennessey* (1989) it was held that automatism resulting from a state of hyperglycaemia which can occur when diabetes is not controlled by insulin is regarded as caused by an internal factor – the 'disease' itself – and falls within the *M'Naghten Rules*.

If Samson chose to plead insanity, then, as there is a presumption of sanity, he would have the burden of proving the defence on a balance of probabilities (*M'Naghten* (1843)).

Although insanity is a defence, a successful plea does not result in a complete acquittal. Where a defendant is found not guilty by reason of insanity, the judge must make one of a number of various orders. These include a hospital order, which may be made with or without restrictions on discharge (s 5 of the Criminal Procedure (Insanity) Act 1964, as substituted by Sched 1 to the Criminal Procedure (Insanity and Unfitness to Plead) Act 1991).

Consequently, Samson may choose not to raise the defence of insanity. If, however, he puts his state of mind in issue by raising automatism, the judge may rule that his condition amounts to insanity (*Sullivan* (1984); cf *Thomas (Sharon)* (1995)). Thus, if Samson wishes to avoid an acquittal on the grounds of insanity, he has no alternative but to plead guilty to the offences charged.

QUESTION 19

Smart held a party, during which he laced Tippsy's lemonade with a drug. Tippsy began to feel strange and so decided to leave the party. He drove part of the way home but then, as he began to have hallucinations, he parked his car, got out and started to walk the remainder of the journey. As Tippsy approached his house he saw Shifty. Tippsy was convinced that Shifty was about to mug him and so he hit him on the head with his umbrella. In fact, Shifty was waiting for his friend Godot and had no intention of 'mugging' Tippsy.

Shifty had an extremely thin skull and died from the blow.

Tippsy collapsed from the effects of the drug and suffered damage to his kidneys which necessitated a long period of hospitalisation and treatment.

▶ Advise Smart and Tippsy about their criminal liability.

How to Answer this Question

This question raises issues concerning a number of offences against the person, including poisoning offences, and an offence contrary to the Road Traffic Act 1988. The legal treatment of a drunken mistake relevant to an issue of defence is raised with respect to Tippsy's liability.

The principal issues are:

* ❖ the 'egg shell skull' principle;
* ❖ self-defence and mistake: the rule in *Williams* (1983) and *Beckford* (1988); s 76 of the Criminal Justice and Immigration Act 2008;

❖ administration of a 'noxious' thing contrary to ss 23 and 24 of the Offences Against the Person Act 1861;
❖ the *mens rea* requirement of s 23;
❖ s 4(1) of the RTA: driving while unfit; and
❖ liability of the 'procurer' of an offence.

Applying the Law

intoxication

Tippsy's liability   Smart's liability

Homicide	s 18 OAPA 1861
Legal causation	s 20 OAPA 1861
Egg shell skull	s 23 OAPA 1861
Mens rea	s 24 OAPA 1861
Murder	s 4 RTA 1988
Manslaughter	
Self-defence	
Mistaken belief	

This two part flow chart shows the main legislation and principles needed to assess the liability of both Tippsy and Smart.

ANSWER

TIPPSY

MURDER AND MANSLAUGHTER

The *actus reus* of both murder and manslaughter require that D's acts were a legal cause of the death of V, a human being. This requirement is satisfied in Tippsy's case. The fact that Shifty had a thin skull rendering him more vulnerable to fatal injury does not prevent the attribution of the death to Tippsy. There is a principle in English law to the effect that 'one must take one's victim as one finds him'. This means that a defendant whose actions are a cause of death may not point to a peculiar vulnerability of the victim as breaking the chain of causation (*Martin* (1832)).

Whether Tippsy may be convicted of either murder or manslaughter (or neither), depends on his intent at the time of striking the blow. A conviction for murder requires proof that D either intended unlawfully to kill or to cause grievous bodily harm (*Moloney* (1985)). The approach to intention has been a matter of much debate and the position can be summarised as follows.[9]

If Tippsy's aim or purpose was to kill or cause grievous bodily harm, then he intended to kill or cause grievous bodily harm. If it was not his aim or purpose, but he was aware that either death or grievous bodily harm was virtually certain to result from the attack, then the jury may find that he intended death or grievous bodily harm (*Hancock and Shankland* (1986); *Nedrick* (1986); *Woollin* (1998); *Matthews and Alleyne* (2003)).

Constructive manslaughter requires proof that D intentionally committed an unlawful act which was dangerous and was the legal cause of V's death (*Goodfellow* (1986); *Jennings* (1990)).

The battery committed against Shifty amounts to an unlawful act (*Larkin* (1943)) and it is clear from the facts that Tippsy applied force intentionally.

The requirement of dangerousness is satisfied on proof that all sober and reasonable people would recognise that striking Shifty with the umbrella was likely to subject him to the risk of some harm (*Church* (1966); *Goodfellow* (1986)). It is not necessary to show that there was a risk of serious harm, nor is it necessary to prove that the defendant was aware of any risk of harm (*Lipman* (1970)) (Think Point (1)).

---

9   Where the facts of the question do not disclose the intent with which D acted consider the alternatives by explaining the requirements of the relevant offences. Where it is not possible to come to a conclusive answer do not attempt to provide one!

Now, the facts of the question do not disclose Tippsy's intent. It is not clear whether he intended to cause grievous bodily harm, some lesser harm or merely to apply force without causing harm. But, whatever Tippsy intended, both murder and manslaughter require an intent to cause the defined consequence *unlawfully*. And in *Williams* (1983) it was decided that a mistaken but genuine belief in facts which, if true, would justify self-defence negatives that intent to act unlawfully (*Beckford* (1988); now codified by s 76(3) and (4) of the Criminal Justice and Immigration Act 2008).[10]

Furthermore, although it seems that a mistaken belief in the need to use force may not be relied upon if it was a result of voluntary intoxication (*O'Grady* (1987); *Hatton* (2005); s 76(5) of the Criminal Justice and Immigration Act 2008), a mistaken belief resulting from involuntary intoxication may excuse. The exclusionary rule regarding voluntary intoxication and offences of basic intent is based on the principle of prior fault. The person who has made a mistake as a result of self-induced intoxication is regarded as blameworthy because he is responsible for his condition. The involuntarily intoxicated individual who makes a legally relevant mistake is not responsible for his condition. It is fair, therefore, that he be allowed to rely on the mistake (see *DPP v Majewski* (1977); *Hardie* (1984); *Kingston* (1994)).[11]

Thus, whether charged with murder or manslaughter, Tippsy should be acquitted unless the prosecution prove that Tippsy did not use such force as was reasonable in the circumstances as he believed them to be (*Abraham* (1973); *Shannon* (1980); *Stripp* (1978); *Scarlett* (1994); *Oatridge* (1991)). The question whether the force was reasonable is one solely for the jury (*Owino* (1996)).

It should be noted that force may be used to ward off an attack which the defendant anticipated; a pre-emptive strike may be justified (*Attorney General's Reference (No 2 of 1983)* (1984)).

SMART

SECTIONS 18 AND 20 OF THE OFFENCES AGAINST THE PERSON ACT 1861

Under s 20 of the Act, it is an offence 'unlawfully and maliciously . . . to inflict grievous bodily harm upon any other person'. Under s 18, it is an offence 'unlawfully and maliciously to . . . cause grievous bodily harm to any person by any means whatsoever . . . with intent to do grievous bodily harm'. 'Grievous bodily harm' means 'serious bodily harm'. It is a matter for the jury to decide whether the harm caused or inflicted is grievous

---

10 As self-defence is available to murder and manslaughter it is an efficient strategy to deal with it at this stage, having considered the positive ingredients of both offences.

11 As there is no direct authority on the effect of involuntary intoxication where D mistakenly believed in the need to use force in self-defence, relevant legal principle is considered.

(*DPP v Smith* (1961); *Saunders* (1985)), but injuries resulting in lengthy treatment or incapacity are clearly capable of amounting to grievous bodily harm.

Until recently, it was generally accepted that there could be no infliction of grievous bodily harm contrary to s 20 in the absence of an application of force to the body of the victim (see, for example, *Wilson* (1984)). However, in *Ireland; Burstow* (1997), the House of Lords held that there was no 'radical divergence' between the meaning of 'inflict' in s 20 and 'cause' in s 18 and that injury could be inflicted or caused without the application of force (see also *Mandair* (1995)).

Thus, the only significant difference in terms of the ingredients of liability for the two offences relates to their *mens rea* requirements. For s 20, it must be proved that the defendant was reckless with respect to causing some harm (*Mowatt* (1967); *Savage; Parmenter* (1991)).

The *mens rea* requirement for s 18 is relatively high. The prosecution must prove that Smart intended to cause grievous bodily harm (*Belfon* (1976)).

MALICIOUSLY ADMINISTERING A NOXIOUS THING

By virtue of s 23, it is an offence to maliciously administer a poison or other noxious thing to any person so as to endanger the life of such person or to inflict upon him any grievous bodily harm. The maximum punishment is a term of imprisonment not exceeding five years.

By virtue of s 24, it is an offence to maliciously administer a poison or other noxious thing with intent to injure, aggrieve or annoy such person. The maximum punishment is a term of imprisonment not exceeding five years.

In *Harley* (1830), it was held that an offence may be committed where, as in this case, the noxious thing is put into a drink taken by the victim.

The concept of a 'noxious thing' is wide enough to include anything which is even only slightly harmful or which disturbs either physiological or psychological function, bearing in mind not only the quality and nature of the substance, but also the quantity administered (*Marcus* (1981)).

For liability under s 23, the prosecution must prove, as an element of the *actus reus*, that either life was endangered or grievous bodily harm was inflicted.

As far as the *mens rea* is concerned, the authorities are not absolutely clear.

In *Cunningham* (1957), it was held that the prosecution must prove that the defendant either intended or foresaw that the 'particular kind of harm' might result and went on to take the risk of it. In *Cato* (1976), the Court of Appeal interpreted this to mean that although the prosecution were required to prove that the defendant intentionally or recklessly administered the thing knowing at least that there was a risk that it would cause harm (that is, that it was 'noxious'), it was not necessary to prove that the defendant foresaw the risk that it would endanger life or cause grievous bodily harm.

It would seem, however, that the Court of Appeal intended that this restricted form of the *mens rea* would apply only if the noxious thing is applied directly (in *Cato*, heroin was injected). Therefore, if, as in this case, the noxious thing is indirectly administered, the prosecution apparently must prove recklessness not only with respect to the administration of the noxious thing, but also with respect to the risk of endangering life or causing grievous bodily harm.[12]

For s 24, the *mens rea* consists of two elements: (a) intention or recklessness (as above) with respect to the administration of a noxious thing; and (b) an intention to injure, aggrieve or annoy (see *Hill* (1985)).

If Smart is charged with the offence under s 23, but the prosecution fail to prove he acted with the necessary *mens rea*, he may be convicted of the offence under s 24 providing, as the facts imply, that he acted with the *mens rea* for that offence (s 25 of the Offences Against the Person Act 1861).

ROAD TRAFFIC ACT (RTA) 1988
By virtue of s 4(1) of the RTA, a person who drives a vehicle while unfit through drink or drugs commits an offence. The maximum punishment is six months' imprisonment or a £5,000 fine or both. And, unless there are special reasons, the offender must be disqualified from driving for at least 12 months.

By s 4(5) of the Act, a person is taken to be unfit to drive if his ability to drive properly is impaired. Whether a driver's ability is impaired is a question of fact. Medical evidence may be submitted to demonstrate that Tippsy was unfit before he parked the car and decided to walk.

Although the fact that his drink was laced does not absolve him of liability, it may amount to a special reason allowing the court, within its discretion, to refrain from imposing an order of disqualification (*Pugsley v Hunter* (1973)).

Smart, by virtue of s 8 of the Accessories and Abettors Act 1861, may be convicted of 'procuring' the commission of the offence under s 4(1) of the RTA.

12   Note the uncertainty concerning the element of *mens rea* in the s 23 offence.

In *Attorney General's Reference (No 1 of 1975)* (1975), the Court of Appeal held, in a case involving similar facts to the present problem, that 'to procure' means 'to produce by endeavour'. This implies that it is necessary to prove that the defendant intended to bring about the principal offence. In *Blakely and Sutton v DPP* (1991), on the other hand, Lord Bingham understood 'procuring' to involve intention or 'the willing acceptance of a contemplated result'. This implies that advertent recklessness with respect to the central conduct of the *actus reus* will suffice. Such an interpretation is far removed from the ordinary meaning of 'to procure' and, it is submitted, ought not to be followed.

It seems, however, that recklessness will suffice as far as the circumstances of the offence are concerned (*Carter v Richardson* (1976)). In other words, it must be proved that Smart knew that Tippsy was going to drive and was aware that he was probably unfit as a result of the administered drug.

Think Point

1   The rule in *Watson* (1989) and *Dawson* (1985), to the effect that a peculiar vulnerability of the victim is not relevant to the issue of dangerousness unless it would have been apparent to a reasonable observer of the incident, does not apply in this case. The rule applies only where the act of the accused would not otherwise be dangerous as defined.

Aim Higher   ★

In answering a question of this type it is important to appreciate the treatment of legally relevant mistakes arising from involuntary intoxication. Although there is no authority directly dealing with a situation where D, as a result of involuntary intoxication, mistakenly believes that it is necessary to use defensive force, an answer to the problem can be found by considering the principles underlying existing case law.

QUESTION 20

Tosh is a fanatical supporter of the England football team. He did not have a ticket for the match against Malta and so he jumped over the turnstile. He hid in the crowd and watched the match. England were beaten 6–0. Tosh was thoroughly shocked and depressed. As he walked home, he passed by the office of the Malta Tourist Board. He jumped through the plate glass window of the office, smashing it. He claims that he was so shocked by the football result that he felt as though he were 'in another world' and that he did not know what he was doing.

▶ Discuss Tosh's criminal liability.

How to Answer this Question
This question raises issues concerning the distinction between sane and insane automatism and, in particular, the legal categorisation of conditions brought about by 'stress and disappointment'. In addition, it raises a question of liability for the offence of making off without payment contrary to s 3 of the Theft Act 1978.

The principal issues are:

❖   the distinction between sane and insane automatism; internal and external causes; conditions resulting from the 'ordinary stresses and disappointments of life'; and
❖   is there an offence of making off without payment contrary to s 3 of the Theft Act 1978 where payment is expected or required prior to the provision of the service?

The principal authorities are: *R v G and Another* (2003); *Attorney General's Reference (No 2 of 1992)* (1993); *Sullivan* (1984).

Answer Structure

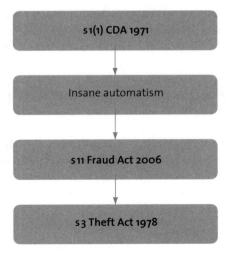

s1(1) CDA 1971

Insane automatism

s11 Fraud Act 2006

s3 Theft Act 1978

ANSWER

CRIMINAL DAMAGE

Tosh may be charged with the offence of criminal damage contrary to s 1(1) of the Criminal Damage Act 1971. By s 4, the maximum punishment for this offence is a term of imprisonment not exceeding 10 years.[13]

The *actus reus* of the offence consists of damaging or destroying property belonging to another. Clearly, Tosh has committed the *actus reus*.

As far as the *mens rea* is concerned, the prosecution must prove that Tosh either intended to cause damage or was reckless with respect to damaging property. In *R v G and Another* (2003), the House of Lords held that a person acts recklessly within the meaning of s 1 of the Criminal Damage Act 1971 when he is aware of a risk of damaging property belonging to another and it is, in the circumstances known to him, unreasonable to take the risk.

However, Tosh may contend that, at the relevant time, he was in a state of automatism, that is, that he had lost control of his actions. If he does wish to raise the 'defence', he is required to produce medical evidence supporting the claim that his actions were not voluntary. Provided he does so, the probative burden lies with the prosecution. That is, the prosecution must prove that, at the relevant time, Tosh did not lack control of his actions (*Hill v Baxter* (1958); *Bratty v Attorney General for Northern Ireland* (1963); *Pullen* (1991)).

It is not clear from the facts of this case whether a plea of automatism would be successful. First, it should be noted that if Tosh knew what he was doing, in the sense that his conduct was within his immediate control but he acted without normal self-restraint, then the defence would not be available to him. There is no general defence of 'irresistible impulse' (*Isitt* (1977)). Secondly, the Court of Appeal held in *Attorney General's Reference (No 2 of 1992)* (1993) that the defence of automatism requires a total destruction of conscious control on the defendant's part. The court even seemed prepared to accept that subconscious control would be enough to preclude the 'defence'. There are, however, many authorities which support the view that a partial loss of control will suffice (see, for example, *Kemp* (1957); *Quick* (1973); *T* (1990)) and it is submitted that this approach is preferable. If the loss of control suffered by Tosh was of such a degree that he could not be said to be responsible for his actions in jumping through the window, then the defence of automatism should be available to him. However, even if the loss of control was sufficient to found a plea of automatism, the judge may rule that Tosh has raised the defence of insanity (*Sullivan* (1984)).

---

13   Any discussion of criminal liability in a problem question should start with identification of the offence under consideration.

The ingredients of the defence of insanity were laid down in the *M'Naghten Rules* (1843). These state that to establish a defence on the ground of insanity, it must be proved that, at the time of committing the act, the party accused was labouring under such a defect of reason, from disease of the mind, as not to know the nature and quality of the act he was doing; or, if he did know that, that he did not know that what he was doing was wrong. Now, by definition, a person who was in a state of automatism was labouring under such a defect of reason as not to know the nature and quality of his act. The crucial issue, therefore, is whether the defect of reason resulted from a disease of the mind. It is this which determines whether the condition amounts to sane or insane automatism.[14]

The significance of the distinction for the defendant is that whereas sane automatism results in a complete acquittal, a verdict of not guilty by reason of insanity may be followed by an order committing the defendant to a hospital and may contain restrictions concerning the minimum period of time for detention. It may specify that the person may be detained until the Home Secretary orders release (s 5 of the Criminal Procedure (Insanity) Act 1964, as substituted by the Criminal Procedure (Insanity and Unfitness to Plead) Act 1991).

Tosh's condition – if it did result in an effective loss of conscious control – would be categorised as an instance of insane automatism. This is because only conditions caused by external factors are regarded as amounting to sane automatism. Psychological states caused by the 'ordinary stress and disappointments of everyday life' are perceived to be a consequence of the predisposing internal factors. Thus, if he did lack control at the time he caused the damage, the proper verdict is not guilty by reason of insanity (Think Point (1)).

OBTAINING SERVICES DISHONESTLY – s 11 FRAUD ACT 2006
A person is guilty of an offence contrary to s 11(1) of the Fraud Act 2006 if he dishonestly obtains services for himself.

'Services' is not defined but presumably it includes admission to a football ground to watch a match. They were made available on the basis that payment was made for them (s 11(2)(a)). Knowing that payment was required (s 11(2)(c)(i)) Tosh obtained them without payment (s 11(2)(b)) and dishonestly intended to avoid payment (s 11(2)(c)(ii)).

The offence under s 11 carries a maximum penalty of five years' imprisonment on conviction on indictment.

MAKING OFF WITHOUT PAYMENT
The offence of making off without payment, contrary to s 3 of the Theft Act 1978, is committed where D dishonestly makes off without payment after having been supplied goods or having had some 'service done'.

14 In questions involving automatism take care to explain, by reference to M'Naghten, the significance of whether D's behaviour resulted from a 'disease of the mind'.

In this case, the service is not 'done' until the game is over and thus, as payment was neither required nor expected at the end of the match, Tosh did not make off 'knowing that payment . . . for a service done was required or expected from him'. Section 3 is worded such that it appears only to apply to situations where payment is expected or required after the service has been provided and not where payment is required in advance.

Think Point

1   See the Canadian case of *Rabey* (1980). In *T* (1990), the defendant's confused state was categorised as sane automatism. The immediate cause, that is, rape, was not an 'ordinary' stress. The condition was regarded as having been externally caused.

QUESTION 21

Does English law recognise a general defence of necessity?

How to Answer this Question

In criminal law, the term 'necessity' is sometimes used in a very general sense, referring to a number of defences which excuse or justify otherwise criminal acts. For example, Lord Simon, in *DPP for Northern Ireland v Lynch* (1975), regarded duress by threats as a particular type of 'necessity' (see also *Martin* (1989); *Conway* (1989); *DPP v Bell* (1992)).

More commonly, 'necessity' is used in a narrower sense to describe those instances of compulsion where the defendant was compelled through force of circumstance to commit a criminal act. Used in this way, necessity is perceived as a species of compulsion comparable to but distinct from duress.

As this essay is concerned with the scope of the defence of necessity, it is proposed to adopt the broader approach and to examine each of the recognised defences of compulsion and the areas of doubt.

The principal issues are:

❖   recognised defences of necessity;
❖   duress by threats;
❖   duress of circumstances; and
❖   concealed defences of necessity.

The principal authorities are: *Howe* (1987); *Graham* (1982); *Willer* (1986); *Conway* (1988); *Dudley and Stephens* (1884); *Bourne* (1938); *Adams* (1957); *Gillick v West Norfolk and Wisbech AHA* (1985); *Bournewood Community and Mental Health NHS Trust* (1998); *Re A (Children) (Conjoined Twins: Medical Treatment) (No 1)* (2000).

Answer Structure

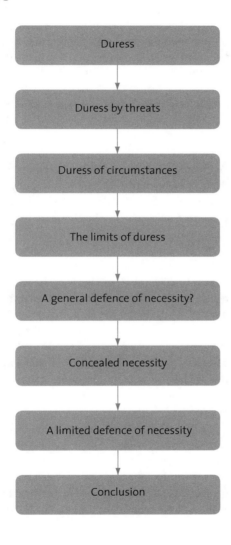

Duress

Duress by threats

Duress of circumstances

The limits of duress

A general defence of necessity?

Concealed necessity

A limited defence of necessity

Conclusion

ANSWER

DURESS

DURESS BY THREATS

It is well recognised that D may be excused if he committed a crime because he believed, on reasonable grounds, that if he did not do so, X would carry out a threat to kill or cause grievous bodily harm to D or another person for whose safety D would reasonably regard himself as responsible and a person of reasonable firmness sharing the characteristics of the defendant would also have given way to the threats (*Graham* (1982); *Howe* (1987); *Martin* (1989); *Wright* (2000); *Hasan* (2005)).

Where duress is raised, the burden of proof is on the prosecution (*Oyouncu* (2001); *Lyness* (2002)).[15]

DURESS OF CIRCUMSTANCES

In a series of decisions in the 1980s, the Court of Appeal recognised a related defence. In *Willer* (1986), D drove along a pavement to escape from a gang of youths who intended violence towards him and his passengers. The Court of Appeal held that the judge had been wrong in refusing to let the defence of compulsion go to the jury and treated the case as one of duress.

Clearly, the facts did not raise the defence of duress of the traditional type discussed above. The youths did not say to Willer, 'drive recklessly or else we will beat up you and your passengers'. The real nature of the defence was explained by the Court of Appeal two years later in the case of *Conway* (1988). This case also concerned reckless driving. D had been urged by his passenger to drive off quickly to escape two youths running towards the car. D feared, apparently with good reason, that the two youths intended a fatal attack upon his passenger. The Court of Appeal held that it was bound by *Willer* to the effect that duress was available as a defence. However, it was stated that the defence was properly termed 'duress of circumstances' – a species of necessity analogous to duress in the traditional sense.

In *Martin* (1989), D was charged and convicted of driving whilst disqualified. At his trial he put forward a plea of necessity, asserting that his wife had threatened to commit suicide if he refused to drive their son to work. The trial judge decided that necessity was not a defence to the crime charged. On appeal, the Court of Appeal held that the defence of duress of circumstances should have been left to the jury. The Court of Appeal held that the ingredients of this defence were equivalent to those of 'duress by threats'. That is, the

---

15   Terminology in this area is not used consistently. As explained in 'How to Answer this Question' it is important to map out the various defences which are sometimes (but not always!) described as defences of necessity.

defence is available if D has acted reasonably in order to avoid a threat of death or serious injury.

THE LIMITS OF DURESS

Both the defences of duress are limited in scope. They have no application in cases of murder or attempted murder (*Howe; Gotts* (1992)), nor do they apply where the defendant was faced with threats of less than serious physical harm (*DPP for Northern Ireland v Lynch* (1975); *Baker and Wilkins* (1997); *Hasan* (2005)).

In *Hasan* Lord Bingham observed in respect of certain features of duress, namely that it operates as a complete defence excusing what would otherwise be criminal conduct in relation to an innocent victim, that the onus is on the Crown to disprove duress and that it is a 'unique defence in that it is so much more likely than any other to depend on assertions which are peculiarly difficult for the prosecution to investigate or subsequently to disprove'. It was this latter feature which justified the defence being confined within strict limits.[16]

A GENERAL JUSTIFYING DEFENCE OF NECESSITY?

What is not clear is whether, in addition to the defences of duress, the English courts recognise a general justifying defence of necessity applying to situations where, faced with a choice of two evils, a person commits an offence to avoid the greater evil.

Consider the following incident reported at the inquest into the deaths resulting from the *Herald of Free Enterprise* disaster. Passengers attempting to escape found their route to safety obstructed by a petrified young man incapable of moving. One of the passengers pushed the man to his certain death. The passenger was not prosecuted for murder but, had he been, might he have been able to take advantage of a defence of compulsion? Duress (of either type) would not have been available to a charge of murder and one of the few authorities in the area would suggest that the courts might be reluctant to acknowledge a general defence of necessity.[17]

In *Dudley and Stephens* (1884), the defendants had been adrift in a small boat with very little food and water. After more than two weeks, they killed the cabin boy and fed on his body until they were rescued. They were convicted of murder. Lord Coleridge rejected the plea of necessity.

The *Herald of Free Enterprise* incident can be distinguished from the facts of *Dudley and Stephens*. First, whereas in *Dudley and Stephens* the appellants deliberately

---

16 Identifying the limits to the defences of duress is important as the question requires consideration of whether there is a general defence which operates outside those limits?

17 It is important to explain why duress would not be available in the circumstances.

chose who was to be the victim, this element of choice was absent in the *Herald* case. Secondly, the immobile passenger was endangering the lives of other passengers, whereas the cabin boy was not. Pushing the young man was the lesser of two evils and was, in the circumstances, justified. The passenger who pushed him out of the way was not morally blameworthy and it is arguable that the utilitarian objectives of punishment would not be served by denying a defence in such a case. Thus, there are strong arguments for allowing a defence in these circumstances and it is arguable that it should be for the jury to determine whether the use of deadly force was justified in the circumstances by balancing the harm caused against the evil averted.[18]

Canadian criminal law recognises the defence in these circumstances. In *Perka et al. v The Queen* (1984), the Supreme Court of Canada held that necessity is an excuse where in situations of emergency the harm inflicted by the defendant is less than the harm threatened.

On a number of occasions, however, the English courts have refused to recognise a general defence of necessity. For example, Lord Denning in *Southwark London Borough v Williams* (1971) expressed the view that hunger could never excuse theft and neither, in a civil context, could homelessness excuse trespass. He said:

> If homelessness were once admitted as a defence to trespass, no one's house could be safe. Necessity would open a door which no man could shut. It would not only be those in extreme need who would enter. There would be others who would imagine they were in need, or would invent a need, so as to gain entry.

And Edmund-Davies stated that:

> [T]he law regards with the deepest suspicion any remedies of self-help, and permits those remedies to be resorted to only in very special circumstances. The reason for such circumspection is clear – necessity can very easily become simply a mask for anarchy.

There are, on the other hand, a number of cases where the courts have, in effect, allowed a defence of necessity. One of the most celebrated is *Bourne* (1938), in which a doctor performed an abortion on a girl. The girl had become pregnant as a result of rape. He was charged with the offence of attempting to procure a miscarriage. MacNaghten J held that an attempt was not unlawful if it was done in good faith for the purpose of preserving

---

18   The difference in rationale underlying the defences of duress and that underlying a general defence of necessity is central to answering the question.

the life of the mother, and this might include protecting her from becoming a 'physical or mental wreck'. And in *Newton and Stungo* (1958), Ashworth J directed the jury that an attempt to procure a miscarriage would not be unlawful if it was done in good faith to preserve the life or health of the woman (Think Point (1)).

CONCEALED NECESSITY

There are, in addition, cases of 'concealed necessity' where the courts have in effect allowed a defence of compulsion by manipulating one or other of the constituent elements of criminal liability. In *Adams* (1957), for example, Devlin J held that a doctor is entitled to take measures to relieve the pain and suffering of a patient even if those measures might shorten life. Provided the steps taken are, from a clinical perspective, reasonable, they will not be regarded as a legal cause of death.

In *Gillick v West Norfolk and Wisbech AHA* (1985), the House of Lords held that a doctor who provides a girl under the age of 16 with contraception does not aid and abet unlawful sexual intercourse unless he intends to encourage the commission of the offence. If the doctor provides the advice and treatment because he believes it necessary for the physical, mental or emotional health of the girl, then he lacks the necessary intent. This implies a very restricted meaning of intention out of line with authority.

The conclusions reached by the courts in *Adams* and in *Gillick* could have been arrived at by openly developing the defence of necessity. This, it is submitted, would have been preferable to distorting orthodox principles of causation and intention.

A LIMITED DEFENCE OF NECESSITY

A defence of necessity was recognised in *F v West Berkshire HA* (1990). The House of Lords held that doctors were justified in carrying out a sterilisation operation on a woman who lacked the mental capacity to consent because there was a serious risk of her becoming pregnant, which would have had grave psychiatric consequences for her. Lord Goff regarded the situation as falling within a general defence which applied where action is taken as a matter of necessity to assist another person without his consent (see also *Bournewood Community and Mental Health NHS Trust* (1998)). Lord Goff's formulation of the defence is very limited; it would not have been available, for example, to the passengers on the *Herald of Free Enterprise*.

There is, however, some recognition of a broader based defence of necessity justifying intentional homicides in certain limited circumstances. In *Re A (Children) (Conjoined Twins: Medical Treatment) (No 1)* (2000), the issue facing the Court of Appeal was whether an operation to separate two conjoined twins should proceed where the inevitable result would be that one of the twins would die. If an operation were not performed, both twins were likely to die within months.

Both Brooke LJ and Ward LJ took the view that the operation was justified as the lesser of two evils. Walker LJ based his decision on the approach in *Gillick*, but was prepared to extend the defence of necessity to cover the case (Think Point (2)). Brooke LJ expressly stated that the separation operation was lawful by reason of the operation of the doctrine of necessity. In his view, there were three requirements for the application of the defence:

(a) the act was needed to avoid inevitable and irreparable evil;
(b) no more would be done than was reasonably necessary for the purpose to be achieved; and
(c) the evil inflicted was not disproportionate to the evil to be avoided.

He carefully considered the decision in *Dudley and Stephens* and identified two objections, based upon policy, to allowing necessity as a defence for the sailors. The first objection was: who is to be the judge of this sort of necessity? By what measure is the comparative value of lives to be measured? The second objection was that to permit such a defence would mark an absolute divorce of law from morality.

Neither of these objections applied to the present case. The weaker twin was 'self-designated for a very early death'; her life could not be extended beyond a short span and the moral issues of saving one life at the expense of another were finely balanced.

Ward LJ, concerned that the decision could become authority for a wider proposition than he intended, formulated the defence in narrower terms reflecting the uniqueness of the case:

(a) it must be impossible to preserve the life of X without bringing about the death of Y;
(b) Y by his or her very continued existence will inevitably bring about the death of X within a very short period of time; and
(c) X is capable of living an independent life but Y is incapable under any circumstances of viable independent existence.

CONCLUSION

While the judgment of Brooke LJ in *Re A (Children) (Conjoined Twins: Medical Treatment) (No 1)* goes some way to recognising a general defence of necessity, broader in scope and application than either of the two well-established forms of duress, Ward LJ's judgment suggests that the defence of necessity is extremely limited, as does that of Walker LJ. There is still some reluctance on the part of the English courts to recognise a justificatory defence based on a balancing of harms. Concern that a defence based upon principles of justification might be abused and that the law might lose much of its force if available continues to inhibit the recognition and development of a general defence of necessity (Think Point (3)).

Think Points

1   The 'defences' to abortion are now limited by s 5(2) of the Abortion Act 1967 to those conditions defined in s 1 of the Act.

2   Walker LJ concluded that the operation would not be unlawful as: Mary's death would not be the purpose of the operation, although it would be its inevitable consequence. The operation would give her, even in death, bodily integrity as a human being. She would die, not because she was intentionally killed, but because her own body cannot sustain her life.

3   In *Shayler* (2001), Lord Woolf CJ, having referred briefly to Brooke LJ's 'thorough-ranging review of the development of the law on necessity' in *Re A (Children) (Conjoined Twins: Medical Treatment) (No 1)* (2000), said:

> Nonetheless the distinction between duress of circumstances and necessity has, *correctly* (emphasis added), been by and large ignored or blurred by the courts. Apart from some of the medical cases like *West Berkshire* the law has tended to treat duress of circumstances and necessity as one and the same ([2001] All ER (D) 99 (Sep), para 55).

> In *Quayle* (2005) and in *Altham* (2006) the Court of Appeal held that a defence of medical necessity was not available to a charge of possession of a controlled drug of Class B contrary to s 5(2) the Misuse of Drugs Act 1971. The appellants had taken cannabis to relieve chronic pain. It was said that the role of defence 'cannot be to legitimise conduct contrary to the clear legislative policy and scheme' and the rejection of the defence was not contrary to Arts 3 and 8 of the ECHR.

Duress

QUESTION 22

Alfred was kidnapped by the global terrorist organisation, SMERSH. Ugly, an agent for SMERSH, contacted Barry, Alfred's brother, and informed him that unless he seriously injured Douglas, an agent for a rival organisation, Alfred would be killed. Ugly told Barry not to contact the police, and to show that the threat was serious he sent Barry a toe severed from Alfred's foot.

Barry knew that Douglas was very strong and would be difficult to deal with on his own, so he approached Colin and asked him to assist him in carrying out Ugly's order. Barry lied to Colin, telling him that SMERSH also held Colin's mother captive and had threatened to kill her. On the strength of this, Colin agreed to help Barry.

They waylaid Douglas on his way home one night. As a result of the attack, Douglas suffered severe injuries.

▶ Discuss the liability of Barry and Colin.

How would your answer differ if:

(a) Douglas had died as a result of the attack?; or
(b) Barry had himself been a member of SMERSH three years previously?

How to Answer this Question

This is a fairly intricate question raising a wide range of issues. There are a number of offences to discuss. As the facts are fairly 'open' with respect to a number of issues, a number of possible resolutions must be considered.

The principal issues are:

❖ the ingredients of the defence of duress and its application;
❖ duress of circumstances;
❖ duress and murder;
❖ duress and membership of a criminal organisation;
❖ the ingredients of the offence of kidnapping; and
❖ threats to kill.

The principal authorities include: *Graham* (1982); *Howe* (1987); *Bowen* (1996); *Sharp* (1987); *Shepherd* (1988).

Applying the Law

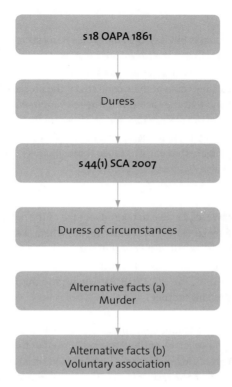

The main legal principles applied in this scenario are outlined here.

ANSWER

CAUSING GRIEVOUS BODILY HARM WITH INTENT

As the facts of the problem state that Douglas suffered severe injuries, it is proposed, first, to consider Barry and Colin's liability for causing grievous bodily harm with intent, contrary to s18 of the Offences Against the Person Act 1861. The maximum punishment for this offence is a term of imprisonment for life.

The facts of the problem imply the necessary intention to cause grievous bodily harm (*Belfon* (1976)) (Think Point (1)). It is not clear from the facts of the problem whether both parties assaulted Douglas. If they did, they may be charged as joint principals. They will be liable as joint principals (provided the relevant *mens rea* can be proved) if the injuries suffered were a result of the aggregate effect of their individual contributions to the attack, even if it could not be proved that their individual contribution would, on its own, have amounted to grievous bodily harm (*Macklin and Murphy's Case* (1838)).

If Colin did not attack Douglas but, say, held him while Barry struck him, he can be convicted as an accomplice (s 8 of the Accessories and Abettors Act 1861). If it could not be established whether both Colin and Douglas took part in the attack, or who had perpetrated the injuries, they could both be convicted if the prosecution could prove that they both participated and that they acted with the relevant *mens rea*. If it was unclear whether Colin perpetrated the offence or acted as an accomplice, he could be indicted for causing the injuries to Douglas (or, in the second part, with his murder), instead of alleging that he aided and abetted Barry to cause those injuries or kill Douglas (*Swindall and Osborne* (1846); see also *Giannetto* (1997)).[19]

DURESS

Barry and Colin may, however, be able to take advantage of the defence of duress. There are two forms of the defence. Duress by threats applies where D was compelled to act as he did because of threats of death or serious injury to himself or someone for whose safety D would reasonably regard himself as responsible (see *Ortiz* (1986); *Martin* (1989); *Wright* (2000); *Shayler* (2001); *Hasan* (2005)). Barry may raise this form of duress in respect of the threat to kill his brother.

Colin, however, cannot rely on duress by threats. He was not ordered to attack Douglas (*Cole* (1994)). He might, however, be entitled to avail himself of the second form of the defence known as 'duress of circumstances'. This applies in situations where objective dangers other than threats of the form 'do this or else ...' compel criminal action (see *DPP v Rogers* (1998); and *Pommell* (1995)) and is subject to the same limiting conditions as duress by threats (see *Graham*, above). Thus it is available if the accused committed an offence in order to avoid circumstances which he reasonably believed presented an imminent danger of death or serious injury to himself or another (*Martin* (1989); *Conway* (1989); *Abdul-Hussain and Others*).[20]

Once raised, the burden of negativing duress rests on the prosecution (*Gill* (1963); *Bone* (1968)).

In *Graham* (1982), Lord Lane CJ held that there were two questions to be considered by the jury:

(a) Was the defendant, or may he have been, impelled to act as he did because, as a result of what he reasonably believed X to have said or done, he had good cause to fear that if he did not so act, X would kill or cause serious injury?

---

19 Ensure that the positive ingredients of liability are considered fully before turning to possible defences.
20 Both forms of duress are raised by this question.

(b)   If so, would a sober person of reasonable firmness sharing the characteristics of the defendant have responded, or might he have responded, to whatever he reasonably believed X said or did by doing as the defendant did?[21]

With respect to the first of the questions above, it is not sufficient for the prosecution to prove that there was not in fact any threat or circumstance giving rise to duress; they must prove that the defendant did not believe, on reasonable grounds, in the existence of the threat or circumstance (*Safi* (2003); *Cairns* (1999)).

The decision in *Graham* was approved by the House of Lords in *Howe* (1987), and again in *Hasan* (2005) the House of Lords reaffirmed that the first question is an objective one. A mistaken belief by D that he is being threatened must be a reasonable one and he must have 'good reason' to fear death or serious injury. Although the House did not refer to the decisions in *Martin (David Paul)* (2000), it is clear that the decision of the Court of Appeal in that case is not to be relied upon.

In *Martin* (1989), it was held that the *Graham* principles applied to duress of circumstances (see also *Cairns* and *Safi*).

Thus, the jury should be directed to consider whether Colin's mistaken belief that SMERSH had kidnapped his mother was, in the circumstances, reasonable.

The second question is framed in objective terms, but allows for the attribution of certain characteristics of the defendant to the reasonable person. In *Bowen* (1996), it was said that, ordinarily, only the age and sex of the defendant will be relevant characteristics. Exceptional vulnerability, timidity or susceptibility to threats are not in themselves characteristics to be imputed to the reasonable person, but physical disability which inhibits self-protection or a recognised psychiatric illness (provided persons generally suffering from such a condition may be more susceptible to pressure and threats) are (see also *Antar* (2004); *Sewell* (2004); *Walker* (2003)).[22]

The jury should be directed to consider whether the threat of imminent death or serious injury was operating on the minds of the defendants so as to overbear their will at the time they attacked Douglas. In *Hasan* it was stated that if there was an opportunity that they might reasonably have taken to avoid committing the crime then the defence should fail. Lord Bingham expressed disapproval of the judgment in *Hudson and Taylor* (1971) and stated that it should be made clear to the jury that if the threat against the defendant or his family or a person for whom he reasonably feels responsible

---

21   Note carefully the combination of 'subjective' and 'objective' elements in the defence of duress.
22   The facts of the question do not disclose any characteristics of Barry and Colin which might be relevant to the second element of duress and so a general account of the relevant principles is sufficient.

is not such as he reasonably expects to follow immediately or almost immediately on his failure to comply, there may be little if any room for doubt that he could have avoided committing the crime charged either by going to the police or by some other means.

Thus, the jury should consider what the likely reaction of the reasonable person would have been to the threat, taking into account the relevant characteristics of the defendants, the circumstances in which they found themselves, the opportunities which existed to avoid it and the risks that they faced.

INTENTIONALLY ENCOURAGING OR ASSISTING AN OFFENCE

Barry may have committed an offence contrary to s 44(1) of the Serious Crime Act 2007. By urging Colin to participate in the attack on Douglas he did an act capable of encouraging the commission of an offence (s 44(1)(a)), he intended to encourage the doing of an act which would amount to the commission of that offence (s 47(3)(a)) and he believed that, were the act to be done, it would be done with the requisite fault (s 47(5)(a)(i)). Barry may have believed that Colin might be excused on the grounds of duress but the statute makes no provision for this and it probably has no impact on liability as a successful plea of duress does not negative fault (Think Point (2)).

DURESS OF CIRCUMSTANCES

Barry could not rely on duress by threats to the charge of intentionally encouraging an offence. He was not ordered to encourage Colin (*Cole* (1994)). He might, however, be entitled to avail himself of 'duress of circumstances' (see discussion above).

ALTERNATIVE FACTS

Part (a) An intention to do grievous bodily harm is sufficient *mens rea* for murder (*Moloney* (1985); *Cunningham* (1982)). According to the House of Lords in *Howe* (1987), duress is no defence to murder, whether as a principal or an accomplice. Consequently, had Douglas died, Barry and Colin would be guilty of murder.

Part (b) In *Hasan* the House of Lords, by a majority, held that if a person voluntarily becomes or remains associated with others engaged in criminal activity in a situation where he knows or ought reasonably to know that he may be the subject of compulsion by them or their associates, he cannot rely on the defence of duress to excuse any act which he is thereafter compelled to do by them (*Baker and Ward* (1999) disapproved).

However, in this case Barry left SMERSH three years previously. He had broken his links with the organisation and its members before the offence was contemplated and therefore the defence ought not to be denied on the grounds of voluntary association.

Think Points

1 In this problem, the facts clearly imply an intention to cause grievous bodily harm and so the lesser offence under s 20 is not discussed.

2 Duress is a defence independent of the *mens rea*. It was held in *Bourne* (1952) that a person might be convicted as an abettor, despite the fact that the 'principal' – a victim of duress – was acquitted. It is arguable, by analogy with that case, that a person may be guilty of encouraging an offence even though he is aware that the person incited would have a defence to liability if he carried out the offence.

Aim Higher

It is important to discuss the alternative possible bases of liability of Colin and Duncan as discussed in the opening paragraphs of the answer before considering the availability of the defence of duress.

QUESTION 23

With reference to the rationale of the defence and its parameters, consider critically the English courts' unwillingness to accept duress as a defence to murder.

How to Answer this Question

This question requires a critical evaluation of the rule that duress is no defence to murder by reference to the rationale of the defence and the limits on its availability.

The principal points to be discussed are:

❖   the rationale of the defence of duress;
❖   the distinction between excuses and justifications;
❖   the objective limiting criteria; and
❖   the arguments for and against allowing duress as a defence to murder.

The principal authorities are: *DPP for Northern Ireland v Lynch* (1975); *Howe* (1987); *Graham* (1982).

Answer Structure

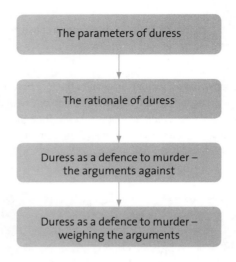

ANSWER

The defence of duress operates where the accused has committed the *actus reus* of an offence with the appropriate *mens rea* but was compelled to act as he did because of threats made by another. Where the defence applies, it is a complete defence.

WHAT ARE THE PARAMETERS OF THE DEFENCE?

The Court of Appeal in *Graham* (1982) held that there are two elements to the defence, the burden of proof being on the prosecution. The jury should consider whether:

(a) the accused was, or may have been, impelled to act as he did because, as a result of what he reasonably believed X had said or done, he had good reason to fear that, if he did not so act, X would kill him or cause him serious injury; and

(b) a sober person of reasonable firmness, sharing the characteristics of the accused, would have responded to whatever he reasonably believed X said or did by acting as the accused did (*Ortiz* (1986); *Martin* (1989); *Wright* (2000); *Shayler* (2001); *Hasan* (2005)).

WHAT IS THE RATIONALE OF THE DEFENCE?

Duress, when it applies, excuses the defendant's conduct; it does not justify the commission of the offence. The distinction is an important one. There is an element of approval or, indeed, encouragement in the case of justifications. Thus, for example, a person who uses force to prevent crime is justified in what he does. He has a 'right' to use force. On the other hand, where behaviour is excused it is neither approved of nor encouraged. The rationale for excuses is quite different from the rationale for justifications. Duress excuses the conduct of the defendant because he was effectively denied a 'fair opportunity' to choose between obeying or disobeying the law (Hart, HLA, *Punishment and Responsibility*, Oxford: OUP, 1968, p 22). Lord Morris in *DPP for Northern Ireland v Lynch* explained that the law would be 'censorious and inhumane' were it not to recognise the 'powerful and natural' instinct of self-preservation.

In addition, not only would it be unfair to punish the accused for failing to resist the threat if the person of reasonable steadfastness would have done likewise but, also, it is arguable that punishment would serve no rational purpose. If D acted as an ordinary person would have acted in the circumstances, then it folows that the threat of punishment would not influence his decision, or that of the ordinary person, to observe the law in a similar situation in the future.[23]

The defence is not available, however, either to murder (*Howe* (1987)) or attempted murder (*Gotts* (1992)).

Prior to *Howe*, a distinction was drawn between principals and accomplices to murder. Whilst the defence was not available to the actual perpetrator (*Abbott v R* (1977)), it was available to the accomplice (*DPP for Northern Ireland v Lynch*). The distinction drawn between accomplices and perpetrators of murder was criticised as illogical and unsatisfactory. Professors Smith and Hogan point out that it is not always true that the perpetrator is more blameworthy than an accomplice. There may be little or no moral difference between them. Professor Williams agreed and pointed out that there is no moral distinction between, for example, the individual who is forced to drive a bomber to a pub and the person who is forced to carry the bomb into the pub. When the matter came before the House of Lords in *Howe*, their Lordships agreed that there was no valid distinction between the perpetrator of murder and an accomplice to it and overruled the decision in *DPP for Northern Ireland v Lynch*, holding that duress was not a defence to murder, irrespective of the degree of participation.

WHY SHOULD THE DEFENCE NOT BE AVAILABLE TO A PERSON ACCUSED OF MURDER?

Lord Hailsham regarded it as neither good law nor good morals nor, perhaps more importantly, good policy to suggest that the ordinary man of reasonable fortitude is not capable of heroism. He added that the object of the criminal law was to protect ordinary lives and to set a standard of conduct which ordinary men and women are expected to observe if they are to avoid criminal liability. In his Lordship's opinion, it was not 'just or humane' to withdraw the protection of the criminal law from an innocent victim and in the name of 'a concession to human frailty' to offer protection to the 'coward'.

23 The first step in answering this question is defining the parameters of the defence and its rationale.

It is submitted, with respect, that this appears to require unrealistic heroism and overlooks the fact that an appropriate standard is set by the second limb of the defence. Only if the jury believe that a person of reasonable fortitude would have or might have yielded to the threat will the defence succeed. As Lord Morris pointed out in *DPP for Northern Ireland v Lynch*, standards of heroism should not be demanded – in the 'calm of the courtroom' – when they could not have been expected of the reasonably resolute person when the threat was made (Think Point (1)). Furthermore, the argument advanced by Lord Hailsham would apply equally to other crimes of violence, for example, wounding with intent – a crime for which his Lordship accepted the defence of duress would, in appropriate circumstances, be available.[24]

In *Abbott v R*, Lord Salmon stated that allowing the defence would invite the danger of providing a 'charter for terrorists, gang leaders and kidnappers'. D, if he were allowed to go free, might be approached again by the terrorist group and, having gained relevant experience and expertise, commit a further murder.

The Court of Appeal in *Gotts* gave a further reason for restricting the defence: Lord Lane thought that the defence was easy to raise and difficult for the prosecution to disprove beyond reasonable doubt.

Again, however, these arguments are arguments against the defence generally and do not justify the special treatment of murder and attempted murder. In any case, is there reason to suppose that the jury would be any less capable of recognising a bogus claim of duress than one in respect of, say, self-defence?

In *Howe*, Lord Hailsham advanced a further argument. He stated that where the accused faced the choice between the threat of death or serious injury and deliberately taking an innocent life, a reasonable man might reflect that one innocent life is at least as valuable as his own or that of his loved one. In such a case, if the man chooses to kill, he cannot claim that he is choosing the lesser of two evils.

There are two objections to this point.

First, and most importantly, the defence of duress is not based upon the idea that the defendant chose the lesser of two evils. The error lies in regarding duress as a justification. As explained above, duress is a defence because, if D was subject to immediate threats which were so powerful that the reasonable man would have acted in a similar fashion, the law would lack deterrent force and it would be unconscionably harsh to punish D.

---

24 Evaluation of the arguments advanced in the English courts is a necessary next step.

As Lord Edmund-Davies correctly observed in *DPP for Northern Ireland v Lynch*, to allow a defence is not necessarily to approve of the defendant's conduct, but simply to recognise that it is not deserving of punishment. Secondly, to give way to the threat might amount to choosing the lesser of two evils, where, for example, the threat is to kill a large number of people, say, the defendant's family, unless he kills one individual.[25]

Two additional arguments were put forward to justify the refusal of the defence in cases of murder.

Lords Bridge and Griffiths said that Parliament's failure to enact the recommendation of the Law Commission made 10 years previously was an indication that Parliament had rejected the proposal. However, as Professors Smith and Hogan have pointed out, the matter has not been put before Parliament for its consideration.

Lords Griffiths and Hailsham felt that the interests of justice would be served in hard cases, especially those involving secondary participation in murder under duress, by leaving issues relating to the culpability and punishment of those involved to administrative discretion. It would be 'inconceivable', according to Lord Griffiths, that, for example, a woman who was forced to act as a getaway driver for the principal offender would be prosecuted. In other cases, the Parole Board might be expected to weigh fairly the relative culpability of the defendant and, where appropriate, advise the Home Secretary that an early release would be justified.

However, leaving the fate of the defendant to discretionary executive action is unacceptable, as the outcome is by no means certain and neither early release nor the granting of a royal pardon would remove the stigma of a criminal conviction for what most people regard as the most heinous crime.

The decisions in *Howe* and *Gotts* mean that, when charged with murder or attempted murder, it is no excuse that, in the face of threats, the accused behaved with what a jury would consider to be reasonable fortitude. The law seems to require suicidal heroism (Think Point (2)).

Think Points

1   In *Horne* (1994), the Court of Appeal expressed approval of the trial judge's description of the reasonable person as an average member of the public; neither a hero nor a coward, but just an average person.

---

25   The difference between 'justifications' and 'excuses' is an important one.

2 A compromise solution would be for duress, in cases of murder, to operate as a partial defence, reducing liability, when successfully pleaded, to manslaughter. Recognising duress as a partial defence to murder would allow the gravity of the duress and its effect on the culpability of the accused to be taken into account at the sentencing stage, rather than to convict of murder and leave it to executive discretion to order early release.

This compromise was, however, rejected in *Howe* (1987). Lord Griffiths said that it would be 'anomalous' for the defence of duress to operate as a form of mitigation for the crime of murder alone, but this is precisely the effect of a successful plea of the analogous defence of provocation.

In *Hasan* (2005) Lord Bingham noted, in passing, that the Law Commission ('Criminal Law. Report on Defences of General Application' (Law Com No 83, Cm 556, 1977, paras 2.44–2.46)) recommended that the defence should be available to all offences, including murder and observed that 'the logic of this argument is irresistible'.

QUESTION 24

In what circumstances will a mistake relieve a defendant of criminal liability?

How to Answer this Question

The principal issues are:

- the effect of mistakes negativing *mens rea*;
- the inconsistent treatment of mistakes relevant to defences;
- mistakes induced by voluntary intoxication;
- mistakes resulting from 'a defect of reason caused by a disease of the mind'; and
- mistakes of law.

The principal authorities are: *DPP v Morgan* (1976); *Williams* (1983); *Howe* (1987); *DPP v Majewski* (1977); *M'Naghten* (1843).

Answer Structure

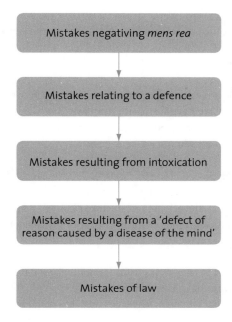

ANSWER

In discussing the effect of mistake upon criminal liability, it is important to appreciate that there are different types of mistake. A mistake may negative the *mens rea* for the offence charged. Alternatively, a mistake may relate to an issue of relevance to a particular defence. Thirdly, a mistake may be one of law. In addition, the causes of any mistake will have a bearing on its effect on liability. Mistakes caused by the voluntary consumption of alcohol or drugs, for example, are subject to special legal treatment.[26]

MISTAKE NEGATIVING *MENS REA*

For most crimes, the prosecution must prove not only that D performed the *actus reus* of the offence, but that he did so with the appropriate *mens rea*. For example, a person is guilty of murder if he kills a human being, intending to kill or cause grievous bodily harm to a human being (*Moloney* (1985)). Thus, if a person, whilst hunting, shoots and kills what he believes to be a bear, he cannot be convicted of murder if it transpires that he

---

26 As the introduction explains there are many different types of legally relevant mistake. This brief outline maps the structure of the answer.

has killed a human being. His mistake as to the nature of his target negatives the appropriate *mens rea*.[27]

In *DPP v Morgan* (1976), the House of Lords held that where the law requires intention, knowledge or recklessness with respect to the *actus reus*, a mistake, whether reasonable or not, which negatives the *mens rea* will excuse.

The case concerned the offence of rape, the *mens rea* for which at the time was an intention (or recklessness) to have sexual intercourse with a woman without her consent. The trial judge, however, had informed the jury that only a reasonable mistake as to whether the woman was consenting would excuse.

The House of Lords disapproved of the trial judge's direction and held that 'as a matter of inexorable logic', any mistake which negatives the *mens rea* requirement of the offence must result in an acquittal. Since an honest mistake clearly negatives the *mens rea*, the reasonableness or otherwise of that mistake is no more than evidence for or against the view that the mistake was made.

From the above, it should be clear that mistake is not really a 'defence'. The burden of proving *mens rea* lies with the prosecution (*Woolmington v DPP* (1935)). The accused does not even bear an evidential burden in respect of mistakes going to the *mens rea* (*DPP v Morgan*, per Lord Hailsham).

In *Kimber* (1983), D was charged with the (now repealed) offence of indecent assault contrary to s 14(1) of the Sexual Offences Act 1956. He alleged that he thought the woman was consenting. The Court of Appeal held that the *mens rea* for indecent assault is an intention to apply unlawful personal violence. As violence would not be unlawful if the woman consented to it, D should be acquitted if he mistakenly believed she was consenting. Observing the logic of the House of Lords judgment in *Morgan*, the Court of Appeal in *Kimber* held that the burden lay with the prosecution to prove that D did not believe the woman was consenting.

Where negligence is the basis of liability (see, for example, s 25 of the Firearms Act 1968), only a reasonable mistake will excuse. This follows because an unreasonable mistake is, by definition, a negligent mistake (see *Tolson* (1889)).

A crime of strict liability is one for which neither *mens rea* nor negligence need be proved with respect to one or more of the elements in the *actus reus*. It follows that no mistake

---

27 In this section of the answer the point is made that whether a mistake negatives the *mens rea* for an offence depends on the *mens rea* requirement of that particular offence.

with reference to that element will excuse, even if it is a reasonable mistake. For example, in *Cundy v Le Cocq* (1881), the defendant was convicted of selling intoxicating liquor to a drunken person contrary to s 13 of the Licensing Act 1872. The Divisional Court held, as a matter of construction, that the offence was one of strict liability and, therefore, it was unnecessary to prove that D knew the customer to be drunk. Logically, then, it was legally irrelevant that D mistakenly believed that the person served was sober, and this was true even though his mistake was a reasonable one.

Thus, whether a mistake will excuse depends on the *mens rea* requirement of the particular crime with which the accused has been charged. In *Ellis, Street and Smith* (1987), the defendants were charged with an offence contrary to s 170(2) of the Customs and Excise Management Act 1979, under which there are a number of offences of being knowingly concerned in the fraudulent evasion of a prohibition on the importation of various types of contraband, including controlled drugs and obscene material. The defendants imported drugs, mistakenly believing that they were importing prohibited obscene material. The Court of Appeal held that they had sufficient *mens rea* – knowledge that they were importing a prohibited good – despite their mistake as to the nature of the prohibited goods.

In *Forbes* (2001), the appellant had flown from Amsterdam to Heathrow airport where he was stopped by customs officers and found to be in possession of two video tapes, falsely labelled as 'Spartacus' and 'The Godfather Part 2'. On inspection by the officers, it was found that both tapes contained footage of indecent photographs of teenage boys under the age of 16. The appellant gave evidence to the effect that a man he met in a bar in Amsterdam had asked him to take the videos to London and to deliver them to another man in London. The appellant claimed that he was told when given the videos that they were recordings of two films called 'The Exorcist' and 'Kidz' and that he had assumed they were prohibited films. That belief, he explained, was the reason he had behaved suspiciously upon his arrival in the UK. In fact, neither 'The Exorcist' nor 'Kidz' is indecent or obscene and their importation is not prohibited.

The trial judge directed the jury that if an accused person knew that the activity he was engaged in was the evasion of a prohibition against importation and he knowingly took part in that operation, his conviction would be justified under s 170(2) even if he did not know precisely what kind of goods were being imported. In addition, he explained to the jury that unless they were sure that the defendant's explanation that he believed the films were 'The Exorcist' and 'Kidz' was untrue, they should acquit. The defendant appealed. He contended that the trial judge ought to have directed the jury that the prosecution were required to prove that the appellant knew that the videos contained indecent photographs of young persons under 16.

The House of Lords dismissed the appeal. It was not necessary to prove that the defendant knew that the goods were indecent photographs of children; indeed, it was not even necessary to prove that he knew they were photographs.

The appellant's defence was based on the decision in *Taaffe* (1984). In that case, the defendant was charged with having been knowingly concerned in the fraudulent evasion of the prohibition on the importation of cannabis resin. His defence was that he believed the goods to be currency, which he wrongly believed to be subject to a prohibition on importation. The judge ruled that those facts afforded no defence. His conviction was quashed. The House of Lords held that being 'knowingly concerned' involved not merely knowledge of a smuggling operation, but also knowledge that the substance in question was one of which importation was prohibited and thus he was to be judged on the facts as he believed them to be.

The judge in *Forbes* directed the jury in accordance with *Taaffe*, but the jury clearly did not believe the appellant's account. Having rejected his explanation, the only issue for the jury was whether the appellant was aware that the goods which he was transporting were subject to a prohibition. The prosecution were not required to prove that the accused knew what the goods were; it was sufficient to prove that he knew that they were prohibited goods.

MISTAKE RELATING TO A DEFENCE

There is another type of situation where the accused may have made a relevant mistake and that is where, if the facts had been as he believed them to be, he would have been entitled to a defence. For example, if D intentionally wounded another because he mistakenly believed that the other was about to attack him, will the mistake excuse?[28]

In *Albert v Lavin* (1981), the Divisional Court held that a mistaken belief in the necessity for self-defence will only excuse if it was reasonable. The court proceeded on the basis that the *mens rea* for assault was an intent to apply force and drew a distinction between the case where D's mistake relates to a defence element and the situation where the mistake relates to an element of the *actus reus*, as, for example, in *DPP v Morgan*.

The decision in *Albert v Lavin* was disapproved in *Williams* (1983). D was charged with an assault occasioning actual bodily harm to a man whom he mistakenly believed was unlawfully assaulting another man. The Court of Appeal held that the mental element necessary for an assault is the intent to apply unlawful force to the victim. Force used in defence of oneself or others or to prevent crime is not unlawful force (s 3 of the Criminal Law Act 1967). Therefore, as D acted to prevent what he mistakenly believed to be an unlawful attack on another, he did not intend to apply unlawful force.

In these circumstances, the reasonableness or unreasonableness of D's mistake is material only to the credibility of the assertion that he made the mistake. If the mistaken

---

28 In this section of the answer the point is made that the legal treatment of a mistake relevant to the availability of a defence depends on the precise formulation of the elements of the defence in question.

belief was, in fact, held, its unreasonableness is irrelevant. In *Beckford* (1988), the Privy Council endorsed this approach in a case where D, having mistakenly believed that his life was in danger, acted in self-defence. By treating unlawfulness as a definitional element of the *actus reus* to which the accused must have *mens rea*, the distinction drawn in *Albert v Lavin* disappears (Think Point (1)).

This approach has not been adopted with respect to all defences. In *Graham* (1982), the Court of Appeal held that the defence of duress is available only where D reasonably believed that he was being subjected to duress. It was stated that where D has committed the *actus reus* of the offence with the requisite *mens rea*, a mistake relating to a defence must be reasonable. The court did not treat duress as relating to the element of unlawfulness in the *actus reus*.

The approach in *Graham* was subsequently endorsed by the House of Lords in *Howe* (1987) and in *Hasan* (2005) and the Court of Appeal in *Martin* (1989) adopted the same approach to the defence of duress of circumstances. In *Baker and Wilkins* (1997) and *Rogers* (1998), it was held that duress of circumstances would be available if the defendant genuinely believed that commission of the offence was necessary to avoid death or serious injury. However, these decisions are out of line with the previous authorities and although the issue did not arise for decision in *Safi* (2003), the Court of Appeal proceeded on the basis that the defendant's belief that he faced death or serious injury had to be a reasonable one.

The courts were prepared, however, to allow the defence of provocation where the accused mistakenly believed, without reasonable grounds, that he was being provoked (*Letenock* (1917); *Luc Thiet Thuan* (1996)).

This lack of consistency is unacceptable and it is submitted that, as far as crimes of *mens rea* are concerned, the accused should always be judged on the basis of what he actually believed without a requirement of reasonableness. The effect of the rule in *Graham* is to convict D on the basis of negligence and not on the basis of subjective fault even where the offence may be one requiring *mens rea*.

MISTAKES AND INTOXICATION[29]

If a relevant mistake of the defendant was induced by alcohol or drugs voluntarily consumed, then the treatment of the mistake varies depending upon whether the mistake negatives the *mens rea* or relates to a defence element.

---

29 Here it is necessary to distinguish intoxicated mistakes which negative the *mens rea* of an offence from intoxicated mistakes relating to a defence.

(A) MISTAKE NEGATIVING THE *MENS REA*

In this case, although a mistake induced by voluntary intoxication will excuse, it will only do so for crimes of 'specific intent' (for example, murder) but not crimes of 'basic intent' (for example, manslaughter) (*DPP v Majewski* (1977)). In cases of involuntary intoxication, however, a lack of *mens rea* will excuse all crimes *(Kingston* (1994)) (Think Point (2)).

(B) MISTAKE RELATING TO A DEFENCE

In *O'Grady* (1987), the Court of Appeal held that in relation to self-defence, a mistake of fact which has been induced by voluntary intoxication cannot be relied upon by the defendant even for crimes of specific intent. The court held that the decision in *Williams* was of no application where the mistake was caused by voluntary intoxication. Although *obiter*, this decision was regarded as binding by the Court of Appeal in *O'Connor* (1991) (Think Point (3)).

In *Richardson and Irwin* (1999), the Court of Appeal took a different approach to a drunken mistake as to whether the victim consented to horseplay. The defendants, after a drinking session, went with a friend to a flat belonging to one of the defendants. As a prank, the defendants lifted their friend over the edge of the balcony. He fell about 10 or 12 ft and sustained serious injuries. The defendants were convicted of inflicting grievous bodily harm contrary to s 20 of the Offences Against the Person Act 1861. The defendants claimed that their friend had consented to the horseplay and that his fall was an accident. The Court of Appeal allowed their appeal on the grounds that the trial judge had not directed the jury to take account of the evidence that the defendants' minds were affected by alcohol when considering whether they believed their friend was consenting. This is a very strange decision. The offence under s 20 is an offence of basic intent. The decision means that an intoxicated mistake relieves the prosecution of having to prove foresight that some harm might result, but not that the defendant believed that the victim consented.

In the case of those defences for which only reasonable mistakes will excuse – for example, duress – an intoxicated mistake will not excuse.

There is, however, some authority for the proposition that, where a statute provides that a belief shall afford a defence to a particular offence, a mistake induced by intoxication may be considered. This is a matter of statutory construction. Thus, for example, in *Jaggard v Dickinson* (1981), the court held that the defendant could rely on the 'lawful excuse' defence in s 5(2) of the Criminal Damage Act 1971 even though she had made a drunken mistake. Section 5(3) of the statute provides that 'it is immaterial whether a belief is justified or not if it is honestly held'. The court was of the opinion that, as a matter of statutory construction, no exception could be made to this rule even where the mistake was caused by voluntary intoxication.

MISTAKES RESULTING FROM A 'DEFECT OF REASON CAUSED BY DISEASE OF THE MIND'

If the defendant's mistake is a result of a 'defect of reason due to disease of the mind', and the mistake is such that the defendant either did not know the 'nature and quality' of his act or did not know that 'he was doing wrong', then, in legal terms, the defendant is not guilty by reason of insanity and entitled only to a qualified acquittal (*M'Naghten Rules* (1843)).

MISTAKES OF LAW

The general rule is that it is no excuse that the defendant mistakenly believed his conduct to be lawful (see, for example, *Esop* (1836); *Attorney General's Reference (No 1 of 1995)* (1996); *Hipperson v DPP* (1996); *Lee* (2000)).

However, there are exceptions. Firstly, where because of a mistake as to law the defendant lacks the *mens rea* for the offence charged, then, of course, the mistake excuses. In *Smith* (1974), for example, D was not guilty of intentionally or recklessly damaging property belonging to another as he mistakenly believed that as a matter of law the property which he damaged belonged to him. See also s 2(1)(a) of the Theft Act 1968, which provides that an appropriation of property belonging to another is not dishonest and hence not theft if the defendant does so in the mistaken belief that he has in law the right to deprive the owner of it.

Secondly, where D makes a mistake of law as a result of a defect of reason caused by a disease of the mind, then D is not guilty by reason of insanity (*Windle* (1952)).

Think Points

1   Whilst a mistake as to the necessity for force is legally relevant, a mistake as to what constitutes reasonable force in the circumstances is not. A person may use such force as is objectively reasonable in the circumstances as he subjectively believes them to be (*Owino* (1996)).

2   In *McKnight* (2000), the Court of Appeal held that the test was whether drunkenness had rendered the defendant incapable of forming the necessary specific intent. This is inconsistent with authority (see, for example, *Pordage* (1975)). The issue is not whether D was capable of forming the intent, but whether the necessary *mens rea* was in fact formed.

3   This part of the decision of the Court of Appeal in *O'Connor* (1991) was also *obiter dicta*; see also *Hatton* (2005). This rule has now been codified in s 76 of the Criminal Justice and Immigration Act 2008.

QUESTION 25

Jeremy is a well-known practical joker. One day, he went into the office of a colleague, Robin, and pointed a water pistol at him. He was about to fire it in Robin's face when Robin, irritated by Jeremy's constant joking, threw an ashtray at him which hit Jeremy in the face, resulting in the loss of an eye. The water pistol was found to contain ammonia and Jeremy has admitted that he intended to injure Robin by spraying it in his face.

▶ Discuss the criminal liability of Jeremy and Robin.   *Jeremy*

How to Answer this Question

This question concerns the availability of self-defence where the defendant is unaware of the justifying circumstances. There is an almost total lack of authority as far as this issue is concerned.   *Robin x sure·*

The principal issues are:

❖ the *Dadson* (1850) principle;
❖ liability for attempts;
❖ the ingredients of liability for burglary under s 9 of the Theft Act 1968; and
❖ possession of an offensive weapon – the meaning of 'public place'.

Applying the Law

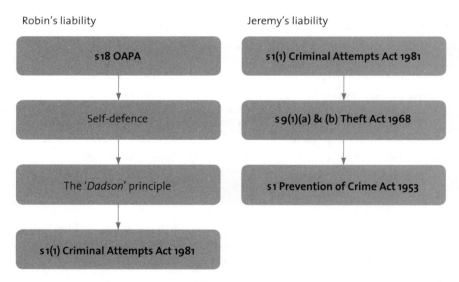

This two part diagram shows the main legislation and principles to apply in assessing the liability of Robin and Jeremy.

ANSWER

ROBIN

S18 deel

CAUSING GRIEVOUS BODILY HARM WITH INTENT

As the facts of the problem state that Jeremy lost an eye, it is proposed to consider Robin's liability for causing grievous bodily harm with intent, contrary to s 18 of the Offences Against the Person Act 1861, and maliciously inflicting grievous bodily harm, contrary to s 20 of the same Act. 'Grievous bodily harm' means 'serious bodily harm' (*DPP v Smith* (1961); *Saunders* (1985)) (Think Point (1)).

To establish liability under s 18, the more serious offence, the prosecution is required to prove that Robin intended to cause serious harm. Recklessness will not suffice (*Belfon* (1976)).

If it was Robin's aim or purpose to cause serious harm, then he intended grievous bodily harm. If Robin did not desire to cause serious harm but he knew that serious harm was a virtually certain result of his actions, then the jury may find that he intended it (*Woollin* (1998); *Matthews and Alleyne* (2003)).

If intention cannot be proved, then liability under s 20 should be considered.

The *mens rea* requirement for the offence under s 20 is recklessness with respect to some harm. This means that it must be proved that when he threw the ashtray, Robin was aware that Jeremy might suffer some harm, albeit not serious harm (*Savage; Parmenter* (1991)).

The maximum penalty for the offence under s 20 is a term of imprisonment not exceeding five years and, under s 18, life imprisonment.[30]

Now, it would appear that, had he acted in response to Jeremy's intended attack upon him, Robin would have been able to avail himself of the defence of self-defence. Robin, however, was not aware of the facts which would have justified his conduct and, thus, it is necessary to consider whether a defence is available where the defendant is unaware of the facts upon which a plea may be founded.[31]

In the nineteenth-century case of *Dadson* (1850), the defendant was a constable whose duty was to guard a copse from which wood had been stolen. V emerged from the copse

---

30 As the intent with which Robin acted is not disclosed the requirements of **s18** and **s20** are explained.
31 Identifying the issue raised by a problem is a useful step in answering a question, particularly one where the law is uncertain.

carrying stolen wood. Dadson shouted at him to stop. V refused to do so and started to run away. Dadson shot him in the leg.

Dadson was convicted of unlawful wounding with intent to cause grievous bodily harm. It was not unlawful to wound an escaping felon, but stealing wood was not in itself a felony, unless the thief had at least two previous convictions. In fact, V had numerous previous convictions for theft. Dadson, however, did not know of the circumstances making V a felon and it was held that, as a consequence, he could not take advantage of the defence.

The decision has been criticised. Professor Williams argued that Dadson did not unlawfully wound V, as the element of unlawfulness which appears in the definition of most offences against the person is a component of the *actus reus* and, therefore, the lawfulness or otherwise of the defendant's behaviour may be assessed without reference to the defendant's beliefs or knowledge. Thus, if a person assaults or wounds or, indeed, kills another in unknown circumstances of justification, the assault or wounding or killing is lawful (Williams, G, *Criminal Law: The General Part*, 1961, p 22).

Professor Smith, on the other hand, took the view that the word 'unlawfully' in the definition of a crime means simply 'in the absence of a recognised defence', but does not imply anything about the requirements of any particular defence. It is a matter of policy whether any given defence requires knowledge of the relevant circumstances and, in *Dadson*, Professor Smith argued, the court came to the 'perfectly reasonable conclusion' that the particular defence in that case should not be available unless the defendant was aware of the circumstances justifying his actions (Smith, JC, *Justification and Excuse in the Criminal Law*, London: Stevens, 1989, p 31). Should self-defence be subject to the *Dadson* principle?

Professor Smith believes that it should and argued that the existing law as expressed in *Williams* (1983) and *Beckford* (1988) supports this conclusion.

Those cases dealt with the situation where D mistakenly believed that he was justified in using force and, therefore, they were not directly concerned with the matter currently under discussion. However, in both cases, the court expressed the opinion that a person may use such defensive force as is reasonable in the circumstances as he believes them to be. It would appear to follow that if the defendant does not believe it is necessary to use defensive force – if he does not intend to defend himself – then the defence is not available to him. If this analysis is correct, Robin will not be able to take advantage of self-defence.

Professor Williams disagreed with such a conclusion. He drew a distinction between 'justifications' and 'excuses'. There is an element of approval or indeed encouragement in the case of the former. For example, a person who uses force to prevent crime is justified in what he does. An 'excuse', on the other hand, does not exist to promote the conduct in question. Duress, for example, excuses. It does not justify (Williams, G, *Criminal Law: The General Part*, 1961, p 25).

In Professor Williams' view, as justifications are concerned with the promotion of particular consequences, they should be available even if the defendant is unaware of the justifying circumstances.

Self-defence is a justification. Thus, if Professor Williams' analysis is correct and, provided the force used was, in the circumstances, reasonable, Robin will escape liability for the injuries inflicted on Jeremy (Think Point (2)).[32]

ATTEMPT

However, even if self-defence is available, Robin might be guilty of an attempt to cause grievous bodily harm contrary to s 1(1) of the Criminal Attempts Act 1981. This is because s 1(2) of the Act provides that a person can be convicted of an attempt to commit an offence even though the facts are such that the offence is impossible to commit. This is reinforced by s 1(3), which provides that the question whether the defendant has the necessary intent for an attempt is to be answered by reference to the facts as he believed them to be (see *Shivpuri* (1987)).

For attempt, the prosecution must prove an intention on the part of the accused as to the consequence defined in the *actus reus*. Thus, for an attempt to commit the offence under s 18, it must be proved that the defendant intended grievous bodily harm (*Millard and Vernon* (1987)). Intention in this context bears the same meaning as discussed above (*Walker and Hayles* (1990)).

If Robin intended to cause harm but not serious harm, then he may be convicted of an attempt to commit the offence under s 47 of the Offences Against the Person Act 1861.

Professor Smith argues that Professor Williams' analysis leads to an absurd conclusion, that is, that the defendant was justified in causing grievous bodily harm, but may be convicted of an attempt unlawfully to cause grievous bodily harm! See Smith, JC, *Justification and Excuse in the Criminal Law*, London: Stevens, 1989, p 43.

It is submitted that Professor Smith's analysis is preferable to that of Professor Williams and that, as it is sound in principle to limit defences justifying or excusing the use of force to those occasions where the defendant is aware of the justifying or excusing

---

32 Where there is a lack of authority or the authorities are uncertain arguments in favour of one or more approach to the problematic issue should be explained.

circumstances, the defence of self-defence ought not to be available to Robin in respect of either the substantive offence of causing grievous bodily harm with intent or an attempt.

JEREMY'S LIABILITY

ATTEMPT

Jeremy may be convicted of an attempt to cause grievous bodily harm contrary to s 1(1) of the Criminal Attempts Act 1981 (Think Point (3)).

The facts of the problem indicate that he had the requisite intent. Thus, the only issue is whether he has done 'an act which is more than merely preparatory' to the commission of the offence (s 1(1)).

Provided there is sufficient evidence of acts capable in law of amounting to an attempt, the question whether those acts are more than mere preparation is a question to be left to the jury (s 4(3)).

It is submitted that in this case, there is clear evidence of an attempt. In *Jones* (1990), the defendant jumped into P's car and pointed a loaded sawn-off shotgun at his face. P managed to grab hold of the gun and throw it out of the window. Although the safety catch of the gun was on, and D would have had to put his finger on the trigger and pull it, the Court of Appeal upheld his conviction for attempted murder.

BURGLARY

Jeremy may be guilty of an offence contrary to s 9(1)(a) of the Theft Act 1968.

This provides that a person is guilty of burglary if he enters a building, or part of a building, as a trespasser, intending to commit therein one of a number of offences including the infliction of grievous bodily harm (s 9(2)).

A person enters as a trespasser if he enters without the occupier's consent.

The facts of the problem do not state whether Jeremy had permission to enter Robin's office. However, even if he did, presumably the permission granted was, expressly or impliedly, limited to particular (lawful) purposes. As Jeremy entered the office intending to cause grievous bodily harm, he entered in excess of that permission and thus entered as a trespasser (*Jones and Smith* (1976)). As he was aware of the facts that made his entry trespassory, he is guilty of burglary (*Collins* (1973)).

He also committed burglary contrary to s 9(1)(b). This section provides that a person is guilty if, having entered a building or part of a building as a trespasser, he attempts to inflict grievous bodily harm on any person therein.

For this form of burglary the prosecution have to prove, in addition to the elements of attempt (discussed above), that D entered as a trespasser (as above) and that he knew, or at least was reckless with respect to, the facts that made his entry trespassory (*Collins*).

As he intended to cause grievous bodily harm when he entered the office, the above criteria are satisfied.

Jeremy may be convicted and sentenced to a term of imprisonment not exceeding 10 years for each offence of burglary (s 9(3)(b)).[33]

POSSESSION OF AN OFFENSIVE WEAPON

Section 1 of the Prevention of Crime Act 1953 provides that any person who has with him in a public place any offensive weapon is guilty of an offence punishable with up to two years' imprisonment. 'Offensive weapon' is defined to include things intended to cause injury and thus the water pistol would qualify (s 1(4), as amended by s 40(2) and Sched 2 to the Public Order Act 1986).

The only unclear issue is whether Jeremy had the offensive weapon with him in a public place.

By s 1(4), this includes any highway and any premises to which the public have access.

The facts do not state whether or not the public have access to this workplace but, even if it is not a public place, the jury are entitled to draw the inference, if the evidence permits, that Jeremy brought the ammonia-filled water pistol to work and that he necessarily had it with him on the public highway (*Mehmed* (1963)).

Think Points

1   The Code for Crown Prosecutors, Offences Against the Person, June 1994, para 2.15, advises prosecutors to treat any injury 'resulting in permanent disability or permanent loss of sensory function' as grievous bodily harm.

2   The question of whether the force used was, in the circumstances, reasonable is a matter for the jury (*Attorney General's Reference for Northern Ireland (No 1 of 1975)* (1977)).

3   The Code for Crown Prosecutors (see point 1) additionally advises prosecutors to treat 'permanent, visible disfigurement' as grievous bodily harm.

---

33 Deal with each instance of burglary separately and chronologically.

QUESTION 26

Bodie and Doyle, two armed plain clothes policemen, saw someone they believed to be Budgie, a dangerous escaped criminal, driving through the town. In fact, the occupant of the car was Hilton, who bore a remarkable resemblance to Budgie.

Bodie and Doyle stopped the car and approached it.

Hilton made to switch off his car radio. Doyle, mistakenly believing that he might be reaching for a weapon, fired at the car. He aimed to miss Hilton but the bullet ricocheted and struck Hilton in arm, wounding him.

Hilton, fearing for his life, and believing that Bodie and Doyle were criminals intent on attacking him, drove his car at them. The car struck Doyle, who was seriously injured. The car collided with a lamp post and came to a stop.

Bodie ran to the car and pulled Hilton out. Hilton, fearing attack, punched Bodie. Bodie, still believing him to be Budgie, hit Hilton over the head with his gun, intending to incapacitate him. Hilton suffered serious injuries.

▶ Discuss the liability of the parties.

Would your answer differ had Hilton been aware that he resembled Budgie and had realised, as he drove at them, that Bodie and Doyle were plain clothes policemen who had mistakenly thought him to be the dangerous criminal?

[Ignore issues of accessorial liability and liability for offences of criminal damage.]

How to Answer this Question

This is a fairly complex question involving issues relating to the lawful use of defensive force. A wide variety of offences under the Offences Against the Person Act 1861 provides the context for the defence. The bases of liability for these offences must be discussed before tackling the defence issues.

The principal issues are:

❖   ss 47, 20, 18 and 38 of the Offences Against the Person Act 1861; s 89 of the Police Act 1996;
❖   force used in self-defence and in effecting a lawful arrest;
❖   the effect of a mistake upon the defences; and
❖   force used against an attack known in the circumstances to be lawful.

Applying the Law

The liability of Bodie and Doyle	Hilton's liability
s18/s20 OAPA 1861	Assault with intent to resist arrest – s38 OAPA 1861
↓	↓
s3 CLA 1967 – prevention of crime	s18 OAPA 1861
↓	↓
Reasonable force – s76 CJIA 2008	Assault on pc in execution of duty – s89 Police Act 1996

This diagram shows the main legislation and principles to apply in assessing the liability of Bodie and Doyle first, then Hilton.

ANSWER

BODIE AND DOYLE

Doyle may be charged with the offence contrary to s 20 of the Offences Against the Person Act 1861 in respect of the bullet wound sustained by Hilton (*Moriarty v Brookes* (1834)). For this offence, it must be shown that the defendant was reckless with respect to some harm resulting. Thus, the prosecution would be required to prove that, although aiming to miss, Doyle foresaw a risk that some harm might result (*Savage; Parmenter* (1991).

However, a person is only liable for an offence under s 20 if he '*unlawfully* . . . wounds'. Similarly, although Bodie intentionally caused Hilton grievous bodily harm, his liability for an offence contrary to s 18 of the 1861 Act will depend upon whether there he intended *unlawfully* to cause grievous bodily harm.

By virtue of s 24 of the Police and Criminal Evidence Act 1984, a police constable may arrest without warrant anyone whom he, with reasonable cause, suspects to have committed, be in the act of committing or be about to commit an arrestable offence. In addition, by virtue of s 3 of the Criminal Law Act 1967, 'a person may use such force as is reasonable in the circumstances in the prevention of crime, or in effecting the lawful arrest of offenders or suspected offenders or of persons unlawfully at large'. Similarly, the common law defence of 'private defence' allows the use of reasonable force in defence of one's person or that of another (Think Point (1)).

Whether the force used was reasonable is an objective question but if, as in this case, the defendant mistakenly believed that the circumstances were such that force was required to effect arrest, or to defend against an attack – present or imminent – the jury must decide whether the force used was reasonable by reference to the circumstances as the defendant believed them to be (*Williams* (1983); *Beckford* (1988); *Owino* (1996); **Criminal Justice and Immigration Act 2008 s 76(3)–(8)**).

Force may be used, as in this case, to ward off an attack which the defendant anticipated. If the defendant genuinely but mistakenly believed he was in imminent danger, the mistake need not be a reasonable one (*Beckford*).

If the jury believed that, in the heat of the moment, Doyle and Bodie did what they honestly believed to be necessary, then that would be 'potent evidence' (but no more than that) that the force used was reasonable (*Palmer* (1971); *Attorney General's Reference for Northern Ireland (No 1 of 1975)* (1977); s 76(7)(b)). In addition, although there is no duty to retreat, a failure to do so is a factor that might be taken into account when assessing the reasonableness of the defendant's actions. It is generally accepted, however, that police officers attempting to effect an arrest may advance, using such defensive measures as are reasonable, as they do so (*McInnes* (1971); *Finch and Jardine* (1983)).[34]

HILTON

There are a number of offences with which Hilton may be charged:

(a) assault with intent to resist arrest contrary to s 38 of the 1861 Act;
(b) causing grievous bodily harm with intent to resist arrest contrary to s 18 of the 1861 Act.
(c) assault on a police constable in the execution of his duty contrary to s 89 of the Police Act 1996;

(It shall be assumed that the attempted arrest was lawful, that is, that Bodie and Doyle had reasonable grounds for suspicion.)

As far as s 38 and s 18 of the OAPA 1861 are concerned, it must be shown that there was an intent to resist arrest and, as Hilton did not know they were police officers he should, on that basis alone, be acquitted (see *Brightling* (1991)).

A police officer making a lawful arrest is acting in the execution of his duty for the purposes of s 89 (*Waterfield* (1964)). According to *Forbes and Webb* (1865), the only *mens rea* required for this offence is that required for a common assault. As explained above,

---

34 It should be noted that the question whether force used was reasonable is one for the jury and to explain, by reference to the facts of the question, the factors which may be taken into account.

however, a defendant may rely upon a mistaken belief in circumstances which, if true, would render the use of force lawful (*Gladstone Williams* (1987)).

This 'defence' applies to all offences and thus, provided the use of force was reasonable, Hilton should, despite his mistake, be acquitted of all three offences.

ALTERNATIVE FACTS

Although Hilton knew that the men were police officers who suspected he was a dangerous criminal, he may have mistakenly believed that the arrest was unlawful. This mistake, however, being a mistake of law, would not excuse him (*Bentley* (1850); *Lee* (2000); *Hewitt v DPP* (2002)) (Think Point (2)).

Is he entitled, however, to take advantage of self-defence even though he knows the officers are acting in circumstances that make their use of force lawful? May one use force lawfully against a lawful attack?[35]

(Clearly, Hilton cannot rely on s 3 of the Criminal Law Act 1967 – force used 'in the prevention of crime' – if he knows that Bodie and Doyle are acting lawfully.)

In *Browne* (1973), the Court of Appeal in Northern Ireland stated, *obiter*, that when an officer is using lawful force in effecting the arrest of a suspect, self-defence against him is not lawful. It was said that this was the case even if, as in the present problem, according to the true facts, the police were acting without justification.

In *Fennell* (1971), on the other hand, Lord Widgery implied that where a person honestly believes that he, or another person, is in imminent danger of injury from an arresting officer, he may use reasonable force in defence. This statement was *obiter*. It is also ambiguous – it is not clear whether it was meant to apply to the situation where the defendant, as in Hilton's case, knows of the circumstances making the police officer's behaviour lawful.

Professor Smith argued that the wide *dicta* in *Browne* should not be followed. He pointed out that although an innocent person must submit to arrest, it is unreasonable to expect him to do nothing in the face of a serious attack. Thus, he suggested that an otherwise innocent person should not be convicted of an offence for taking reasonable defensive action, even though he knows that the police officer he assaults or injures has reasonable grounds for suspicion and is, therefore, acting lawfully (Smith, JC, *Justification and Excuse in the Criminal Law*, London: Stevens, 1989, p 26).

It is submitted that this view is preferable to that expressed in *Browne* and that Hilton should be acquitted provided the force he used was, in the opinion of the jury, reasonable in the circumstances.

....

35 A clear exposition of the issue under consideration provides focus.

Think Points

1 In *Finch and Jardine* (1983), the trial judge agreed with the submission of the prosecution that force that is reasonable in self-defence may be excessive if done in order to effect an arrest. Thus, Bodie and Doyle might be advised to rely on self-defence.

2 In *Lee* (2000), it was said that a mistaken belief that the victim was not a police officer might afford a defence in relation to assault with intent to resist arrest or assaulting an officer in the execution of his duty; in *McKoy* (2002), it was held that the trial judge had erred when instructing the jury that a defendant who mistakenly believed he was being arrested was not entitled to use force to free himself.

Modes of Participation, Inchoate Offences and Vicarious Liability

4

INTRODUCTION

In this chapter will be found questions where the principal issues relate to one or more of the following topics: accessorial liability; attempts; conspiracy; incitement; and vicarious liability. These topics also arise as subsidiary matters in a number of other questions in other chapters.

Checklist ✔

The following issues are covered in this chapter:

- modes of participation: liability as an accomplice; **s 8** of the **Accessories and Abettors Act 1861**; aiding, abetting, counselling, procuring; joint unlawful enterprises; the *mens rea* requirement of accessorial liability; the offence of aiding and abetting a suicide contrary to **s 2** of the **Suicide Act 1961**;

- attempts: the **Criminal Attempts Act 1981**; the rationale for the punishment of attempts; the *actus reus* of attempt; the *mens rea* for attempts; attempting the impossible;

- conspiracy: statutory conspiracy – the **Criminal Law Act 1977**; the *mens rea* for conspiracy; exemptions from liability for conspiracy; common law conspiracy to defraud; conspiring to do the impossible

- vicarious liability: the 'delegation' principle and the principle of 'extensive construction'; corporate liability; the liability of unincorporated associations.

- offences of 'encouraging or assisting' – the **Serious Crime Act 2007**.

QUESTION 27

Maxwell, walking Sweet home, pushed her to the ground. He told her that he intended to have sexual intercourse with her and warned her that he would hurt her severely if she resisted. He told her to undress. Sweet was extremely frightened and so did as she was told. Maxwell was about to have sexual intercourse with Sweet when suddenly he felt extremely guilty. He decided not to have sexual intercourse with her. He dressed himself and went home.

▶ Discuss the criminal liability of Maxwell.

How to Answer this Question
This question involves Maxwell's liability for offences of attempted rape and attempted assault by sexual penetration. The principal issue concerns whether or not his acts were 'more than merely preparatory' to the commission of the full offence. In addition, his liability for assault and indecent assault is discussed.

The principal authorities are: *Becerra and Cooper* (1975); *Whitefield* (1984); *Attorney General's Reference (No 1 of 1992)* (1993); *Haughton v Smith* (1975).

Answer Structure

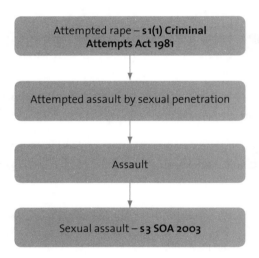

ANSWER

ATTEMPTED RAPE
Maxwell may be guilty of attempted rape contrary to s1(1) of the Criminal Attempts Act 1981. The subsection provides that a person is guilty of an attempt if, with intent to commit an indictable offence, he does an act which is more than merely preparatory to the commission of that offence.

Rape is an offence contrary to s1(1) of the Sexual Offences Act 2003, which provides that a person (A) is guilty of rape if: (a) he intentionally penetrates the vagina, anus or mouth of another person (B) with his penis; (b) B does not consent to the penetration; and (c) A does not reasonably believe that B consents.

Section 74 provides that a person consents if he 'agrees by choice, and has the freedom and capacity to make that choice'.[1]

Had Maxwell had sexual intercourse with Sweet, he would have been guilty of rape. Sweet did not freely agree to sexual intercourse and Maxwell acted with the appropriate *mens rea* for attempted rape – he intended to have sexual intercourse with Sweet knowing that she did not consent (Think Point (1)). However, as far as the *actus reus* of attempted rape is concerned, it is not clear that his acts were more than merely preparatory.

In *Gullefer* (1990), it was held that if there is evidence on which a jury could reasonably arrive at the conclusion that the defendant had done acts which were more than merely preparatory and had 'embarked on the crime proper', then it is for the jury to decide whether the defendant did in fact go beyond mere preparation. Lord Lane added that there may be evidence of an attempt even though the defendant had not performed the last act prior to the commission of the substantive offence (see also *Jones* (1990)).

Following this approach, the Court of Appeal in *Attorney General's Reference (No 1 of 1992)* (1993) held that in the case of attempted rape, it is not necessary to prove that the defendant had gone as far as to attempt physical penetration of the vagina. It is sufficient if there is evidence of acts which a jury could properly regard as more than merely preparatory to the commission of the offence. In that case, the evidence that the defendant had dragged the woman up some steps, lowered his trousers, got on top of her and interfered with her private parts, together with his statements to the police and the evidence that she was partly undressed and in a state of distress, was thought to be sufficient to justify leaving the question to the jury. It was a matter then for the jury to decide whether they were sure that those acts were more than merely preparatory.

The facts of Maxwell's case are, of course, different from the facts involved in the *Attorney General's Reference*. There is no suggestion, for example, that Maxwell touched Sweet after pushing her to the ground. Might there nonetheless be sufficient evidence of an attempt to rape to leave the matter to the jury? Unfortunately, the expression 'embarking on the crime proper' is not sufficiently clear to allow one to answer that question with certainty (Think Point (2)).[2]

....

1   When answering questions concerning liability under **s1(1)** of the **Criminal Attempts Act 1981**, start by explaining the elements of the substantive offence that D may have attempted.

2   Indicate where the application of the law to the facts is not straightforward.

Provided that there is sufficient evidence and the jury conclude that Maxwell's acts were more than merely preparatory, he may be convicted of attempted rape – the fact that Maxwell changed his mind about raping Sweet has no effect upon his liability. Withdrawal is not possible after the stage where a more than merely preparatory act has been performed (*Taylor* (1859); *Lankford* (1959); *Haughton v Smith* (1975)). The fact that his decision to abandon the attempt was voluntary may, however, mitigate the penalty imposed.

The maximum penalty for attempted rape is a term of imprisonment for life (s 4(1) of the Criminal Attempts Act 1981; s 1(4) of the Sexual Offences Act 2003).

ATTEMPTED ASSAULT BY SEXUAL PENETRATION

Section 2 of the Sexual Offences Act 2003 creates the offence of assault by sexual penetration. The title of this offence is misleading. An assault in the strict sense of causing V to apprehend immediate violence will not suffice – there must be actual penetration of the vagina or anus.

As penetration may be by any part of the defendant's body including the penis and as this offence includes similar requirements as to lack of consent and absence of reasonable belief in consent to those required for rape, there is overlap between the two offences.

Provided, therefore, that the acts of Maxwell are more than merely preparatory (as discussed above), he will also be guilty of attempting to commit the s 2 offence. The maximum penalty for this offence is the same as for attempted rape, a term of imprisonment for life (s 4(1) of the Criminal Attempts Act 1981; s 2(4) of the Sexual Offences Act 2003).[3]

ASSAULT

Maxwell is guilty of an assault contrary to s 39 of the Criminal Justice Act 1988. He intentionally caused Sweet to apprehend the application of immediate, unlawful force (*Venna* (1976)). The maximum penalty for this offence is a term of imprisonment not exceeding six months or a fine not exceeding level 5 on the standard scale or both.

Maxwell, however, did not commit the offence of sexual assault defined in s 3 of the Sexual Offences Act 2003. Like the s 2 offence, the title of this offence is misleading. An intentional non-consensual touching is required (s 3(1) of the Sexual Offences Act 2003).

---

3   There is no need to repeat the discussion of whether D's acts were more than merely preparatory.

Think Points

1   By virtue of s1(3), a presumption as to lack of consent and lack of reasonable belief in consent applies where certain facts are proved. These include where violence was being used against the complainant or the complainant was caused to fear that immediate violence would be used against him (s75(2)). The presumption is rebutted by adducing sufficient evidence to raise an issue as to whether the complainant consented or the defendant reasonably believed that the complainant consented.

2   Lord Lane thought his formulation of the test was 'perhaps as clear a guidance as is possible in the circumstances'. It is true that the nature and variety of attempts and the complex and sometimes conflicting reasons for their punishment make precise formulation difficult. However, other than the obscure requirement that the defendant must have 'embarked on the crime proper', the law as it is currently formulated gives the judge very little positive guidance. The decisions of the Court of Appeal give illustrations of the evidence which is not necessary for liability. There is, however, no precise explanation of the type of evidence that is necessary and/or sufficient. Each case is 'merely an example' (per Lord Taylor in *Attorney General's Reference (No 1 of 1992)* (1993)). It is up to the judge, therefore, to decide intuitively whether or not he feels there is sufficient evidence to allow the matter to go the jury. If he is 'wrong' – that is, if the intuitions of the Court of Appeal do not correspond with those of the trial judge – an appeal will be successful (see *Geddes* (1996) and commentary thereto).

It might be thought that the problem is not a major one as the judge is simply concerned with the threshold question of whether there is prima facie evidence of attempt and the jury have the task of deciding whether the acts were in fact more than merely preparatory. It is worth noting, however, that in most of the leading cases in this area, the jury found the defendant guilty of attempt, but the Court of Appeal held that there was not sufficient evidence from which a reasonable jury could conclude that there was an attempt.

Aim Higher ★

It is important to acknowledge that it is not possible to come to a conclusive answer in respect of the question whether Maxwell has committed an offence of attempted rape. You should explain the principle by reference to which the jury should decide whether his act was more than merely preparatory.

QUESTION 28

Why is an attempt to commit an offence punished? Should attempts be punished as severely as the full offence?

How to Answer this Question

A straightforward question concerning the policy underlying the punishment of attempts. The principal issues are:

❖ the distinction between 'complete' and 'incomplete' attempts;
❖ the justification for the punishment of attempts – 'utilitarian' and 'desert' theories; and
❖ arguments for and against the equal punishment of attempts and the full offence.

Answer Structure

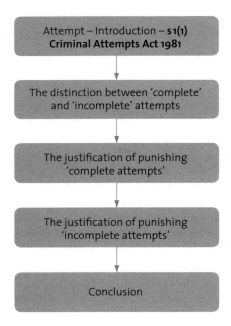

Attempt – Introduction – **s1(1)**
Criminal Attempts Act 1981

The distinction between 'complete' and 'incomplete' attempts

The justification of punishing 'complete attempts'

The justification of punishing 'incomplete attempts'

Conclusion

ANSWER

INTRODUCTION

Section 1(1) of the Criminal Attempts Act 1981 provides that a person is guilty of an attempt if, with intent to commit an offence triable on indictment, he does an act which is more than merely preparatory to the commission of that offence.

The question of whether an act is more than merely preparatory is a question of fact for the jury and not a question of law for the judge (s 4(3)). If, however, there is insufficient evidence or it would be unsafe to leave the evidence to the jury, the judge can rule that there was no attempt and direct a verdict of not guilty (*Campbell* (1991)). In *Gullefer* (1987), it was held that if there is evidence on which a jury could reasonably arrive at the conclusion that the defendant had gone beyond preparation by having 'embarked on the crime proper', then it is for the jury to decide whether the defendant did, in fact, go beyond mere preparation. Lord Lane added that there may be evidence of an attempt, even though the defendant had not performed the last act prior to the commission of the substantive offence (see also *Jones* (1990); *Geddes* (1996)).

As far as the *mens rea* requirement for an attempt is concerned, the prosecution must prove that the accused intended the result defined in the *actus reus* of the full offence (s 1(1) of the 1981 Act; *Pearman* (1985); *Walker and Hayles* (1990)). It would appear, however, that if recklessness as to circumstances in the *actus reus* will suffice for the full offence, it will also be sufficient for an attempt (*Khan* (1990); *Attorney General's Reference (No 3 of 1992)* (1994)).[4]

The maximum penalty for an attempt is generally the same as for the complete offence (s 4(5) of the 1981 Act). However, normally, a person convicted of attempt can expect a lesser sentence than he would have had he been successful.

Before discussing the justifications for the punishment of attempts, a distinction must be drawn between two types of attempt, both of which attract criminal liability.

First, there are those attempts where the person has done all that he believes is necessary to achieve the intended object but fails for some reason. These may be termed 'complete attempts'. An 'incomplete attempt', on the other hand, occurs where although he has done an act that is more than merely preparatory, the defendant has not yet taken the step which would amount to the commission of the full offence.[5]

COMPLETE ATTEMPTS

An example of a complete attempt is where the defendant has detonated a bomb, intending to kill, but the bomb fails to explode. In such a case, the defendant has engaged in conduct with a manifestly blameworthy intent and so it is generally accepted that such a person is as much in need of rehabilitation or restraint or deterrence as if he had been

---

4   Before evaluating the law relating to criminal attempts it is necessary to provide a summary of the ingredients of liability.
5   When evaluating the law relating to attempts and the policy underlying it is often helpful to distinguish complete attempts from incomplete attempts.

successful. There is a danger that, if unpunished, he might try to commit the offence again (and, perhaps, with some success the next time).

From a utilitarian standpoint, the punishment of an attempt is justified in terms of general deterrence, just as it is where the full offence is committed. Others who might be more successful should be discouraged from attempting to commit the crime.

Should the person who is guilty of a 'complete' attempt be punished to the same extent as he would have been had he been successful, or does the fact that there was a failure to cause the defined harm justify a lower penalty?

First, the fact that the specific harm intended has not occurred does not mean that no harm at all has been caused by the behaviour of the defendant. The 'complete attempt' is a threat to the general security of the members of society and to that extent is harmful. It is arguable, however, that the social consequences of criminal activity which results in specific harm are qualitatively different from the situation where no specific harm results (even if by accident) and that the equal treatment of attempts and consummated crimes cannot be justified on the basis of 'equal harm'. The equal treatment of the failed attempt and the completed offence may, however, be justified on the basis that a person who attempts to cause harm but fails is as culpable as the person who succeeds. According to this 'subjectivist' view, the influence of morally neutral chance elements is minimised. The failed attempt 'deserves' the same degree of punishment as the complete offence (Think Point (1)).

Indeed, as the *mens rea* for attempts is based upon an intention to commit the *actus reus*, it is arguable that, in some cases, the degree of culpability of the attempter is greater than that of the person who commits the full offence. For example, whereas a person may be guilty of murder 'merely' on proof of an intention to cause grievous bodily harm, attempted murder requires proof of an intention to kill (*Cunningham* (1982); *Whybrow* (1951)).

Professor Williams, on the other hand, cautioned that the equal treatment of attempts and consummated crimes might result in the law losing public support. He argues that, from the crudely retributive perspective adopted by much of the general public, according to which punishment should relate to the harm done, the equal treatment of attempts and consummated crimes might appear harsh (Williams, G, *Textbook of Criminal Law*, 2nd edn, 1983, London: Sweet & Maxwell, p 405).

There may be additional 'emotional' reasons justifying a lesser punishment for attempts. Professor Hart, for example, argued that a greater punishment is necessary to deprive the successful offender of the 'illicit satisfactions' and gratification that follows success. He also argues that the retributive 'instinct' of the victim is stronger and the demand for revenge is greater where harm has actually been caused than in cases where the intended victim has escaped harm (Hart, HLA, *Punishment and Responsibility*, Oxford: OUP, 1968, p 1314).[6]

. . . .

INCOMPLETE ATTEMPTS

An example of an 'incomplete' attempt is where the defendant has planted a bomb and is apprehended as he is about to detonate it.

The requirement of acts that are more than 'merely preparatory' should ensure that attempts of this sort are not simply 'thought crimes'. The law insists upon some conduct because an individual who has taken steps to achieve the prohibited result has manifested a 'firm resolve' and may be regarded as more disposed to criminal activity than one who merely expresses an intention to commit a crime without acting on that intent. In addition, there is a greater degree of psychological commitment to completing the crime concerned as one approaches its actual commission. The person who sets out to commit an offence becomes progressively less likely to change his mind the more steps he takes.

Many of the arguments in favour of punishing complete attempts apply, with equal force, to this type of attempt. In addition, the criminalisation of the incomplete attempt enables and justifies law enforcement officials to intervene before any real harm has been caused.

Does the person who makes an 'incomplete attempt' deserve equal punishment to the person who consummates the crime?

Arguments in favour of relative leniency may be advanced in the case of incomplete attempts that do not apply to completed attempts. As it is conceivable that the interrupted attempter might have changed his mind and not gone through with his intentions to the point of consummation, his 'moral blameworthiness' may be less than that of either the complete attempter or the person who commits the full offence. As liability for an attempt attaches before the commission of the last act, there must always be some doubt that the accused had the necessary firm resolve. In addition, the less severe punishment of incomplete attempts may provide some incentive to stop at the last moment. If a person gives up after having done an act that is more than merely preparatory then, although it does not negative his liability, it may affect the level of punishment that the court imposes (*Taylor* (1859)).

In conclusion, therefore, it may be said that although the punishment of attempts is justified, there are utilitarian arguments in favour of relative leniency, especially in the case of 'incomplete' attempts.

. . . .

6   This question, like many requiring evaluation of a controversial issue in criminal law, requires consideration of the objectives of punishment.

Think Point

1   Note s 1(2) of the 1981 Act: a person may be guilty of attempting to commit an offence even though the facts are such that the offence is impossible. Does the degree of incompetence of the individual who sets out to achieve an event which fails through impossibility justify a lesser punishment than that given to the successful offender or the chance failure? Does the person who attempts to kill by poisoning, but who uses a substance which he does not realise is innocuous, present the same danger as the person who administers a poisonous substance but fails in his attempt to kill due to the intervention of a doctor?

Aim Higher

There is more to this question than meets the eye. To answer it effectively requires a good understanding of the objectives of punishment and how they are served by the criminalisation of the conceptually distinct 'complete' and 'incomplete' attempts.

QUESTION 29

PART (A)

Although Paula did not consent, Cliff, who was drunk, tried unsuccessfully to have sexual intercourse with her.

PART (B)

Anson had sexual intercourse with Hilda. He was not sure whether or not she had consented. In fact, she had consented.

PART (C)

Sam and Dave agreed to sell a necklace left to them by their grandmother. They agreed to advertise the necklace as being made of pure gold. In fact, as Sam knew, it was gold-plated. Dave suspects that it was not pure gold but is not sure.

▶   Consider the criminal liability of Cliff, Anson, Sam and Dave.

How to Answer this Question

The three parts of this question involve issues of attempt and conspiracy. There is a lack of authority regarding some of the issues. The principal issues are:

❖   attempts and intoxication;
❖   attempts and impossibility – s 1(3) of the Criminal Attempts Act 1981;

❖   'recklessness' and statutory conspiracy – s1(2) of the Criminal Law Act
     1977; and

❖   'recklessness' and common law conspiracy to defraud.

Answer Structure

(a)   (b)

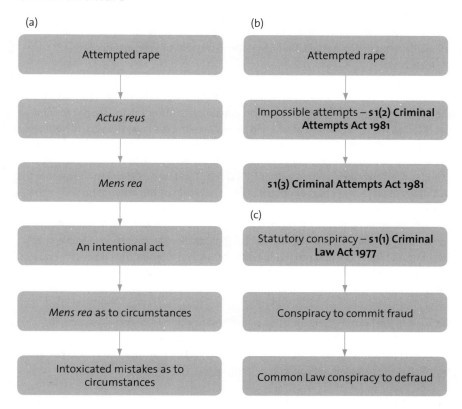

(a) flow	(b)/(c) flow
Attempted rape	Attempted rape
Actus reus	Impossible attempts – s1(2) Criminal Attempts Act 1981
Mens rea	s1(3) Criminal Attempts Act 1981
An intentional act	(c) Statutory conspiracy – s1(1) Criminal Law Act 1977
Mens rea as to circumstances	Conspiracy to commit fraud
Intoxicated mistakes as to circumstances	Common Law conspiracy to defraud

ANSWER

PART (A)

ATTEMPTED RAPE

Cliff may be convicted of attempted rape contrary to s1(1) of the Criminal Attempts
Act 1981. This provides that if, with intent to commit an offence, a person does an act
which is more than merely preparatory to the commission of the offence, he is guilty of
attempting to commit the offence.

Section 4(3) of the 1981 Act provides that where there is evidence that the defendant had done something that was more than 'merely preparatory', the question whether it does or does not amount to an attempt is left to the jury (*Jones* (1990)). We are not told exactly what Cliff did, but it shall be assumed that his acts were more than 'merely preparatory'.[7]

As far as the *mens rea* of attempt is concerned, the prosecution must prove that the acts of the defendant were intentional, that is, he was not an automaton and, as far as result crimes are concerned, that he intended the relevant consequence (*Pearman* (1985)).

However, it was held in *Khan* (1990) that if recklessness as to circumstances suffices for the full offence, then recklessness as to circumstances suffices for an attempt to commit the offence. The case involved attempted rape. When the case was decided, the offence of rape was defined in s 1 of the Sexual Offences Act 1956, as substituted by s 142 of the Criminal Justice and Public Order Act 1994. This provided that rape was committed where D had sexual intercourse with V without V's consent and was reckless with respect to the lack of V's consent. The Court of Appeal in *Khan* held that as the attempt related to the physical activity, the intent that had to be proved for attempted rape was an intention to have sexual intercourse with V, the defendant either being aware that V was not consenting, or being reckless with respect to that fact. Recklessness bore a 'subjective' meaning and therefore for both the full offence and the attempt the prosecution was required to prove that D was aware there was a possibility that V was not consenting (*S (Satnam and Kewal)* (1983); *Breckenridge* (1984)).

Section 1 of the Sexual Offences Act 2003, which came into force on 1 May 2004, redefined rape. The defendant must intentionally penetrate the vagina, anus or mouth of another person with his penis. In addition, there must be an absence of 'a reasonable belief' that the complainant consented (s 1(1)(c)).

The latter requirement postulates an objective negligence based test. What is not clear is whether a lack of reasonable belief will now suffice for attempted rape or whether subjective recklessness is still required.

In *Attorney General's Reference (No 3 of 1992)* (1994), the Court of Appeal held that recklessness would suffice for an offence of attempted aggravated arson. Schiemann J said that in order to succeed in a prosecution for attempt, it must be shown that the defendant intended to achieve that which was missing from the full offence. If the defendant would have been guilty of the full offence had he achieved what he intended, then he is guilty of an attempt to commit the offence. If this approach is followed for

---

7   Where crucial facts are not disclosed, make an assumption that will allow progress to the next relevant issue.

attempted rape, then the prosecution would have to prove that Cliff intended to have sexual intercourse and lacked a reasonable belief that Paula consented.

Section 1(2) of the Sexual Offences Act 2003 provides that whether a belief is reasonable is to be determined having regard to all the circumstances, including any steps taken to ascertain whether V was consenting. Although most commentators are of the view that the circumstances may include psychological or intellectual characteristics of the defendant which might have limited his ability to appreciate the lack of consent, it is submitted that the defendant's intoxication ought not to be taken into account. A drunken belief is not a reasonable belief. If correct, this approach would mean that the jury should be directed to consider whether the defendant believed that V consented and whether, objectively, there were reasonable grounds for the belief (Think Point (1)).

If convicted of attempted rape, Cliff will face a maximum penalty of life imprisonment (s 4(1) of the Criminal Attempts Act 1981).

PART (B)

ATTEMPTED RAPE

Clearly, Anson cannot be convicted of rape. Although he acted with the *mens rea*, he did not commit the *actus reus* of rape as Hilda had, in fact, consented to the intercourse.

Can he be convicted of attempted rape?

He did not believe that Hilda consented and, therefore, it is submitted that he acted with the *mens rea* of attempted rape (see discussion in part (a) above).

Furthermore, according to s 1(2) of the Criminal Attempts Act 1981, a person may be guilty of attempt even though the facts are such that the commission of the offence is impossible. Thus, it is submitted that Anson may be convicted of attempted rape although he was unsure whether she consented and although the commission of rape was, in the circumstances, impossible.

Professors Smith and Hogan have argued that such a conclusion is neither desirable nor inevitable. They suggest that s 1(3) requires us to assess the defendant's liability by reference to the facts 'as he believed them to be'. The reckless defendant does not believe that the woman is not consenting; he merely believes she might not be consenting. Thus, they conclude that the rules relating to impossibility do not apply to the reckless defendant.

With respect, it is submitted that their argument is fallacious. Section 1(3) only applies where otherwise a person's intention would not be regarded as having amounted to an intent to commit an offence. Anson's intention in this case is to have sexual intercourse with a woman who, he believed, might not be consenting. That is sufficient *mens rea* for rape and attempted rape and thus there is no need to rely upon s 1(3) (Think Point (2)).

PART (C)

STATUTORY CONSPIRACY

The offence of statutory conspiracy is defined in s 1 of the Criminal Law Act 1977, as amended by s 5 of the Criminal Attempts Act 1981. It provides that a person is guilty of conspiracy if he agrees with any person or persons to pursue a course of conduct which, if carried out as intended, will necessarily amount to the commission of an offence by one or more of the parties to the agreement.

CONSPIRACY TO COMMIT FRAUD

Had Sam and Dave advertised the necklace as agreed they would both have been guilty of fraud, contrary to s 1(1) of the Fraud Act 2006. Fraud by false representation in breach of s 1(2) of the Fraud Act 2006 is committed where D, dishonestly and with an intention to make a gain in terms of money or other property or an intention to cause loss to another or expose another to a risk of loss in terms of money or other property, makes a false representation. It is not necessary to prove that D knew the representation to be untrue; knowledge that it *might* be untrue is sufficient (s 2(2)(b)).[8]

However, they are not guilty of a statutory conspiracy to commit fraud. A person cannot be guilty of a statutory conspiracy to commit an offence unless he has knowledge of all the defined circumstances. This is the effect of s 1(2) of the 1977 Act. The subsection provides that even when the full offence does not require knowledge of a circumstance, conspiracy requires that the defendant and at least one other party to the agreement know that any relevant circumstance will exist when the conduct constituting the offence is to take place.

Thus, as Dave does not know that the necklace is gold plated – he merely suspects that it might be – he is not guilty of conspiracy. Neither is Sam. Although he knows the necklace is not made of solid gold there is no other party to the agreement who knows that. There is no conspiracy.

COMMON LAW CONSPIRACY TO DEFRAUD

In *Scott v Metropolitan Police Commissioner* (1975), the House of Lords stated that an agreement by two or more people by dishonesty to deprive a person of something which is his constitutes a conspiracy to defraud.

---

8   When discussing liability for conspiracy, the substantive offence agreed to must be identified and its ingredients of liability summarised.

Dishonesty is determined in accordance with the *Ghosh* (1982) test; that is, if what the accused did was in accordance with the ordinary standards of reasonable people or he mistakenly believed that it was, then it was not dishonest.

The law is not clear, however, as to whether a reckless deception will suffice for common law conspiracy to defraud. In *Wai Yu-Tsang* (1991), the House of Lords, whilst stating that they did not wish to become enmeshed in a distinction between intention and recklessness, said, *obiter*, that it is enough that the conspirators have dishonestly agreed to bring about a state of affairs which they realise will or may result in the victim being deceived. Furthermore, as recklessness sufficed for attempt at common law, it would be remarkable were it not sufficient for common law conspiracy (see *Pigg* (1982)).

The maximum punishment for a common law conspiracy to defraud is a term of imprisonment not exceeding 10 years (s 12 of the Criminal Justice Act 1987).

Think Points

1   In *Woods* (1982), the Court of Appeal took a similar approach as far as the 'old' offence of rape was concerned. Section 1(2) of the Sexual Offences (Amendment) Act 1976 provided that where the jury were required to consider whether the defendant had acted with the necessary *mens rea*, they were to have regard to the reasonableness of the defendant's belief and 'any other relevant matters'. The court held that self-induced intoxication was not a legally relevant matter and should be ignored by the jury, but that they should consider all the other relevant evidence. Where a defendant introduced evidence that he was so intoxicated that he lacked the *mens rea* for rape, the jury were to be directed to consider whether he was reckless disregarding the evidence that he was drunk.

2   As Professors Smith and Hogan acknowledge elsewhere, subs (3) 'does nothing'. It simply spells out what is obvious from subss (1) and (2), that is, that liability for attempts depends upon the intent of the defendant even if founded upon some mistake or misunderstanding.

QUESTION 30

PART (A)

Criminal law regards a person as responsible for his own crimes only ... *Qui peccat per alium peccat per se* is not a maxim of criminal law.

Per Lord Diplock in *Tesco v Nattrass* (1972)

▶ What are the exceptions to this 'rule'?

PART (B)

Matthew sold Chump a gun and ammunition. Although nothing was said, Matthew thought that Chump intended to use it to kill his neighbour, Funny. Matthew was aware that Chump and Funny had had a series of disputes. In fact, Chump had bought the gun as he intended to kill himself. His girlfriend, Chagrin, had left him. He returned home, put the gun to his head, and pulled the trigger. The gun jammed. He decided to hang himself. He tied a rope to the ceiling and stood on a chair. Just as he was about to jump, Funny peered through the window. He smiled to himself when he realised that Chump was about to commit suicide. Chump, who had not seen Funny, jumped from the chair. The rope broke. Funny was disappointed. Later that evening he gave Chump a leaflet, published by an organisation called JUMP (an unincorporated association), which explained some tried and tested methods of suicide. He hoped that this would strengthen Chump's resolve to kill himself. Chump, however, was no longer interested in committing suicide. Chagrin had realised that Chump was the most lovable man in the world and had decided to marry him.

▶ Discuss the liability of Matthew, Funny and JUMP.

How to Answer this Question

The first part of this question concerns the exceptions to the general rule of English law that one person is not liable for the criminal acts of another. These exceptions define vicarious liability and the liability of corporations. The second part concerns the offence of aiding and abetting a suicide contrary to s 2 of the Suicide Act 1961. It also raises the issue of criminal liability of an unincorporated association.

The principal issues are:

❖ vicarious liability;
❖ the delegation principle;
❖ the 'extensive construction' principle;
❖ liability of corporations;
❖ aiding and abetting a suicide;
❖ attempting to aid and abet (s 1(4)(b) of the Criminal Attempts Act 1981); and
❖ criminal liability of an unincorporated association.

Answer Structure

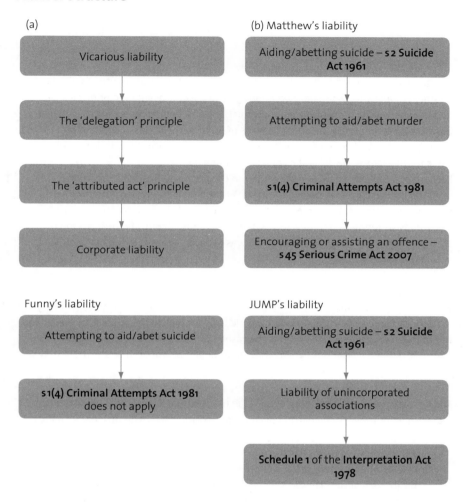

(a)

- Vicarious liability
- The 'delegation' principle
- The 'attributed act' principle
- Corporate liability

(b) Matthew's liability

- Aiding/abetting suicide – s2 Suicide Act 1961
- Attempting to aid/abet murder
- s1(4) Criminal Attempts Act 1981
- Encouraging or assisting an offence – s45 Serious Crime Act 2007

Funny's liability

- Attempting to aid/abet suicide
- s1(4) Criminal Attempts Act 1981 does not apply

JUMP's liability

- Aiding/abetting suicide – s2 Suicide Act 1961
- Liability of unincorporated associations
- Schedule 1 of the Interpretation Act 1978

ANSWER

PART (A)

VICARIOUS LIABILITY

The general rule in criminal law that a person is not liable for the unauthorised acts of another is subject to two major exceptions. The first is the 'delegation principle'. This applies where a statutory offence imposes liability on a person occupying a particular position, for example, the owner or licensee of premises, who has delegated the management of the premises to another. The owner or licensee will be vicariously liable for the acts of the delegate. For example, in *Allen v Whitehead* (1930), the licensee of a cafe employed a manager to run the premises. Despite instructions from the licensee not to allow prostitutes to enter, the manager permitted women he knew to be prostitutes to meet on the premises. The licensee was convicted of 'knowingly suffering prostitutes' to meet on the premises, contrary to s 44 of the Metropolitan Police Act 1839. The licensee was liable on account of the manager's acts and knowledge.

Were it not for the principle allowing vicarious liability, in such a case the legislation would be devoid of effect, as it (in common with many other statutory offences applying to licensed premises) creates an offence which applies only to the licensee or keeper and not to the manager. However, even in the case of offences which impose personal liability upon the manager, vicarious liability may, additionally, be imposed on the delegator (see, for example, *Howker v Robinson* (1972)).

The delegate need not be an employee of the licensee. The licensee will be vicariously responsible for the acts of a partner or co-licensee committed in his absence (*Linnett v MPC* (1946)).

The principles whereby delegation will be found to have taken place are not totally clear. The absence of the licensee is, however, of great importance as this is consistent with delegation of authority. In *Vane v Yiannopoullos* (1965), a licensee was charged with an offence contrary to s 161(1) of the Licensing Act 1964 of 'knowingly selling or supplying alcohol' contrary to the conditions of his licence. A waitress, contrary to the licensee's instructions, served drinks illegally while he was in the basement of the restaurant. The House of Lords held that the licensee was not guilty of the offence. Lord Hodson held that the principle imposing vicarious liability applies only where there is a complete delegation of authority, which had not occurred in this case. Lord Reid based his decision on the fact that the licensee had not left the premises in the charge of the waitress.

In *Howker v Robinson*, the Divisional Court held that whether or not there has been delegation is a question of fact. In that case, a licensee who was serving in the public bar was found to have delegated authority to a barman in the lounge bar. There was complete delegation as far as that part of the premises was concerned.

In *Winson* (1969), Lord Parker pointed out that the delegation principle applies only where the statutory offence requires *mens rea*. In cases of strict liability, the second of the two exceptions to the general principle of personal liability may come into play.[9]

This second exception – the attributed act principle – is based on the construction of certain verbs used in penal statutes. For example, where the *actus reus* of an offence consists of 'selling' goods of some description then, as the legal transaction of sale is made by the owner of the goods, the employer and not the assistant commits the offence (*Coppen v Moore (No 2)* (1898)).

The principle has been held to apply to statutes imposing liability for, among other things, 'supplying goods' (s 1 of the Trade Descriptions Act 1968) and 'using a motor vehicle' (Motor Vehicles (Construction and Use) Regulations 1972).

Vicarious liability based on this construction principle does not allow for the attribution of the employee's intent to the employer. The principle is limited to offences of strict liability unless it can be proved that the employer acted with the relevant intent (*Winson*). For this reason, there can generally be no vicarious liability for aiding and abetting an offence nor for an attempt to commit an offence (*Ferguson v Weaving* (1951); *Gardner v Ackroyd* (1952)).

The justification for vicarious liability is pragmatic. The offences concerned are of a regulatory nature, concerned with the sale and supply of food, drugs and alcohol. Were it not for the principle of delegation, a licensee could avoid responsibility for an offence requiring *mens rea* by turning the management over to an employee. The manager himself would escape liability where the offence strikes at the licensee.

By imposing liability on the employer for the acts of an employee, it is hoped that the employer will be encouraged to take steps to prevent the commission of offences by his staff.

This solution, however, involves, in the case of the delegation principle at least, interpreting statutes in clear contradiction of the words used. A licensee may be convicted of an offence of 'knowingly allowing, etc' even though he neither allowed it nor was aware of it, and despite expressly instructing his employee to observe the

....

9   Vicarious liability for the acts of another based on the delegation principle should not be confused with liability based on the construction of particular verbs used in penal statutes.

legislation. A fairer solution would be to impose liability on the employer for the unauthorised acts of an employee only where the employer was negligent. Ineffectual legislation should be redrafted rather than applied by imposing a fictitious interpretation on it.

CORPORATE LIABILITY

There is one further situation in which one person may be responsible for the acts of another, and that concerns the liability of corporations. A corporation is, in English law, a legal person distinct from its members or directors.

In addition to those situations where a company might attract liability vicariously for the acts of its employees, there is a more direct form of liability which may be imposed on a corporation for the unlawful acts of an employee or officers. In this situation, the corporation is regarded as having primary responsibility for the offence.

For whose acts might the corporation be criminally liable? In *Lennard's Carrying Co Ltd v Asiatic Petroleum Co Ltd* (1915), it was held that criminal liability may be attributed to the corporation for the acts of those individuals who could be identified with the company itself – those employees and officers who individually or collectively constituted the 'directing mind and will' of the company.

In *Tesco Supermarkets Ltd v Nattrass* (1972), Lord Reid explained that a corporation, although a separate entity, acts through living individuals. The controlling officer is an embodiment of the company. His acts are the acts of the company and his mind is the mind of the company. This would include directors and others to whom management authority has been delegated. Lords Diplock and Pearson stated that the constitution and organisation of the corporation should be considered.

This rule has a fairly restricted range of application. Liability will only be attributed if a senior manager committed the *actus reus* of the offence with *mens rea*.

In *Meridian Global Funds Management Asia Ltd v Securities Commission* (1995), the Privy Council examined the authorities, including *Tesco Supermarkets* and *Lennard's Carrying Co*, and concluded that there had been 'some misunderstanding of the true principles' upon which they were decided. In his advice, Lord Hoffmann stated that whether criminal acts of an employee should be attributed to a company is a matter of interpretation of the particular substantive rule and, in particular, the policy underlying it. The fundamental question is: '. . . whose act (or knowledge, or state of mind) was for this purpose intended to count as the act of the company?' (Think Point (1)).

For which offences might a corporation be criminally liable?

Criminal liability for most offences may be attributed to a company. These include serious offences carrying heavy penalties. In *ICR Haulage Ltd* (1944), the company's conviction for common law conspiracy to defraud was upheld. It is also clear that a corporation can be convicted of manslaughter if the way in which its activities are managed or organised causes a person's death, and amounts to a gross breach of a relevant duty of care owed by the organisation to the deceased – s1(1) **Corporate Manslaughter and Corporate Homicide Act 2007.** The way in which its activities are managed or organised by senior management must be a substantial element in the breach – s1(3).

Those crimes which cannot be committed by a coroporation include murder, where the mandatory form of punishment is inappropriate, and crimes like bigamy and rape which, because of their personal nature, cannot be committed by a company.

It is sometimes argued that holding a corporation criminally liable is pointless or unjust. The expense is either borne by the shareholders or employees or passed on as a cost to the consumer. On the other hand, it is arguable that the behaviour of the officers of the corporation may be shaped by the subculture of the organisation as a whole and that, in order to influence the behaviour of the group, it may be necessary to punish the corporation. In addition, the potential of bad publicity resulting from a conviction might encourage good practice. In any case, the officers of the company can, as an alternative, be convicted personally as perpetrators or, if the company is convicted as perpetrator, the officers can be convicted as accessories. Further, offences of omission – where there is a duty on the company to perform some act – may not attach to individual officers. If the company could not be convicted, the law would be ineffective.

PART (B)

MATTHEW

Section 2 of the **Suicide Act 1961** provides that it is an offence to aid, abet, counsel or procure the suicide of another or the attempt by another to commit suicide. The maximum punishment is a term of imprisonment not exceeding 14 years.

The words 'aid and abet', etc, have the same meaning for this offence as they do for the general law relating to the liability of accomplices to crime (*Reed* (1982)).

Has Matthew intentionally helped the attempted suicide by Chump?

Supplying a gun is clearly capable of amounting to assistance (*NCB v Gamble* (1959)), but Matthew mistakenly believed that Chump was going to murder Funny. In *Bainbridge* (1960), the Court of Criminal Appeal held that a person may be liable as an accomplice even if he did not know the particular crime intended. It was enough that he knew the type of crime intended. This decision was referred to with approval in *Maxwell v DPP for Northern Ireland* (1979).

However, although murder and suicide both involve the intentional killing of a human being, they are not similar types of crime. This is because, although aiding a suicide is a crime, neither suicide nor attempted suicide is (s 1 of the Suicide Act 1961). Thus, the principle in *Bainbridge* does not apply in this case and Matthew is not guilty of an offence contrary to s 2.[10]

Nor can Matthew be convicted of attempting to aid and abet murder (s 1(4)(b) of the Criminal Attempts Act 1981).

He is, however, guilty of an offence of 'encouraging or assisting an offence believing it will be committed' contrary to s 45 of the Serious Crime Act 2007.

He did an act – supplying the gun – which was 'capable of assisting the commission of an offence' (the murder of Funny) – s 45(a). He believed that a murder would be committed by Chump and that supplying the gun would assist its commission – s 45(b). The fact that Chump did not murder Funny and had never contemplated doing so has no bearing on Matthew's liability – s 49(1).

A person convicted of encouraging or assisting murder is liable to imprisonment for life – s 58(2).

FUNNY

Funny's deliberate failure to attempt to save Chump's life when he saw him about to hang himself does not amount to aiding and abetting his attempted suicide. It is only where a person has a duty to act, or controls the actions of another, that he can be regarded as assisting through inactivity (*Russell* (1933); *Tuck v Robson* (1970)).

However, when Funny gave Chump the JUMP leaflet, intending unsuccessfully to encourage Chump to commit suicide, Funny committed an offence contrary to s 1(1) of the Criminal Attempts Act 1981.

Section 1(4) of the 1981 Act states that a person may be convicted of attempting to commit any offence which, if it were completed, would be triable on indictment and s 1(4)(b) (mentioned above in relation to Matthew's liability) does not apply in this case because 'aiding, etc, a suicide', triable on indictment, is the substantive offence.

In *Attorney General v Able* (1984), it was held that, although the distribution of a book explaining methods of suicide is not in itself an offence, an offence would be committed if the distributor intended that the booklet would encourage or assist someone who was

---

10 The question whether crimes are of the same 'type' is fraught with difficulty and so the reasons for distinguishing suicide and murder are provided.

contemplating suicide and that the person was in fact assisted or encouraged by the book.

JUMP

In *Attorney General v Able*, Woolf J stated that an unincorporated association could not be guilty of an offence. However, unincorporated associations are 'persons' as far as statutory offences passed since 1889 are concerned (s 19 of the Interpretation Act 1889 and Sched 1 to the Interpretation Act 1978).

Section 2 of the 1961 Act imposes liability on any 'person', as does s 1 of the Criminal Attempts Act 1981 and it is submitted therefore that JUMP may be prosecuted for the full offence provided someone has, in fact, committed or tried to commit suicide, having been assisted or encouraged by the leaflet, or an attempt to commit that offence if it cannot be proved that anyone has committed or tried to commit suicide.

The prosecution would have to prove that a 'controlling official' was responsible for the distribution of the leaflet and had the appropriate *mens rea* defined and explained above (Think Point (21)).

Think Points

1 See also *Re Supply of Ready Mixed Concrete (No 2)* (1995).

2 Although the question does not raise the issue, members or controlling officials of JUMP may, of course, be personally responsible either as perpetrators or accessories depending on their involvement in the production of the leaflet and their own *mens rea*.

QUESTION 31

Charles was angry at his girlfriend, Josephine, as she had been unfaithful. Charles asked Andrew, who had recently discharged himself from a psychiatric hospital, to rape Josephine. Andrew agreed. He lay in wait for her near her house. He saw a woman approach and, believing her to be Josephine, he attacked and raped her. In fact, the woman attacked was not Josephine, but her neighbour, Kathy. When arrested, Andrew maintained that, although he was aware that Kathy had not consented to sexual intercourse, he did not know that rape was against the law.

▶ Discuss the criminal liability of Andrew and Charles.

How to Answer this Question

This question raises the defence of insanity and issues concerning conspiracy and accessorial liability where one of the parties is insane.

The principal issues are:

❖ the defence of insanity and the requirement that D knew the act was wrong;
❖ liability for conspiracy where one of the parties is insane;
❖ accessorial liability where the perpetrator is not guilty by reason of insanity;

The principal authorities are: *Sullivan* (1984); *Windle* (1952); *Bourne* (1952); *Cogan and Leak* (1975); *DPP v K and C* (1997); *Whitehouse* (1977).

Answer Structure

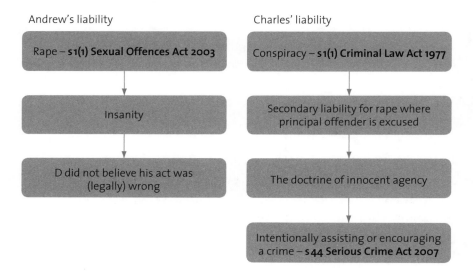

Andrew's liability

| Rape – s1(1) Sexual Offences Act 2003 |
| Insanity |
| D did not believe his act was (legally) wrong |

Charles' liability

| Conspiracy – s1(1) Criminal Law Act 1977 |
| Secondary liability for rape where principal offender is excused |
| The doctrine of innocent agency |
| Intentionally assisting or encouraging a crime – s44 Serious Crime Act 2007 |

ANSWER

ANDREW – RAPE

Rape is an offence contrary to s1 of the Sexual Offences Act 2003. The maximum punishment is life imprisonment (s1(3)).

Although ignorance of the law is no excuse (*Esop* (1836)), Andrew may be able to take advantage of the common law defence of insanity. The criteria of the defence are set out in what are known as the *M'Naghten Rules* (1843). These were accepted by the House of Lords in *Sullivan* (1984) as providing the authoritative definition of insanity in English criminal law.

The *M'Naghten Rules* provide that to establish a defence on the ground of insanity, it must be proved that, at the time of committing the act, D was:

> . . . labouring under such a defect of reason, from disease of the mind, as not to know the nature and quality of the act he was doing or if he did know that, he did not know that what he was doing was wrong.

A person is presumed sane unless the contrary is proved to the jury's satisfaction on 'a balance of probabilities' (*Bratty v Attorney General for Northern Ireland* (1963)).

There is no suggestion in this case that Andrew did not know the nature and quality of his act and, thus, it is proposed to consider the alternative limb: that, at the time he raped Josephine, he was labouring under a defect of reason caused by a disease of the mind such that he did not know that what he was doing was wrong.

Whether Andrew suffers from a condition amounting to a 'disease of the mind' is not a medical question, but a question of law (*Kemp* (1957); *Bratty*). Any disease, whether organic or functional, that results in a malfunctioning of the faculties of the mind is a disease of the mind. It matters not whether it is temporary or permanent, curable or incurable (*Kemp*). Lord Denning in *Bratty* said that any condition which has 'manifest itself in violence and is prone to recur' is a disease of the mind.

The requirement of a 'defect of reason' means that it must be proved that there was a deprivation of cognitive ability (*Clarke* (1972)).

We are told that Andrew maintained that he did not realise rape was a crime. Provided it can be proved that he genuinely held that belief, it would seem, on the strength of *obiter* statements made by the Court of Criminal Appeal in *Windle* (1952), that the second limb of the defence is satisfied even if he believed that it was morally wrong to commit an act of rape.[11]

If the defence is successful, Andrew will be found not guilty by reason of insanity (s 1 of the Criminal Procedure (Insanity) Act 1964) and, by virtue of the Criminal Procedure (Insanity and Unfitness to Plead) Act 1991, the court may make a hospital order with or without a restriction as to discharge, a guardianship order, a supervision and treatment order, or an order of absolute discharge.

CONSPIRACY

As far as Charles' liability for conspiracy to rape is concerned, the central issue is whether a person can be guilty of conspiracy where the alleged co-conspirator is insane within the *M'Naghten Rules*.[12]

---

11 Where appropriate, acknowledge that a judicial statement was made by way of *obiter dicta*.

12 Clear identification of the issue in the question is the first step in its resolution.

Section 1(1) of the Criminal Law Act 1977 provides that a person is guilty of conspiracy if he agrees with another to pursue a course of conduct which, if carried out as intended, will necessarily amount to the commission of an offence by at least one of the parties.

In this case, the agreement was that Andrew should rape Josephine. If he was insane, the agreement was not one which, if carried out as intended, would 'necessarily amount to the commission of an offence' by him. And, as it appears to have been accepted that 'commission of an offence' in s1 means commission of an offence as a principal, and not as a secondary party, neither would it have amounted to an offence by Charles (see the decision of the Court of Appeal in *Hollinshead* (1985); the House of Lords did not consider it necessary to decide the matter).

There is therefore no conspiracy between Andrew and Charles.

SECONDARY LIABILITY

Section 8 of the Accessories and Abettors Act 1861 provides that a person who aids, abets, counsels or procures the commission of an offence is liable to be tried and punished for that offence as a principal offender.

Charles has 'counselled', that is, encouraged the commission of the offence (*Calhaem* (1985)). The fact that he asked Andrew to rape Josephine but Andrew raped Kathy has no effect upon Charles' liability. It would be different if Andrew had intentionally deviated from the agreed plan to rape Josephine (see, for example, *Saunders and Archer* (1573)).

The principal issue concerns whether Charles may be convicted as an accomplice if the alleged principal offender, Andrew, is not guilty by reason of insanity.[13]

The traditional view is that accessorial liability is derived from the liability of the principal and that, unless there was a perpetrator responsible for the offence, there is no basis for the conviction of the accomplice (*Thornton v Mitchell* (1940)).

In *Bourne* (1952), however, the Court of Appeal held that a person may be guilty as a secondary party even though the 'principal offender' is excused. In that case, the principal was excused as she had been the victim of duress. The Court of Appeal stated that despite the duress, there had been an offence committed to which the other party could be an accessory.

The decision has been criticised by the supporters of the traditional view as being based on the conceptually improper notion of an 'excused offence'. However, in *Cogan and Leak* (1975), the Court of Appeal gave some support to the decision in *Bourne* by holding, *obiter*, that a man could be convicted as an accessory to rape even though the 'perpetrator' was acquitted due to a lack of *mens rea*. In *DPP v K and B* (1997), the Divisional Court held that

---

13   Again, identifying the relevant issue is an important step in resolution.

a person could be convicted of rape as a procurer, despite the fact that the prosecutor had failed to rebut the presumption of *doli incapax* in respect of the alleged principal (see also *Millward* (1994)) (Think Point (1)).

Although there are difficulties with the reasoning in these cases, it is submitted that the outcome is correct and that despite Andrew's lack of capacity, Charles may be convicted of rape as a procurer.

Alternatively, there is some authority to suggest that Charles might be convicted as the principal offender acting through the innocent agency of Andrew.

The doctrine of innocent agency states that a person may be regarded as the perpetrator of an offence where he intentionally causes the *actus reus* of an offence to be committed by a person who is himself innocent because of a lack of *mens rea* or lack of capacity (*Anon* (1634)). Indeed, the main ground for the decision in *Cogan and Leak* was that a man might be convicted of rape through an innocent agent.

However, this reasoning has been strongly criticised. It is generally accepted that the doctrine of innocent agency applies only where it is possible to say that the defendant performed the *actus reus* and that there is no room for its application where, as in the case of rape, the offence is specified in terms implying personal conduct on the part of the offender (see, for example, *Thornton v Mitchell* and *DPP v K and B*).

INTENTIONALLY ASSISTING OR ENCOURAGING A CRIME

Charles may be convicted of an offence of intentionally encouraging Andrew to commit an offence contrary to s 44 of the **Serious Crime Act 2007** (Think Point (2)).

He encouraged Andrew to commit rape and he intended to encourage the commission of rape – s 44(1). In addition, he believed that Andrew would act with the fault required for rape – s 47(5)(a). The fact that Andrew may have lacked capacity on the grounds of insanity has no bearing on Charles's liability – it matters not whether an offence is committed s 49(1)).

Think Points

1   The Divisional Court treated the concept of *doli incapax* as a 'presumption concerning *mens rea*'. It was, more accurately, a presumption of incapacity. The presumption and the defence of *doli incapax* were abolished by s 34 of the **Crime and Disorder Act 1998**. See *R v T* [2008] EWCA Crim 815.

2   The fact that the crime was committed is no defence to a charge of intentionally assisting or encouraging a crime – s 49 SCA 2007.

Common Pitfalls ✗

You need to be careful with this type of question. The law concerning the possible secondary liability of Charles is not entirely clear and you should acknowledge that in your answer.

QUESTION 32

Dougal had been persistently making advances to Susan, Simon's girlfriend. He had phoned her up on a number of occasions to invite her out. When Simon found out, he was extremely angry and decided to visit Dougal. He asked his brother, Peter, to accompany him. They decided they would 'warn' Dougal that if he did not agree to stop making advances towards Susan, they would smash up his flat, and they agreed that if Dougal 'gave them lip', they would beat him up.

They visited Dougal and told him that they wanted him to stop making advances towards Susan, and that if he did not agree to stop visiting her, they would smash up his flat. Dougal responded by saying that he would not be intimidated and had no intention of changing his behaviour. He said that Susan preferred him to Simon and that she would be happier if Simon left her alone. At this, Simon flew into a rage. He pulled out a knife and, intending serious injury, stabbed Dougal in the right eye.

Dougal fell to the floor, unconscious. He was taken to hospital where it was discovered he had suffered severe brain damage. In addition, a medical examination revealed that he had a duodenal ulcer. The doctors decided that because of the brain damage they could not operate on the ulcer. Two weeks later, while still unconscious, Dougal died when the ulcer burst.

Discuss the criminal liability of Simon and Peter. (Ignore offences under the Prevention of Crime Act 1953 and the Criminal Justice Act 1988.)

How to Answer this Question

The principal issues are:

❖ principles of causation where injuries prevent medical treatment;
❖ the defence of loss of self-control;
❖ accessorial liability: the effect upon secondary liability where the principal is provoked to kill; and
❖ conspiracy and conditional intention.

The principal authorities are: *McKechnie* (1992); *Pearson* (1992); *Ahluwalia* (1992); *DPP v Camplin* (1978); *Powell and Another; English* (1997); *R v Rafferty* (2007); *Rahman* (2008) UKHL 45.

Answer Structure

Simon's liability

Murder
↓
Loss of control – **s54(1) Coroners and Justice Act 2009**
↓
Loss of self-control
↓
Qualifying trigger – **s55**
↓
Person with normal degree of tolerance and self-restraint might have reacted in a similar way
↓
Threats of damage – **s2 Criminal Damage Act 1971**

Peter's liability

Murder – liability as a secondary party
↓
The use of the knife – a fundamentally different act?
↓
Foresight of principal's intent
↓
The effect of a loss of self-control by principal on secondary liability
↓
Conspiracy

ANSWER

SIMON

MURDER

It is proposed to consider Simon's liability for murder.

First, the prosecution must prove that Simon's actions were a legal cause of Dougal's death.

In *McKechnie* (1992), the Court of Appeal held that it must be proved to the jury's satisfaction that the injuries significantly contributed to the victim's death and, where they prevent life saving medical treatment, injuries will be regarded as a significant contribution if the prosecution prove that the decision not to operate was reasonable and competent. It is unnecessary for the prosecution to prove that the decision not to operate was the only decision that a competent doctor might arrive at, nor that it was necessarily the correct one.

Provided Simon's actions were a legal cause of death, as the facts state that he intended to cause serious injury, he will be convicted of murder unless he can take advantage of the defence of loss of self-control (*Moloney* (1985)). The partial defence of loss of control replaces the common law partial defence of provocation abolished by s 56 of the Coroners and Justice Act 2009 and, like the common law defence, a successful plea reduces liability from murder to manslaughter – s 54(7).[14]

Section 54(1) of the Coroners and Justice Act 2009 sets out the ingredients of the defence. It provides that where a person ('D') kills another ('V'), D is not to be convicted of murder if D's acts and omissions resulted from D's loss of self-control, the loss of self-control had a qualifying trigger, and a person of D's sex and age, with a normal degree of tolerance and self-restraint and in the circumstances of D, might have reacted in the same or in a similar way to D.

The defendant bears an evidential burden in respect of the defence (s 54(6)). Only where, in the opinion of the judge, a jury properly directed could reasonably conclude the defence might apply should it be left for their consideration. Provided this threshold requirement is met, the burden of proof rests with the prosecution and the jury must assume that the defence is satisfied unless the prosecution proves beyond reasonable doubt that it is not (s 54(5)).

Thus the prosecution must prove that (a) Simon's fatal act did not result from a loss of self-control and/or (b) the loss of self-control was not a result of a 'qualifying trigger' as defined in s 55 and/or (c) a person of Simon's sex and age, with a normal degree of tolerance etc would not have reacted in the same or similar way to Simon.[15]

LOSS OF SELF-CONTROL

What amounts to a loss of self-control is not defined. At common law it was not necessary that D suffered such a complete loss of self-control that he was not aware of what he was doing (*Richens* (1994)). It was sufficient that he could not restrain himself and that, presumably, is what is required for the new defence. The fact that Simon flew into a rage in response to Dougal's comments and there was no delay between the comments and the stabbing is evidence that Simon suffered a loss of self-control at the time of the fatal act but ultimately the question whether he did is one for the jury in the light of all the evidence.

---

14 Before considering any available defences it is important to identify the offence of which D may be guilty and to discuss any relevant issues in respect of its *actus reus* and *mens rea*.

15 Clarity in exposition is best achieved by expressing the ingredients of the defence of loss of control in terms of what the prosecution must prove.

QUALIFYING TRIGGER

The qualifying triggers in s 55 include a thing or things done or said (or both) which (a) constituted circumstances of an extremely grave character and (b) caused D to have a justifiable sense of being seriously wronged (s 55(4)). This bears some similarities with the old defence of provocation. However, whereas *anything* said or done could qualify as a trigger for provocation, the new defence is limited to things of an *extremely grave* character. This is, presumably, an objective question. Similarly, whether D had a *'justifiable* sense of being seriously wronged' implies an objective evaluation. The question whether Dougal's comments were a qualifying trigger is again one for the jury and they may take into account the effect of his earlier behaviour as it may have contributed to Simon's loss of control (Think Point (1)).

It is submitted that if, as a result of a qualifying trigger the defendant loses his self-control and kills with malice aforethought, the fact that the defendant had a conditional intention to cause grievous bodily harm prior to the provocation should be no bar to the defence. The prior intention may not have been carried out. Provided the jury are satisfied that the murderous attack was, or may have been, a result of a loss of self-control, the causal nexus between the loss of self-control and the fatal attack is satisfied. A sense of being seriously wronged by a thing done or said is not justifiable by virtue of s 55(6) only where D incited the thing to be done or said for the purpose of providing an excuse to use violence. That limitation does not apply in this case.

A PERSON WITH A NORMAL DEGREE OF TOLERANCE

It is for the jury to decide what powers of self-control one might reasonably expect from an ordinary man of Simon's age but no allowance should be given for characteristics of D which might have made him abnormally volatile – s 54(3).[16]

Simon may also be convicted of the offence, contrary to s 2 of the Criminal Damage Act 1971, of making threats to destroy or damage property belonging to another. It is unnecessary to prove that Dougal actually feared Simon would damage his property. It is sufficient that Simon intended Dougal to fear that his property would be damaged. The maximum penalty for this offence is 10 years' imprisonment.

PETER

MURDER

Section 8 of the Accessories and Abettors Act 1861, as amended by the Criminal Law Act 1977, provides that a person who aids, abets, counsels or procures the commission of an indictable offence is liable to be tried, indicted and punished as a principal offender (Think Point (2)).

---

16 Where the jury is required to make an objective evaluation of the defendant's conduct it is not necessary to predict the jury's decision. It is necessary and sufficient to explain how the jury should approach the task and the facts that may be taken into account.

Where, as in this case, two persons embark on a joint unlawful enterprise, each of the parties is equally liable for the consequences of such acts of the other as are done in the pursuance of that joint enterprise and also for the unforeseen consequences of the other's acts done in pursuance of their agreement (*Anderson and Morris* (1966)). If an accomplice lends himself to a criminal enterprise on the understanding that grievous bodily harm should, if necessary, be inflicted, he will be guilty of murder if the principal kills in accordance with the plan (*Hyde, Sussex and Collins* (1990)). So, if Dougal had died as a result of the intended beating, Peter would have been guilty of murder as an accomplice.

What difference might it make that death resulted from the use of the knife? The issue has been considered by the House of Lords in *Powell and another; English* (1997) and the Court of Appeal in *Uddin* (1998) and *Greatrex* (1998) (see also *Hyde, Sussex and Collins; Hui Chi-Ming* (1992); *Roberts* (1993); *Cairns* (2002); *McCarthy* (2003)). In these cases, the courts identified a number of principles, the relevance of which depends upon elements of the secondary party's *mens rea*. As Peter's *mens rea* is not fully disclosed, there are a number of possible outcomes in this case. The following summary deals with the most likely:

(a) A secondary party is not responsible for an act which is of a fundamentally different type from that foreseen by the secondary party. It would appear that the question whether one attack is different in type from another is a matter for the jury and they might conclude that an attack by using a knife is different from an attack with fists (see also *O'Flaherty and Others* (2004); *Rahman* (2008); *Rafferty* (2007); *Mendez* (2010)).

(b) If Simon's act was fundamentally different from any foreseen by Peter, then Peter is not a party to the death, and is neither guilty of murder nor of manslaughter (*Uddin* (1998); *English; Anderson and Morris* (1966); *Attorney General's Reference (No. 3 of 2004)* (2005); *Robinson v R* (2011)).

(c) If Peter knew that Simon had the knife and that he might use it with an intention to do grievous bodily harm, then he is guilty of murder unless the contemplated use of the knife was fundamentally different from the way in which it was in fact used.

(d) If Peter knew that Simon had a knife but foresaw that he might use it with an intent to cause less serious harm than grievous harm then Peter is guilty of manslaughter (*Roberts, Day and Day* (2001); *D* (2005); *Rahman* (2008); *Carpenter* (2011)).[17]

How might a finding that Simon lost his self-control affect Peter's liability? In *McKechnie* (1992), the principal killed V, having been provoked to lose his self-control whilst carrying out a joint enterprise. The Court of Appeal held that the loss of self-control

---

17 In a question where significant facts are not disclosed do not guess what the facts might have been. Consider the possibilities and explain the alternative outcomes.

was incompatible with a joint enterprise to cause grievous bodily harm to the deceased. Thus, although the principal was guilty of voluntary manslaughter, the other parties were neither guilty of homicide nor of causing grievous bodily harm with intent.

In his commentary to *McKechnie* in the Criminal Law Review, Professor Smith suggests that the decision implies that a loss of self-control brings a prior joint enterprise to an end. However, it is submitted that it is not at all clear that this is what the court intended. The Court of Appeal appeared to take the view that the jury's finding that the principal was provoked ruled out the possibility that there was, prior to the provocation, a joint enterprise to cause grievous bodily harm to which the other defendants could have been parties. The court added that if the principal had been labouring under long-term provocation and the parties had agreed upon a joint enterprise to do serious harm prior to the final act of provocation, then, although the principal would have been guilty of manslaughter, the other parties would have been guilty of murder. And in *Pearson* (1992), the Court of Appeal, distinguishing *McKechnie*, held that a loss of self-control does not necessarily terminate a joint enterprise. In that case, both parties were provoked prior to undertaking the joint enterprise and, although it is not clear from the judgment, it is submitted that the possible basis of the distinction is that, in *Pearson*, there was evidence that both parties intended to kill or cause serious harm from the outset (see *Uddin*). In addition, it was said in *Hui Chi-Ming* that if two men embark upon a robbery and the principal is carrying a weapon which he intends to use merely to frighten if they meet resistance but, through panic at the scene, changes his mind and uses it with malice aforethought, then the secondary party will be guilty of murder if he foresaw at the outset that the principal might use the weapon with malice aforethought.

It is submitted, therefore, that the question of secondary liability where the principal is provoked to kill depends primarily upon whether the secondary party had the appropriate *mens rea* prior to the loss of self-control. If Peter was aware that Simon carried a knife and foresaw that he might use it with an intention to do grievous bodily harm, then he may be convicted of murder, although Simon might be guilty only of manslaughter (Think Point (3)).

(If, however, Professor Smith's analysis of *McKechnie* is correct and Simon's loss of self-control terminates the joint enterprise, then Peter will incur no liability for the homicide or for grievous bodily harm with intent, even if he foresaw the possibility that Simon might use the weapon with malice aforethought.)

In addition, Peter may be convicted as an accomplice to the offence, perpetrated by Simon, of making threats contrary to s 2 of the **Criminal Damage Act 1971**.

CONSPIRACY
Did Peter and Simon conspire to cause grievous bodily harm? It is submitted that they did not.

Section 1(1) of the **Criminal Law Act 1977** provides that a person is guilty of statutory conspiracy if he agrees with another that a course of conduct shall be pursued which, if the agreement is carried out as intended, will necessarily amount to the commission of an offence by at least one of the parties to the agreement. As their agreed course of conduct would not necessarily involve the infliction of grievous bodily harm, they did not conspire to commit that offence (*Reed* (1982)).

They are, however, guilty of a conspiracy to make threats to damage property belonging to another (Think Point (4)).

Think Points

1   Section 55(6)(c) provides: In determining whether a loss of self-control had a qualifying trigger . . . the fact that a thing done or said constituted sexual infidelity is to be disregarded. Dougal's comments do not constitute sexual infidelity nor do they disclose sexual infidelity.

2   In *Concannon* (2001), it was held that a conviction for murder and the resulting imposition of a mandatory life sentence where the offender was a secondary party was not in breach of **Art 6 of the European Convention on Human Rights**.

3   See also *Dunbar* (1988) and *Mitchell and King* (1999); cf *Roberts, Day and Day* (2001). In *Uddin* (1998), it was said that if D2 continues to participate in an attack after becoming aware that D1 has produced a weapon, he will be guilty of murder if the weapon is used to kill V: see *Cairns* (2002).

4   Where the defendants have been charged with a substantive offence, the prosecution may not also proceed with a charge of conspiracy to commit it, unless they can satisfy the judge that the interests of justice demand it (*Practice Note* (1977)).

Common Pitfalls

This is a fairly complicated question raising a variety of issues, including those relating to the effect of provocation upon the liability of an accessory. The most common error in answering this type of problem is to attempt to come to a definite conclusion on the parties' liability. It is not clear, for example, whether Peter knew Simon had a knife and, if so, whether he might use it, and so you should explain the alternative outcomes consistent with the disclosed facts.

QUESTION 33

Martin's mother was dying from cancer. He was extremely depressed. Explaining that he intended to kill his mother he asked Shona, a chemist, for some cyanide. Shona agreed to do so but supplied him, as she had always intended, with a quantity of a non fatal substance. He put it in his mother's tea. She fell asleep without drinking the tea and died from a heart attack during the night.

▶ Discuss the parties' criminal liability.

How to Answer this Question

This question requires an examination of inchoate offences and accomplice liability. It is necessary to consider attempting the impossible in relation to murder and the offence contrary to s 23 of the Offences Against the Person Act 1861. The question also raised issues in respect of offence of conspiracy and whether criminal liability can lie in respect of aiding and abetting an attempt.

Answer Structure

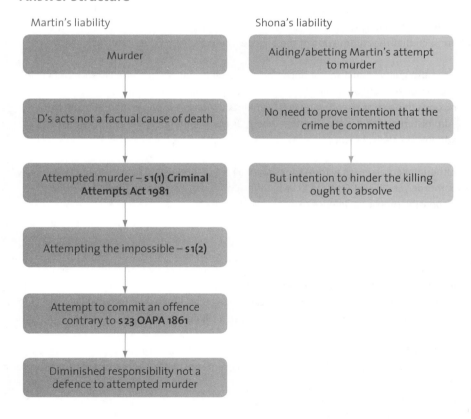

Martin's liability

- Murder
- D's acts not a factual cause of death
- Attempted murder – **s 1(1) Criminal Attempts Act 1981**
- Attempting the impossible – **s 1(2)**
- Attempt to commit an offence contrary to **s 23 OAPA 1861**
- Diminished responsibility not a defence to attempted murder

Shona's liability

- Aiding/abetting Martin's attempt to murder
- No need to prove intention that the crime be committed
- But intention to hinder the killing ought to absolve

ANSWER

ATTEMPTED MURDER

Clearly Martin is not guilty of murder as his acts were not the factual cause of his mother's death. Although he intended to kill his mother and that event occurred his actions were not a *sine qua non* of the event (*White* (1910)).

He is however guilty of attempted murder.

Section 1(1) of the Criminal Attempts Act 1981 provides that a person is guilty of an attempt if, with intent to commit an offence triable on indictment, he does an act which is more than merely preparatory to the commission of that offence.

By virtue of s 4(3), it is a question of fact whether D has done acts which are more than merely preparatory. However, in this case, there can be little doubt that a jury properly directed would conclude that Martin's acts were more than merely preparatory. And, despite the fact that he administered a non lethal substance, he acted with the necessary intent. Section 1(2) provides that a person may be guilty of attempt even though the facts are such that the commission of the offence is impossible (*Shivpuri* (1987)).[18]

He is also guilty of an attempt to commit the offence under s 23 of the Offences Against the Person Act 1861 of administering to or causing to be administered a poison or other noxious thing so as to endanger life. Cyanide is a recognised poison and 'causing to be administered' includes the situation where, as Martin intended, the victim self administers the substance.

Although depression may form the basis of a plea of diminished responsibility to a charge of murder, Sedley J at Stafford Crown Court (*Campbell* (1997)) ruled that diminished responsibility is not a defence to attempted murder.[19]

It is submitted that this is correct.

The defining ingredient of attempt, contrary to s 1 of the 1981 Act is intent. There is no requirement in the statute that had the attempt succeeded it would have constituted the full offence and s 2(1) of the Homicide Act provides that diminished responsibility is available only where a person kills or is party to a killing.

Furthermore, the purpose of the defence of diminished responsibility is to allow the judge to impose a penalty other than the mandatory sentence of life imprisonment in cases

---

18 Where D has made a 'complete' attempt his act is, inevitably, 'more than merely preparatory'.

19 Decisions of Crown Court judges are not binding but may, of course, be referred to when there is a lack of authority.

where a relevant ability of the defendant has been substantially impaired. As there is no mandatory penalty for attempted murder the judge is free to take the condition into account when sentencing.

CONSPIRACY

Section 1(1) of the Criminal Law Act 1977, as substituted by s 5(1) of the Criminal Attempts Act 1981, provides that a person is guilty of conspiracy if he agrees with any other person or persons to pursue a course of conduct which, if carried out as intended, will necessarily amount to the commission of an offence by one or more of the parties to the agreement or would do so but for the existence of facts which render the commission of the offence impossible.

Was there a conspiracy to murder between Martin and Shona despite the fact that Shona supplied him, as intended, with a non fatal substance? Is it necessary to prove for conspiracy that the defendant intended the agreed offence to be carried out?

In *Anderson* (1986), the House of Lords held that it was not necessary to prove that the defendant intended that the substantive offence be committed. In a number of subsequent decisions, however, the Court of Appeal have not applied this rule, holding that an intention to carry out the crime is a requirement of conspiracy (e.g *Edwards* (1991), *Ashton* (1992); *Harvey* (1999). See also the decision of the Privy Council in *Yip Chiu-Cheung* (1994)). As the decision in Anderson has been heavily criticised and, it is submitted, unlikely to be followed, it would appear that there is no conspiracy between Martin and Shona.

AIDING AND ABETTING AN ATTEMPT

Might Shona be convicted of attempted murder as a secondary party?

Section 8 of the Accessories and Abettors Act 1861 provides that a person who aids, abets, counsels or procures the commission of an indictable offence is liable to be tried, indicted and punished for that offence as a principal offender.

In *Dunnington* (1984) it was held that a person can be convicted as a secondary party to an attempt. And, although it is necessary to show that the act which assisted or encouraged the commission of the offence must be done knowingly and deliberately, it is not necessary to prove that the secondary party intended the crime to be committed (*NCB v Gamble* (1959)). Indifference to the result of the crime does not of itself negative aiding or abetting.

In *Bryce* (2004) it was said where D is charged as a secondary party to an offence committed by A the prosecution must prove:

(a)   an act done by D which in fact assisted the later commission of the offence,

(b) that D did the act deliberately, realising that it was capable of assisting the offence,

(c) that D at the time of doing the act contemplated the commission of the offence by A, ie he foresaw it as a 'real or substantial risk' or 'real possibility' and,

(d) that D when doing the act intended to assist A in what he was doing.

Thus, if it is proved that the defendant intentionally did acts of assistance or encouragement it is no defence that he hoped that events might intervene to prevent the crime taking place. Potter LJ, delivering the judgment of the Court of Appeal, explained that the secondary party's guilt springs from the fact that he contemplates the commission of the crime and he intentionally lends assistance (see also *Rook* (1993); *Maxwell* (1979)).

However, it was pointed out that if the intention is to hinder the carrying out of the offence then there can be no liability as a secondary party.

In the instant problem, Shona intentionally lent her assistance to the attempt to kill, she did not intend to assist Martin to kill his mother. She intentionally supplied a substance which she knew was not lethal and that Martin's attempt to kill using it would prove impossible. Martin, as we have seen, is guilty of attempted murder despite the fact that it was impossible to commit murder. Is Shona guilty as a secondary party to the attempt which she knew to be impossible?

It is submitted that she ought not to be. Although Shona intentionally assisted the attempt she intentionally hindered the killing. This ought to absolve her of liability for secondary liability in respect of the attempt.

QUESTION 34

James, Chris and Mike planned to kill John. They arranged to meet later in the evening, then proceeded to John's house where it was intended that James and Chris would restrain John while Mike stabbed him. At the appointed time, Chris and Mike met but James did not turn up. He had changed his mind. He had tried to telephone Chris and Mike to inform them of his decision, but had been unable to make contact. James telephoned John to warn him that Chris and Mike were on their way and that they planned to attack him. As James was explaining the danger, Chris and Mike arrived. Chris grabbed hold of John, whereupon Mike, following the plan, stabbed John in the heart. John died instantly.

▶ Discuss the criminal liability of James, Chris and Mike.

How to Answer this Question

This question raises issues concerning accessorial liability and conspiracy. The principal issue concerns whether James' failed attempt at informing the other parties that he no longer wished to carry out their agreed plan and/or his telephone conversation with John amounted to an effective 'withdrawal', absolving James of liability for the murder.

In addition, the liability of the parties for conspiracy is discussed. For this offence, 'withdrawal' does not negative liability.

Answer Structure

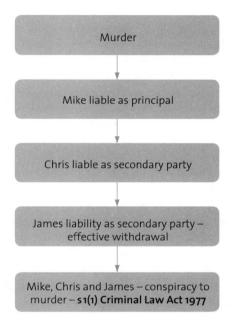

| Murder |
| Mike liable as principal |
| Chris liable as secondary party |
| James liability as secondary party – effective withdrawal |
| Mike, Chris and James – conspiracy to murder – s1(1) **Criminal Law Act 1977** |

ANSWER

MURDER

It would appear that both Chris and Mike are guilty of murder; Mike as principal and Chris as a secondary party. Murder consists of the killing of a human being with either an intention to kill or an intention to cause grievous bodily harm (*Moloney* (1985)). And, by virtue of s 8 of the Accessories and Abettors Act 1861, as amended by the Criminal Law Act 1977, anyone who assists or encourages the commission of an offence is liable to be tried and punished as a principal offender.[20]

The mandatory sentence for those convicted of murder is a term of imprisonment for life (Murder (Abolition of Death Penalty) Act 1965).

20 When tackling a question involving secondary liability always deal first with the liability of the principal.

Whether James is also guilty of murder is less clear. A person can escape secondary liability for an offence by withdrawal before the offence is committed, but what amounts to effective withdrawal depends on the circumstances of the case. In *O'Flaherty* (2004) it was said that D had to do enough to demonstrate that he or she was withdrawing from the joint enterprise. That was a question of fact and degree for the jury which had to take account of the nature of the assistance and encouragement already given.

Where the mode of participation consists merely of counselling or encouraging the commission of the offence, it is generally accepted that communication to the other parties of the intention to abandon the common purpose will suffice. The communication must be timely and must serve unequivocal notice to the others that if they proceed, they do so without the assistance or encouragement of the party seeking to withdraw (*Whitehouse* (1941); *Whitefield* (1984); *Rook* (1993); *Bryce* (2004)). Even where the mode of participation consists of giving material assistance, communication of withdrawal may be effective (*Grundy* (1977)).

James tried but failed to communicate his intention to the other parties, but it is arguable that a reasonable attempt to communicate withdrawal is sufficient.

Alternatively, his telephone call to John might amount to an effective withdrawal. In *Becerra and Cooper* (1975), the Court of Appeal quoted with approval a passage from the decision of the Court of Appeal of British Columbia in *Whitehouse*, in which it was stated that communication to the other parties is essential only where it was 'practicable and reasonable' (see also *Mitchell and King* (1998); *Mitchell* (2008)) and it has been suggested that, where communication with the other parties is either not practicable or not reasonable, timely notification of the proposed offence to the police would suffice. Presumably, timely notification to the intended victim will also suffice (Think Point (1)).

If so, the question for the jury is whether, taking into account the nature of James' participation, the timing of the 'withdrawal' and all other relevant circumstances, what he did was sufficient to amount to an effective withdrawal (Think Point (2)).[21]

CONSPIRACY
Even if James' withdrawal is adjudged to be effective such that he attracts no criminal liability for the murder of John, it would appear that he is guilty of conspiring to murder him. An agreement between two or more persons to commit a crime is a statutory conspiracy defined in s 1(1) of the **Criminal Law Act 1977**. As conspiracy is complete the

---

21   As it is not possible to come to a conclusive answer in respect of the effectiveness of James' attempt to withdraw an explanation of the relevant principles is sufficient.

moment the parties agree to commit an offence, subsequent 'withdrawal' does not negative liability (*Barnard* (1979)). It may, however, be a relevant factor in mitigation (*Gortat and Pirog* (1973); *Davies* (1990)).

By virtue of s 3(2)(a), the maximum penalty for a conspiracy to murder is a term of imprisonment for life.

Chris and Mike could also be charged with conspiracy in addition to murder. However, such a practice is discouraged and the prosecution are required to satisfy the judge that the interests of justice demand charging with both offences (*Practice Note* (1977)).

Think Points

1 In *Rook* (1993), the Court of Appeal stated that communication of withdrawal to the other parties was 'the minimum necessary'. In that case, however, the defendant had not made any attempt to tell the others that he no longer wished to take part in an agreed murder nor did he do anything to stop them carrying out the agreement. He simply failed to turn up at the appointed place.

2 It is obviously not necessary that the defendant successfully prevents the commission of the offence. The issue of secondary liability would not arise at all if the offence were prevented. In *Rook* (1993), Lord Lloyd was not prepared to endorse the view that aid already afforded had to be neutralised. He stated, *obiter*, that it might be enough that the defendant 'did his best' to prevent the commission of the offence.

Offences Against Property

INTRODUCTION

Most criminal law examination papers include a number of questions raising issues in respect of the major property offences. As problem questions are often constructed to test your knowledge of a number of offences, most of the questions in this chapter require discussion of the defendant's potential liability for more than one offence. Occasionally issues relating to the offences against the person are included.

The principal statute in this area is the Theft Act 1968. In addition, this chapter deals with offences created by the Theft Act 1978, the Theft (Amendment) Act 1996, the Fraud Act 2006 and with the major offences of criminal damage under the Criminal Damage Act 1971.

Checklist ✔

Theft and related offences

One of the major current issues concerns the meaning of an appropriation for the purposes of theft and, in particular, the question whether there can be an appropriation of property belonging to another if the owner consents to what D does in relation to the property. It is important that you have a good understanding of the decisions of the House of Lords in *Gomez* (1992) and *Hinks* (2000).

In addition, as most of the offences in this section are offences of 'dishonesty', it is most important that you are well acquainted with the decision of the Court of Appeal in *Ghosh* (1982) and later cases concerning the meaning of that concept.

Issues of civil law – for example, rules concerning the passing of ownership – are of relevance to the law of theft, and the basic principles should be learnt.

The following offences are dealt with (references are to the **Theft Act 1968** unless otherwise stated):

- theft: **s 1**;
- robbery: **s 8**; assault with intent to rob: **s 8(2)**;
- blackmail: **s 21**;
- burglary: **s 9(1)**;

- making off without payment: **s 3** of the **1978 Act**;
- handling stolen goods: **s 22**;
- aggravated burglary: **s 10**;
- taking a conveyance: **s 12**; aggravated vehicle-taking: **s 12A**;
- abstracting of electricity: **s 13**;
- false accounting: **s 17**;
- going equipped: **s 25**;
- fraud: **s 1(1) Fraud Act 2006**;
- obtaining services dishonestly: **s 11 Fraud Act 2006**;
- possession of articles for use in frauds: **s 6 Fraud Act 2006**;
- making or supplying articles for use in frauds: **s 7 Fraud Act 2006**.

Offences of damage: the **Criminal Damage Act 1971**

With regard to criminal damage, you should be familiar with:

- 'simple' damage: **s 1(1)**;
- 'dangerous' damage: **s 1(2)**;
- arson: **s 1(3)**;
- threats to destroy or damage property: **s 2**; and
- defences of 'lawful excuse' in **s 5(2)**.

A number of the problem questions raise issues dealt with in earlier chapters.

QUESTION 35

Innit, via the internet, downloaded anti-virus software onto his computer. There was a charge for the software which Innit paid for using false credit card details.

He then went to a restaurant for lunch. Innit paid for the meal by cheque. He knew that the there were no funds in his bank account and the cheque would be unpaid.

On leaving the restaurant he decided to take a walk. By chance he met an acquaintance, Wottevah. Wottevah owed Innit £50 and had made numerous excuses to avoid repayment of the loan.

Innit asked Wottevah for the money owed but Wottevah refused saying that he was broke. However, as a favour to Innit, he offered to sell his expensive watch to him for just £30. Innit agreed to buy the watch and gave Wottevah a cheque in payment.

Innit then went to the local leisure centre. The adult entry fee was £5 except for the unemployed, for whom there was no charge. Innit presented a forged unemployment card to the cashier and was given access free of charge to the centre, wherein he used the sauna.

▶ Discuss Innit's criminal liability.

How to Answer this Question

This question raises issues concerning a number of offences under the Fraud Act 2006. These include fraud contrary to s 1, obtaining services dishonestly contrary to s 11, possession of articles for use in frauds contrary to s 6.

Applying the Law

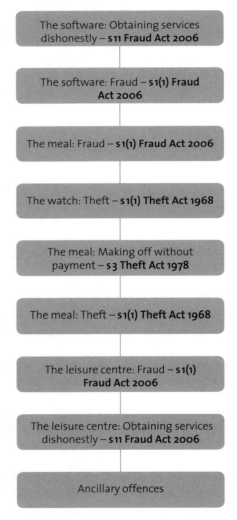

The software: Obtaining services dishonestly – **s 11 Fraud Act 2006**

The software: Fraud – **s 1(1) Fraud Act 2006**

The meal: Fraud – **s 1(1) Fraud Act 2006**

The watch: Theft – **s 1(1) Theft Act 1968**

The meal: Making off without payment – **s 3 Theft Act 1978**

The meal: Theft – **s 1(1) Theft Act 1968**

The leisure centre: Fraud – **s 1(1) Fraud Act 2006**

The leisure centre: Obtaining services dishonestly – **s 11 Fraud Act 2006**

Ancillary offences

This flow chart highlights the main legislation you need to apply in answering this question.

ANSWER

THE SOFTWARE: OBTAINING SERVICES DISHONESTLY – s 11 FRAUD ACT 2006

A person is guilty of an offence contrary to s 11 if, dishonestly intending to avoid payment, he obtains services for which payment is required.

'Services' is not defined but it was intended to include the provision of software by internet download.

Dishonesty is also undefined. The framers of the Act intended that the issue be approached by reference to the test established in the case of *Ghosh* (1982). There is no suggestion in the facts that the downloading of the material was other than dishonest and so fuller discussion of the *Ghosh* test is postponed until a later stage of this answer.[1]

The maximum custodial sentence for an offence contrary to s 11 is five years.

THE SOFTWARE: FRAUD – s 1(1) FRAUD ACT 2006

The offence of fraud can be committed in three ways. All three forms require proof of dishonesty and an intention to make a gain in terms of money or other property or an intention to cause loss to another or expose another to a risk of loss in terms of money or other property.

The downloading of the software amounts to the variant of fraud termed 'fraud by false representation' (s 1(2) Fraud Act 2006).

A fraudulent representation is an assertion which is untrue or misleading and which the person making it knows is or might be untrue or misleading (s 2(2)). It may be implied by conduct, there is no need to prove that anyone was actually deceived by the representation and by s 2(5) a representation may be regarded as made if it is submitted in any form to a system designed to receive, convey or respond to communications. This includes representations made to machines and/or over the internet to activate a piece of software to accept a payment.

Innit falsely made a false representation that he was authorised to use the credit card and as he did so dishonestly with a view to gain he is guilty of an offence of fraud.[2]

The maximum custodial sentence for an offence of fraud is 10 years.

---

1   It is not necessary to discuss in detail an element of an offence which is not a live issue.
2   When considering this form of fraud it is important to identify the fraudulent representation which was made by D.

THE MEAL: FRAUD – s 1(1) FRAUD ACT 2006

Innit is also guilty of fraud in respect of the meal he ordered at the restaurant. The drawer of a cheque impliedly represents that the cheque will be met on presentment (*MPC v Charles* (1977)). As Innit knew that it would not be met he knowingly made a false representation and did so with a view to gain.

THE MEAL: THEFT – s 1(1) THEFT ACT 1968

Can Innit be convicted of stealing the meal contrary to s 1(1) of the Theft Act 1968?

Prior to *Gomez* (1992), although the law was not clear, the balance of authority supported the conclusion that, if a cheat deceived another into selling him something, the victim intending to transfer his entire proprietary interest, the cheat got a voidable title and could not be convicted of theft because he was the owner of the thing. In addition, Lord Roskill in *Morris* (1984) stated that a person did not appropriate property unless he did something in relation to it that he was not authorised to do. If the owner had consented to the act, there could be no appropriation, even where that consent was obtained by fraud.

The House of Lords in *Gomez* disagreed. Lord Keith stated that, although the actual decision in *Morris* was correct, it was unnecessary and erroneous to suggest that an authorised act could never amount to an appropriation. His Lordship quoted with approval a passage from the judgment of Lord Parker in *Dobson v General Accident Fire and Life Assurance Corp plc* (1990), in which it was stated that appropriation can occur even if the owner consents, and it is no defence to say that the property passed under a voidable contract. It was felt to be wrong to introduce, into this branch of criminal law, questions of whether particular contracts are voidable on the ground of fraud.[3]

This decision means that practically all cases where D, intending permanently to deprive, dishonestly obtains property as a result of a false representation amount to theft (Think Point (1)).

And thus, as Innit dishonestly intended not to pay for the meal, he committed theft when he consumed it.

By s 7 of the 1968 Act, as substituted by s 26 of the Criminal Justice Act 1991, the maximum penalty for theft is seven years' imprisonment.

---

3   The issues of whether Innit appropriated the meal and whether it belonged to another at the time of the appropriation are addressed. The remaining elements of theft are referred to but require no detailed discussion as they are clearly satisfied.

THE MEAL: MAKING OFF WITHOUT PAYMENT – s3 THEFT ACT 1978

Whether Innit might be convicted of 'making off without payment' contrary to s3 of the Theft Act 1978 is not clear.

It remains to be authoritatively decided whether a person can be said to have 'made off without having paid as required or expected' if he left with the consent of the creditor, that consent having been obtained by deception.

A circuit judge at Lincoln Crown Court held that there is no 'making off' if the creditor consents to the defendant's leaving in circumstances such as those in the present problem (*Hammond* (1982)). It was said that a person who takes a cheque without a cheque card is aware of the risk of non-payment and, as he allows D to leave, it cannot be said that D 'makes off'.

It is submitted that this interpretation of the section is wrong. The section is aimed at the bilking customer – it should not matter whether D leaves with stealth or openly, with or without the apparent consent of P.

If this analysis is correct, Innit committed the s3 offence on leaving the restaurant. A stolen cheque does not operate as a conditional discharge of his liability to pay. Innit made off without having paid as expected or required.

THE WATCH: FRAUD – s1(1) FRAUD ACT 2006

Although Innit made a false representation – that the cheque would be met on presentment – and did so with a view to gain the watch, it is arguable that he was not dishonest. Wottevah had persistently refused to pay Innit money he was owed and Innit may have believed that, in the circumstances it was not dishonest of him to dupe Wottevah into parting with his watch.[4]

If Innit does raise evidence that he was not dishonest then the issue is one for the jury which should be directed that a person is not dishonest if what he did was, in the jury's opinion, not dishonest according to the ordinary standards of reasonable people or he mistakenly believed that it was not dishonest according to those standards (*Feely* (1973); *Ghosh* (1982)).

THE WATCH: THEFT – s1(1) THEFT ACT 1968

Although the ownership in the watch transferred to Innit when he purchased it from Wottevah he appropriated property belonging to another and he did so with an intention to permanently deprive (see *Gomez* above).

---

4   It is important to appreciate that the fact that D has made a false representation does not necessarily mean that he is dishonest. By expressly including a requirement of dishonesty the framers of the Act acknowledge that a false representation may be honest.

His liability for theft, as for fraud, will depend on whether he acted dishonestly. But the approach to dishonesty in theft is slightly different from that taken in respect of fraud. Section 2 of the 1968 Act defines three states of mind which are, for the purposes of theft only, not dishonest. These include a belief in a legal right to deprive (s 2(1)(a)). Thus, if Innit believes, albeit mistakenly, that because he is owed money, he is legally entitled to take the watch without paying for it he is not dishonest and therefore not guilty of theft. If, however, he knows that he has no legal right to deprive Wottevah of the watch but believes he was morally entitled to do so then the jury should be directed in accordance with *Ghosh* (above).

THE LEISURE CENTRE: FRAUD – s 1(1) FRAUD ACT 2006

Clearly Innit has committed an offence of fraud by false representation when he presented a false unemployment card to gain entry to the leisure centre.

THE LEISURE CENTRE: OBTAINING SERVICES DISHONESTLY – s 11 FRAUD ACT 2006

Innit is, however, not guilty of an offence contrary to s 11 of the Act. Although he obtained services the section provides that the services obtained must be one which was made available on the basis that payment has been, is being or will be made for or in respect of them. In this case although payment would normally be required, Innit deceived the cashier into waiving the charge and thus the services were not made available on the basis that they had been or were to be paid for (Think Point (2)).

ANCILLARY OFFENCES

Section 6 provides that it is an offence to possess an article for use in the course of or in connection with any fraud. The use of the expression *'any* fraud' in the section is intended to ensure that a general intention to use the article for a fraud will suffice. Section 25 of the Theft Act 1968, as amended, is defined in similar terms in respect of articles in D's possession which he intends to use in connection with a theft or a burglary and in *Ellames* (1974) the Court of Appeal held that the word 'any' in the section indicated that it was not necessary to prove an intention to use the article in connection with a specific burglary or theft (Think Point (3)).

Possession of the cheque book and the unemployment card with the intent to use them in the course of fraud are offences contrary to s 6 and possession of the cheque book with intent to use it in the course of theft is an offence contrary to s 25.

The maximum custodial sentence for an offence contrary to s 6 is five years and for an offence contrary to s 25 is three years.

If Innit forged the unemployment card (Think Point (4)) then he is guilty of an offence contrary to s 7 of the Fraud Act. This provides that it is an offence to make, adapt, supply or offer to supply any article intending it to be used to commit fraud. The maximum custodial sentence for this offence is 10 years.

Think Points

1   Only where the property obtained is land will there be no liability for theft.

2   The Law Commission, *Fraud*, Law Com No. 276, (2002) para 8.14.

3   The s 25 offence applies only when D is not at his place of abode. There is no such limitation in respect of the s 6 offence.

4   It is not clear whether Innit was in possession of the false credit card itself or simply had a record of the card details. If the latter he was not in possession of an article for the purposes of s 6.

Common Pitfalls ✗

One of the most common errors in tackling this type of question is to discuss in detail all the elements of each offence. Do not waste your time. Focus on the issues raised by the question.

QUESTION 36

PART (A)
Critically evaluate the *Ghosh* (1982) test of dishonesty.

PART (B)
Swoop was walking along the empty pier at Mudpool when she found a $50 note. She was delighted and decided to celebrate by having a meal at 'El Caro', a posh restaurant on the front. Sitting back, having consumed her meal, she overheard an American lady at an adjacent table say to her husband that she had lost $50. Swoop nevertheless decided to keep the money.

▶   Discuss Swoop's liability.

How to Answer this Question

PART (A)
A critical evaluation of the *Ghosh* test:

❖   the role of the jury in cases where the issue of dishonesty is raised;
❖   the two-part test enunciated in *Ghosh*; and
❖   the problems of leaving questions of dishonesty to the jury.

PART (B)

A relatively straightforward problem centering on the meaning of dishonesty:

❖   application of s 2(1)(c) of the Theft Act 1968; and
❖   the later assumption principle in s 3(1) of the 1968 Act. Principal authorities: *Feely* (1973); *Ghosh* (1982); *Gilks* (1972).

Applying the Law

(a)   (b)

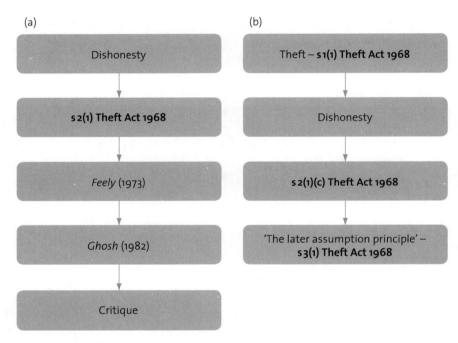

This two part diagram highlights the main legislation and principles to apply in your answer.

ANSWER

PART (A)

Many of the offences under the Theft Acts 1968 and 1978 and the Fraud Act 2006 require the prosecution to prove that D's 'appropriation', 'obtaining' or 'receiving', etc, was 'dishonest'.

For the purposes of theft only, s 2(1) of the 1968 Act specifies three instances of states of mind which as a matter of law are to be regarded as honest. The burden is on the prosecution to prove that D did not have one of the specified beliefs. If the jury have a reasonable doubt that D was dishonest – if the prosecution have failed to prove the absence of an honest belief – then the jury must acquit.

Section 2(1) was intended to be only a partial (negative) definition of dishonesty. The Criminal Law Revision Committee recognised that it would be unwise to attempt an exhaustive list of those states of mind which, in law, might be regarded as honest. The assumption in their Eighth Report seems to have been that in cases not covered by s 2, the issue of dishonesty would be left to the jury to determine as a question of fact. In *Feely* (1973), this course was adopted by the Court of Appeal, which held that as dishonesty was an 'ordinary' word, the jury did not require assistance from the judge as to its meaning. According to the court, the jury would be expected to decide the issue by reference to the 'current standards of ordinary decent people'.

This approach has been criticised by most academic writers as the jury are not only given the task of deciding questions of primary fact (that is, what did the accused believe or intend, etc), but are also left the responsibility of evaluating those beliefs and intentions. In a sense, where dishonesty is a 'live' issue, the jury decide the limits of liability for theft; the *Feely* approach appoints the jury to the role of 'mini-legislators'.

Some later cases went even further than *Feely*. In *Gilks* (1972), for example, the judge directed the jury to consider whether the defendant himself thought he was acting honestly. This implies that the defendant's own standards are applied (see also *Boggeln v Williams* (1978); *McIvor* (1982); *Landy* (1981)). The issue was resolved by the Court of Appeal in *Ghosh* (1982).

Lord Lane CJ, delivering the judgment of the court, stated that, in determining whether the prosecution have proved that the defendant was acting dishonestly, a jury must first of all decide whether, according to the ordinary standards of reasonable and honest people, what was done was dishonest. If it was not dishonest according to those standards, the prosecution fails. If it was dishonest by those standards, then the jury must consider whether the defendant himself realised that what he was doing was, by those standards, dishonest. It is dishonest for the defendant to act in a way which he knows ordinary people consider to be dishonest. If the defendant did not know that, the prosecution fails.[5]

This means that a person is not dishonest if what he did was in accordance with the jury's understanding of ordinary standards or he mistakenly believed that what he did was in accordance with those standards.

5   Note the structure of the **Ghosh** test and take care to express each of the 'if … then' limbs precisely.

The first part of the test corresponds to the *Feely* principle and preserves the principle that the issue of dishonesty is a matter of fact for the jury and not the judge (Think Point (1)).[6]

There are a number of dangers with this approach. There may be considerable variation in standards from one jury to the next. The jury may consist of people who have quite low standards. They may believe, for example, that it is not dishonest to help oneself to the property of an employer. This would mean that some people's property rights would be less well protected than others. In its Consultation Paper, *Legislating the Criminal Code: Fraud and Deception* (Law Com No 155), the Law Commission pointed out that:

> Traditionally, offences consist of objectively defined conduct (or circumstances, or events) and mental states (or other fault elements, such as negligence), subject to objectively defined circumstances of justification or excuse (such as self-defence or duress). In general the fact-finders' task is to determine whether the defendant's conduct falls within the legal definition of the offence, not whether they think it sufficiently blameworthy to be an offence. A requirement that the conduct in question falls short of an undefined moral standard is out of keeping with this approach.
>
> [para 5.11]

It concluded that:

> . . . juries and magistrates should not be asked to set a moral standard on which criminal liability essentially depends. As a general rule, the law should say what is forbidden, and that should be informed by moral insights. A jury or magistrates should then be asked to apply the law by coming to factual conclusions, not moral ones.

The second limb of *Ghosh* presents further problems. Fortunately, it does not go as far as *Gilks*. The defendant is not his own legislator. He is not to be judged by his own standards. However, it does mean that a person who has a low opinion (whether mistaken or not) of the general morality of the community will escape liability for theft. The person who has taken his employer's property and genuinely believes that 'everybody thinks it is all right to steal from their employer' is not dishonest according to *Ghosh*. Again, this means that the proprietary rights of some individuals or groups are, potentially at least, accorded less protection in law than others.

Although much of the criticism regarding *Ghosh* warns that the jury may apply terribly low standards, there is also the danger that they might apply excessively high standards. In crimes of dishonesty other than theft, the issue of dishonesty is exclusively one for the jury – s 2 applies only to theft. Thus, for example, the jury might conclude that a

---

6   This question requires a critical evaluation of the **Ghosh** test. An account of the test is necessary but not sufficient.

defendant who practised fraud to obtain money to which he mistakenly believed he was entitled was dishonest (cf theft, where a mistaken belief that one is legally entitled to the property appropriated is, as a matter of law, an honest state of mind).

In addition, it is debatable whether juries find the test easy to understand. (They must acquit unless they think that the defendant believed that ordinary, reasonable and honest people (like themselves?) would think that what he did, believed and intended was dishonest.)

The task of the jury is made a little easier by the fact that if it is accepted that what D did was dishonest according to ordinary standards, the judge need direct the jury only by reference to the second limb (*Thompson* (1988)). However, if D raises the issue of dishonesty by claiming, for example, that he thought what he was doing was not dishonest according to ordinary standards, the judge should direct the jury in accordance with *Ghosh*, even if the judge believes that D was patently dishonest (*Price* (1989); *Green* (1992); *Clarke* (1996)) (Think Point (2)).

It is submitted that the definition of dishonesty should be a matter of law for the judge, applied, in the ordinary way, by the jury to the facts as they believe them to be. The virtue of this approach would be that the concept might then be refined and developed by analogy with the states of mind specified in s 2 – each of which implicitly recognises the proprietary rights of the owner. This would have the virtue of directing attention towards the victim's property rights and the defendant's attitude towards those rights. This, it is submitted, is preferable to the current approach based on the vague standards of so called 'ordinary people'.

PART (B)

When Swoop discovered the money on the pier, she probably did not commit theft. By virtue of s 2(1)(c), a person does not appropriate property dishonestly if she believes that the person to whom it belongs cannot be found by taking reasonable steps.

However, she may have committed theft when, having overheard the conversation between the Americans, she decided to keep the money. By virtue of s 3(1), a person who originally came by property innocently may be guilty of stealing it on the basis of a later dishonest assumption of a right to it.[7]

Swoop, having heard the conversation, cannot conceivably rely upon s 2(1)(c). If, however, she contends that she thought that keeping the money in those circumstances was in 'accordance with ordinary standards', then the judge would be required to direct the jury in accordance with the *Ghosh* test, explained above (*Price*).

....

7   As all the elements of theft must exist simultaneously, it is necessary to identify the fresh appropriation committed when Swoop decided to keep the money.

Think Points

1 In *Hyam* (1997), it was said that where a *Ghosh* (1982) direction was necessary, the trial judge should use the exact words of Lord Lane's formula.

2 In *Wood* (2002), D claimed that he believed property which he removed from a disused shop had been abandoned. The Court of Appeal pointed out that a *Ghosh* (1982) direction was unnecessary. If the defendant genuinely believed that the goods were abandoned, then he was not, as a matter of law, dishonest, no matter how unreasonable that belief. A *Ghosh* direction should only be given in cases where ordinary people might have differing views from a defendant as to whether what he was doing was dishonest or not. Cf *Rostron* (2003).

Common Pitfalls ✗

The first part of the question requires a critical evaluation of the *Ghosh* (1982) test. An account of the test and its application is necessary, but not sufficient. The main criticisms concern the dangers of leaving the issue of dishonesty to the variable standards of the jury.

QUESTION 37

PART (A)

Samantha borrowed Rachel's recorder without permission. She returned the recorder when the batteries were practically exhausted. Rachel would not have consented to Samantha borrowing the recorder. Assume that the batteries are not rechargeable and that Samantha was aware of that.

▶ Discuss Samantha's criminal liability.

PART (B)

Mark took Henry's cat. He hoped and believed that Henry would assume the cat had strayed and that he would offer a reward to anyone finding it. He intended to return the cat to Henry after a few days, even if no reward was offered.

▶ Discuss Mark's criminal liability. Would your answer differ if Mark had planned to let the cat go free were no offer of reward made for its return?

PART (C)

Dick took Fob's watch and pawned it. He intended to redeem and return it to Fob the following week and, knowing that he will have received his salary by then, he is certain that he will be able to do so.

▶ Discuss Dick's criminal liability.

How to Answer this Question

A three-part problem question involving similar issues and dealing with the offences of theft (s 1) and abstraction of electricity (s 13). The most important issues involve s 6(1) (extended meaning of intention to permanently deprive) and s 4 (property) and, in particular:

❖ the circumstances in which a borrowing is 'equivalent to an outright taking';
❖ the meaning and application of the phrase 'an intention to treat the thing as his own to dispose of regardless of the other's rights';
❖ the definition of 'property'; and
❖ the parting of property under a condition as to its return (s 6(2)).

Applying the Law

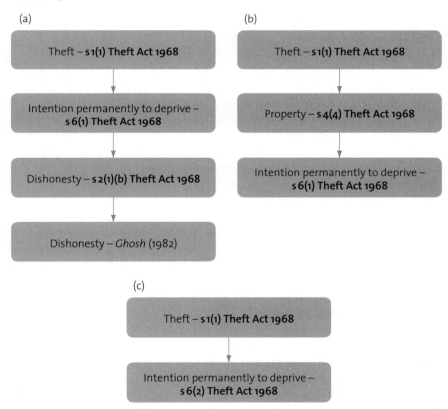

This three part flow chart demonstrates the legislation and principles you need to apply in your answer.

ANSWER

PART (A)

THEFT OF THE BATTERY

It is proposed to consider, first, Samantha's liability for theft, contrary to s 1 of the Theft Act 1968. The punishment for theft is a term of imprisonment not exceeding seven years (s 7 of the 1968 Act, as substituted by s 26 of the Criminal Justice Act 1991).

As Samantha only intended to borrow the recorder, she cannot be convicted of stealing it. Theft requires an 'intention permanently to deprive'. Nor can she be charged with stealing the 'use' or 'enjoyment' of the recorder. Theft is the dishonest appropriation of property belonging to another with the intention of permanently depriving the other of it. The use or enjoyment of a thing is not 'property'.

It is, however, arguable that she is guilty of stealing the batteries despite the fact that she did not intend to keep them. Section 6 of the 1968 Act provides that if certain conditions are satisfied, a person may be regarded as having appropriated property with the necessary intent even though, in a literal sense, he did not intend permanently to deprive.

The necessary conditions are that the accused appropriated the property, intending to borrow it for a period and in circumstances equivalent to an outright taking.[8]

When might these conditions apply?

In *Lloyd* (1985) Lord Lane CJ stated that a mere borrowing is never enough to constitute the necessary *mens rea* unless the intention is to return the thing in such a changed state that it can be said that all its goodness or virtue has gone.

In this case, the batteries are returned with 'practically all' the virtue drained from them. Is this equivalent to an 'outright taking'?

Some commentators take the view that in cases where only some of the virtue is drained from a thing, the question of whether this is to be regarded as amounting to an intention to permanently deprive should be approached as a question of fact for the jury. Others contend that to extend the principle to include cases where D did not intend to drain all the virtue would create difficulties in drawing the line between theft and mere borrowings. It is submitted that, in principle, the latter is the better approach. To

---

8   Note carefully the wording of this part of **s 6(1)**. It is not enough that D borrowed the thing for a period and in circumstances equivalent to an outright taking; it is necessary that D *intended* to borrow the thing for a period and in circumstances equivalent to an outright taking.

conclude otherwise would mean that the mere use of property might, in certain cases, amount to theft. On this basis, Samantha would not be guilty of theft.

However, if the former approach is adopted, and the jury conclude that Samantha's intention was equivalent to an intention permanently to deprive then her liability for theft will depend on whether she *dishonestly* appropriated the batteries. Samantha may have believed, albeit wrongly, that Rachel would have consented to her using the recorder and the batteries. If that were the case, then she was not, as a matter of law, dishonest (see s 2(1)(b)).[9]

If, however, she did not believe that, but raises evidence that she believed that what she did would not generally be regarded as dishonest, then the judge should direct the jury (in accordance with what is known as 'the *Ghosh* test' (*Roberts* (1987)) to consider as a matter of fact whether she was dishonest.

In *Ghosh* (1982), the Court of Appeal held that in determining whether the prosecution have proved that the defendant was acting dishonestly, a jury must first of all decide whether, according to the standards of reasonable and honest people, what was done was dishonest. If it was not dishonest according to those standards, the prosecution fails.

If it was dishonest by those standards, then the jury must consider whether the prosecution have proved that the defendant himself realised that what he was doing was, by the above standards, dishonest. It is dishonest for the defendant to act in a way which he knows ordinary people consider dishonest. If the defendant did not know that, the prosecution fails.

ABSTRACTION OF ELECTRICITY

Samantha cannot be convicted of 'stealing' the electricity in the batteries. Electricity is not 'intangible property' within s 4 of the 1968 Act (*Low v Blease* (1975)).

However, Samantha may have committed an offence contrary to s 13 of the Act, which prohibits the dishonest use of electricity. The punishment is a term of imprisonment not exceeding five years. The offence is not restricted to the dishonest use of mains electricity, but also covers dishonest abstraction from a dry battery.

Section 2 of the Act does not apply to the issue of dishonesty for the purposes of the offence under s 13. Consequently, as far as that offence is concerned, the issue of her dishonesty is exclusively a question of fact for the jury, directed in accordance with *Ghosh* as above.

9   In problems concerning liability for theft which raise the issue of dishonesty always first consider **s 2(1)** of the **Theft Act 1968**. Only where D might not have acted with one of the 3 specified beliefs need the *Ghosh* test be considered.

PART (B)

THEFT

Might Mark be convicted of stealing the cat? He performed the *actus reus* of theft when he took it. Although 'wild' animals are generally not protected by the law of theft – they are not 'property' (s 4(4)) – a domestic pet, being a tame animal, is capable of being stolen.

Mark's dishonesty is not in doubt. The issue is whether it can be said that at the time of appropriation he intended to permanently deprive Henry of the cat. He planned to return the cat in return for a reward which he predicted Henry would offer.

Section 6(1) states that a person may be regarded as intending to permanently deprive if, without meaning the other to lose the thing itself, he intends to treat the thing as his own to dispose of regardless of the other's rights.

Did Mark intend to treat the cat as his own to dispose of?

It is submitted that he did not. Mark did not treat the cat as his own. He did not intend to represent to Henry that he, Mark, was the owner of the cat (see *Holloway* (1849)) (Think Point (1)). Nor did he intend to dispose of the 'thing' regardless of the other's rights. Mark, lacking the necessary intent, is not guilty of stealing the cat.

ALTERNATIVE FACTS

It is submitted that even if his plan had been to get rid of the cat had no reward been offered, he would still have lacked the necessary intent for theft. It could not be said that at the time of appropriating the property, he intended to dispose of the thing as his own regardless of the other's rights. He believed a reward would be offered. This situation is analogous to cases like *Easom* (1971), where it was held that a 'conditional intention' to steal is not sufficient. Furthermore, in *Warner* (1970), it was said that s 6(1) should not be interpreted as 'watering down' the requirement of an intention to permanently deprive in s 1. Recklessness is not sufficient.

PART (C)

THEFT

Again, the issue here is whether it can be said that Dick intended to deprive Fob permanently of his watch.

Section 6(2) provides that a person who parts with property under a condition as to its return that he may not be able to perform is to be regarded as treating the property as his own to dispose of.

The pawning of another's property falls within this section.

It is necessary, however, to consider Dick's intentions. Only if he intended to part with the property under a condition which he might not have been able to perform would he be regarded as having intended to treat it as his own. Thus, arguably, if Dick believed that he would be able to redeem the pledge, he cannot be regarded as having had the necessary intent for theft.[10]

Think Point

1   Cf *Scott* (1987), where D took items from a shop. He returned the next day with the items and asked for a refund. He was convicted of theft. Scott intended to treat the items as his own.

Aim Higher

This question is deceptively complex and requires a very good understanding of **s 6(1)** of the **Theft Act 1968** and the uncertainties concerning its application.

QUESTION 38

Grundy was the manager of the Red Lion Public House. Contrary to his contractual obligations and without the knowledge of his customers, he sold them whisky he had bought from a local off-licence. He kept the profit made from the sale of the whisky. When he was arrested in the public house, he had two bottles of whisky that he had bought from the off-licence.

▶ **Discuss Grundy's criminal liability.**

How to Answer this Question

This question raises issues of liability for theft contrary to s 1 of the Theft Act 1968; fraud contrary to s 1(1) of the Fraud Act 2006; and false accounting contrary to s 17.

---

10   Note carefully the wording of **s 6(2)** and how it relates to **s 6(1)** and the requirement of an *intention* to permanently deprive.

The principal issues are:

- ❖   secret profits and the application of s 5(3) Theft Act 1968;
- ❖   the ingredients of fraud by false representation (s 2 Fraud Act 2006);
- ❖   the ingredients of fraud by abuse of position (s 4 Fraud Act 2006);
- ❖   the ingredients of false accounting (s 17 Theft Act 1968).

Applying the Law

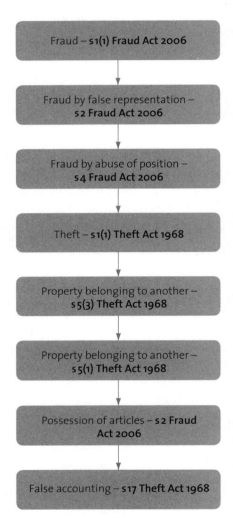

This flow chart highlights the main legislation you need to include in your answer.

ANSWER

FRAUD – s 1(1) FRAUD ACT 2006

Grundy may be convicted of the offence of fraud contrary to s 1(1) of the Fraud Act 2006.

The offence of fraud can be committed in three ways, two of which – fraud by false representation (s 2) and fraud by abuse of position (s 4) – are relevant to the facts of this question.[11]

Both forms require proof of dishonesty and an intention to make a gain in terms of money or other property or an intention to cause loss to another or expose another to a risk of loss in terms of money or other property. These ingredients of liability are satisfied in this case.

As far as fraud by false representation is concerned, a representation may be express or implied by conduct. Grundy impliedly represented that the whisky he offered was his employer's (*Doukas* (1978)) and thus he is guilty of fraud by false representation.

Fraud by abuse of position requires that D occupies a position in which he is expected to safeguard, or not act against, the financial interests of another person (s 4(1)(a)). It is intended to cover a wide variety of situations where D has abused a privileged position including that of an employee, like Grundy, who acts against his employer's interests.

THEFT – s 1(1) THEFT ACT 1968

Although Grundy clearly had a dishonest intent he is not guilty of stealing the money he received or the secret profit he made from the sale of the whisky.

The difficulty in convicting him of theft consists of showing that he appropriated property 'belonging to another'.

By virtue of s 5(3) of the Theft Act 1968, property is to be regarded as belonging to another where it is received on account of another and the recipient is under an obligation to retain and deal with the property or its proceeds in a particular way.

However, in *Attorney General's Reference (No 1 of 1985)* (1986), the Court of Appeal held that an employee who makes a secret profit from his position does not receive the money 'on account of another' and is not under an obligation to 'retain and deal with the property' within the meaning of s 5(3).

---

11   Note that fraud is an offence contrary to s 1(1) of the Act. **Sections 2, 3** and **4** do not create offences – they define the three ways in which the offence under **s 1(1)** may be committed.

Further, although s 5(1) states that property is to be regarded as belonging to any person who has 'any proprietary right or interest in it', the Court of Appeal held that even if an employee holds a secret profit on constructive trust for his employer, this does not amount to a proprietary interest for the purposes of s 5(1) (Think Point (1)).

POSSESSION OF ARTICLES FOR USE IN FRAUDS – s 6 FRAUD ACT 2006

Grundy may also be convicted of an offence of possession of articles, viz the bottles of whisky, for use in frauds, contrary to s 6 of the Fraud Act 2006. The section provides that it is an offence to possess an article for use in the course of or in connection with any fraud. The use of the expression '*any* fraud' is intended to ensure that a general intention to use the article for a fraud will suffice. The maximum custodial sentence for an offence contrary to s 6 is five years.

FALSE ACCOUNTING

Section 17 of the Theft Act 1968 provides that where a person dishonestly and with a view to gain or intent to cause loss falsifies any account or any record or document made for any accounting purpose, he commits an offence punishable with a maximum of seven years' imprisonment.

A person is not guilty of the s 17 offence unless there is a duty to account (*Shama* (1990)).

This is determined by reference to the terms of the contract of employment. If Grundy was under a contractual duty to account for all sales and receipts, his omission to account for the money received for the whisky would amount to a falsification of an account (*Lee Cheung Wing and Lam Man Yau* (1992); s 17(2)).[12]

In addition, the prosecution must prove that Grundy was 'dishonest' and that he falsified the account with a 'view to gain' or 'intent to cause loss' to another. A 'gain' includes a gain by keeping what one has (s 34(2)(a)) and, therefore, there may be a view to gain where the falsification of the account follows the making of a personal profit (and see *Lee Cheung Wing*).

However, if Grundy did not know that he was obliged to account for the personal profit made from sales of the whisky, he could not be convicted of the offence under s 17. There would not, in those circumstances, be a dishonest view to gain.

If Grundy raises evidence that he thought that what he was doing was not dishonest, the judge must direct the jury with respect to the meaning of the term (*Price* (1989); *O'Connell* (1992)).

---

12   As the terms of the contract between Grundy and his employer are not disclosed the question must be approached hypothetically.

In *Ghosh* (1982), the Court of Appeal held that in determining whether the prosecution have proved that the defendant was acting dishonestly, the jury must first of all decide whether, according to the ordinary standards of reasonable and honest people, what was done was dishonest. If it was not dishonest according to those standards, the prosecution fails.

If it was dishonest by those standards, then the jury must consider whether the defendant himself realised that what he was doing was, by those standards, dishonest. It is dishonest for the defendant to act in a way which he knows ordinary people consider to be dishonest. If the defendant did not know that, the prosecution fails.

Think Point

1   Doubt is cast on the decision in the *Attorney General's Reference (No 1 of 1985)* (1986) by that of the Court of Appeal in *Shadrokh-Cigari* (1988). The Court of Appeal held that an equitable interest arising under a constructive trust was a 'proprietary right or interest' under s 5(1). And, in *Attorney General of Hong Kong v Reid* (1994), the Privy Council held that bribes accepted by a New Zealand Deputy Crown Prosecutor during the course of his career were held on constructive trust for the benefit of the person to whom his duties were owed.

QUESTION 39

Frank asked Ike if he could borrow his car. Frank said he needed the car to take his friend Nanook to the railway station (a distance of five miles). In fact, although Frank intended to take his friend to the station, he did not tell Ike that he intended to keep the car for the entire day and use it to visit his friend, Ray, who lived in a town 30 miles away. Ike let him borrow the car on condition that it was returned within an hour. Frank took Nanook to the railway station. Whilst leaving the station car park, Frank collided with a low wall, damaging it, smashing a headlight and denting the front wing of the car. Frank then drove to Ray's house and suggested that they go to the races. Frank said that Ike had let him borrow the car for the day. Although Ray suspected that Ike had not consented to Frank's borrowing the car – he knew that Ike had refused to lend the car to Frank in the past – he asked no questions and got in the car. As they approached the race track, Moon, a six-year-old child, ran out in front of the car. Frank slammed on the brakes. The car stopped short of Moon, who was uninjured, but Ray, who was not wearing a seat belt, lurched forward. His head struck the car window and he sustained a slight injury to his forehead. Ray got out of the car, saying that he no longer felt like going to the races and intended to take a bus home. Frank told Ray that he would meet him later. He was about to drive off when Doreen, a large cat which had been sleeping on a windowsill, fell and landed on the car, causing an enormous dent to the bonnet.

Later that evening, Frank returned the car to Ike.

▶ Discuss the criminal liability of Frank and Ray.

How to Answer this Question

This question concerns the offences of 'taking a motor vehicle or other conveyance without authority' contrary to s 12(1) of the Theft Act 1968 and 'aggravated vehicle-taking' contrary to s 12A of the same Act. Liability for criminal damage contrary to s 1(1) of the Criminal Damage Act 1971, and the offences of 'dangerous driving' and 'careless driving' contrary to ss 2 and 3, respectively, of the Road Traffic Act 1988 are discussed in outline.

Note that s 12(1) creates two offences. If the conditions of liability are satisfied, Frank is guilty of the primary offence of taking a conveyance. Ray, on the other hand, may be liable for the secondary offence in s 12(1) of allowing himself to be carried in the taken vehicle.

As far as Frank's liability is concerned, one of the principal issues raised relates to whether, having induced Ike to part with the car by misrepresenting why he wanted it, Frank took the vehicle without consent. In respect of Ray's liability, the major issue concerns the *mens rea* requirement for the secondary offence. The facts of the question state that he 'suspected' the vehicle was taken without consent. Whether or not that is sufficient for liability is discussed below.

The question raises a number of issues concerning some of the aggravating circumstances in s 12A(2). In particular, the question of whether fault is required with respect to the aggravating circumstances is discussed.

Principal authorities are: *Whittaker v Campbell* (1984); *Peart* (1970); *McKnight v Davies* (1974); *Caldwell* (1982).

Applying the Law

Frank's liability

Ray's liability

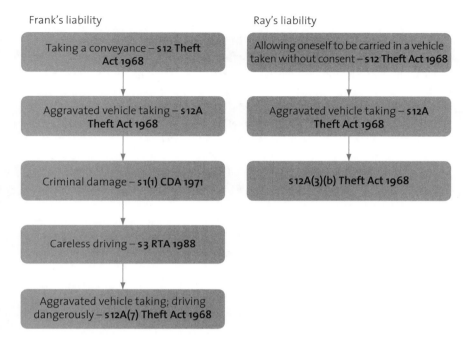

This two part diagram shows the main legislation needed to assess the liability of Frank and Ray.

ANSWER --

FRANK

Section 12 of the Theft Act 1968, as amended by s 37(1) of the Criminal Justice Act 1988, provides that a person is guilty of an offence punishable, on summary conviction, with a fine not exceeding level 5 on the standard scale, imprisonment for up to six months or both, if, without having the consent of the owner or other lawful authority, he takes any conveyance for his own or another's use or, knowing that any conveyance has been taken without such authority, drives it or allows himself to be carried in or on it.

The section creates two offences: the primary offence consists of taking a conveyance and the secondary offence of driving or allowing oneself to be carried in a taken conveyance.

For both offences, the prosecution must prove that the conveyance was taken without the consent of the owner or other lawful authority and, in *Whittaker v Campbell* (1984), the Divisional Court held that consent obtained by means of a deception is nevertheless a valid consent for the purposes of the offence under s 12(1). The Court of Appeal reached a similar conclusion in the case of *Peart* (1970). D had obtained the consent of the owner of a van in Newcastle to lend it to him by pretending that he needed it for an urgent appointment in Alnwick – a town not too far from Newcastle. He knew that the owner would not have lent him the van if he had known of his real intention. Nonetheless, it was held that the taking was with the owner's consent. The Court of Appeal, however, restricted themselves to considering whether there had been a taking without consent when, in Newcastle, Peart initially took possession of the van. For technical reasons concerning the grounds of appeal, the court did not consider whether there had been a fresh taking without consent when he deviated from the route to Alnwick and made for Burnley. In the later case of *McKnight v Davies* (1974), the Divisional Court held that where there is a wholly unauthorised deviation from an authorised route, there is, at that point, a 'taking without consent'. Thus, it would appear that Frank took the conveyance without consent when he left the railway station and, instead of returning the car to Ike, made for Ray's.[13]

Next, it is necessary to consider Frank's liability for the offence of 'aggravated vehicle-taking'. **Section 1** of the **Aggravated Vehicle-Taking Act 1992** inserted a new s 12A after s 12 of the **1968 Act**. This provides that a person is guilty of aggravated vehicle-taking if he commits an offence under s 12(1) and, after the vehicle was taken and before it was recovered, one of a number of aggravating circumstances or events occurred.

Although damage to the vehicle is an aggravating circumstance, there can be no liability for the aggravated offence with respect to the damage to the car caused when leaving the car park of the railway station because, as explained above, that occurred before Frank had committed the *actus reus* of the basic offence. (Note that s 12A(3) of the **Aggravated Vehicle-Taking Act 1992** provides that it is for the defendant to prove (on the balance of probabilities) that the damage or other aggravating circumstance occurred before he committed the basic offence.)[14]

He may, however, be guilty of the offence of criminal damage contrary to s 1(1) of the **Criminal Damage Act 1971**. The maximum punishment for this offence is 10 years' imprisonment (s 4(2)). The prosecution would have to prove that he was at least reckless with respect to causing the damage to the car. In *R v G and Another* (2003), the House of Lords held that a person acts recklessly within the meaning of s 1(1) of the **Criminal Damage Act 1971** when he is aware of a risk of damaging property belonging to another and it is, in the circumstances known to him, unreasonable to take the risk.

---

13   Whether the car was taken without consent or lawful authority is relevant to the liability of both Frank and Ray.
14   As is often the case with criminal liability, the timing of a sequence of events is often crucially important.

In addition, when colliding with the wall, Frank may have committed the summary offence of 'careless driving' contrary to s 3 of the Road Traffic Act 1988, as substituted by s 2 of the Road Traffic Act 1991, punishable with a fine at level 4.

It must be proved that he drove 'without due care and attention'. This involves an objective standard; viz, a failure to exercise the degree of care and attention that a reasonable and prudent driver would exercise in the circumstances (*Simpson v Peat* (1952); *Scott v Warren* (1974)). All the factual circumstances must be considered by the magistrates and although a failure to observe the provisions of the Highway Code may be relied upon as evidence of carelessness, such failure is not conclusive (s 38(7) of the 1988 Act).

Frank may have committed the offence of aggravated vehicle-taking later when approaching the race track. In addition to damage caused to the vehicle, s 12A(2) of the 1968 Act specifies a number of other aggravating circumstances. These include the fact that the vehicle was driven dangerously on a road or other public place.

Dangerous driving is defined in s 12A(7) as driving in a way which falls far below what would be expected of a competent and careful driver and it would be obvious to a competent and careful driver that driving the vehicle in that way would be dangerous. This provision is based on the definition of 'dangerous driving' in s 2 of the Road Traffic Act 1988, as substituted by s 1 of the Road Traffic Act 1991. Section 2A(3) of the 1988 Act provides that 'dangerous' refers to danger either of injury to any person or of serious damage to property. The test is, again, an objective one for the magistrates or jury, who should consider all the relevant evidence. Dangerous driving is punishable with a maximum of two years' imprisonment and, unless there are special reasons, disqualification from driving for not less than 12 months.

A further specified aggravating circumstance is that owing to the driving of the vehicle, an accident occurred by which injury was caused to any person. No fault with respect to the manner of driving is required (*Marsh* (1997)). It is sufficient to prove that the driving was a factual cause of the injury and, consequently, Frank will be liable irrespective of whether an injury was foreseeable and despite the fact that the injury would have been avoided had Ray worn a seat belt.

Furthermore, with respect to the dent caused by the cat, it is sufficient to prove that the basic offence was committed and that damage was caused to the vehicle whilst the defendant was in the vehicle or in its vicinity. For this form of aggravation also, no fault is necessary. Nor is it necessary to show a causal relationship between the taking and the damage (see *Dawes v DPP* (1995)).

The maximum penalty on indictment for the aggravated offence is two years' imprisonment. In addition, by virtue of s 3(1) of the 1992 Act, disqualification from driving for not less than 12 months must be ordered unless there are special reasons for not disqualifying.

RAY

Ray may be guilty of the secondary offence of allowing oneself to be carried in a conveyance taken without consent.[15]

The prosecution must prove that he knew the car had been taken without Ike's consent. The facts of the question state that he suspected that Frank had taken the car without Ike's permission, but did not enquire and cannot be said to have actually known of the lack of consent. Generally, however, where knowledge is an ingredient of liability, 'wilful blindness' will suffice (*Sleep* (1861); *Ross v Moss* (1965)). This means that a person knows a relevant circumstance exists when he is virtually certain that it does or has no substantial doubt that it does and deliberately refrains from enquiring.

Provided the prosecution can prove the necessary *mens rea* for the basic offence, Ray may also be convicted of the aggravated offence. Liability extends to any person who commits the basic offence under s 12(1) of the Theft Act 1968, whether primary or secondary and the same aggravated circumstances apply.

In Ray's case, however, it is not clear whether the injury sustained in the car would amount to an aggravating circumstance. Although the statute provides that an injury caused to 'any person' will suffice, it would indeed be surprising if this were held to apply where the only person injured was the defendant himself. Provided, however, that Ray was still 'in the immediate vicinity' of the vehicle (s 12A(3)(b)) when Doreen fell on the bonnet, then he may be convicted of the aggravated offence. As mentioned above, no fault on the part of the defendant is required with respect to the damage, and it would appear that his apparent withdrawal from the venture has no effect on his liability (Think Point (1)).

> ## Think Point
>
> 1   Note also that s 27 of the Transport Act 1981 made the wearing of seat belts in motor vehicles compulsory.

QUESTION 40

Chump caught a rabbit on Adolf's land. He took it to his houseboat. Flash, who had been observing Chump, followed him. Whilst Chump had a nap, Flash, intending to take the

---

15   The question whether the vehicle was taken without consent or authority was discussed when considering Frank's liability. There is no need to repeat the discussion here.

rabbit, boarded the houseboat. Flash was about to leave with the rabbit when Chump started to wake up. Flash picked up Chump's walking stick, hit Chump over the head with it and left with the rabbit.

▶ Discuss the criminal liability of the parties.

How to Answer this Question

This question raises issues of theft contrary to s 1 of the Theft Act 1968, burglary contrary to s 9(1)(a) and 9(1)(b) of the Act, and aggravated burglary contrary to s 10. Minor questions of liability for criminal damage and the offence of 'going equipped' are raised.

Flash's liability for 'aggravated assaults' is fairly 'open' – that is, we are not told the extent of the injuries sustained nor his *mens rea* at the relevant time. Thus, a full discussion of the ingredients of liability for each of the various offences – under ss 18, 20 and 47 of the Offences Against the Person Act 1861 – is required.

The principal issues are:

❖ the meaning and application of s 4(4) of the 1968 Act – theft of 'wild animals';
❖ liability under s 9(1) – burglary;
❖ the meaning and application of the expression 'has with him' in s 10 – aggravated burglary – and s 25 – going equipped; and
❖ the ingredients of liability for aggravated assaults.

Applying the Law

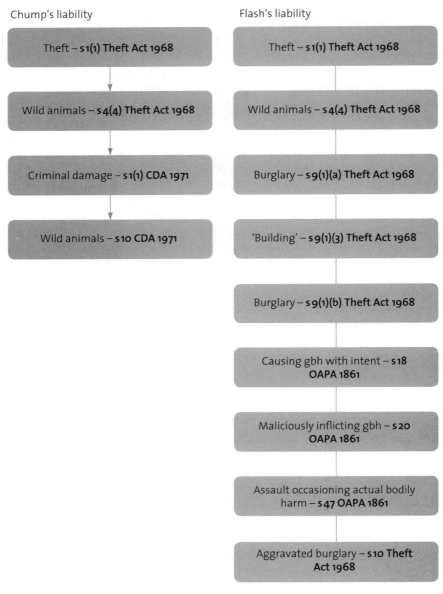

Chump's liability

- Theft – s1(1) Theft Act 1968
- Wild animals – s4(4) Theft Act 1968
- Criminal damage – s1(1) CDA 1971
- Wild animals – s10 CDA 1971

Flash's liability

- Theft – s1(1) Theft Act 1968
- Wild animals – s4(4) Theft Act 1968
- Burglary – s9(1)(a) Theft Act 1968
- 'Building' – s9(1)(3) Theft Act 1968
- Burglary – s9(1)(b) Theft Act 1968
- Causing gbh with intent – s18 OAPA 1861
- Maliciously inflicting gbh – s20 OAPA 1861
- Assault occasioning actual bodily harm – s47 OAPA 1861
- Aggravated burglary – s10 Theft Act 1968

The two parts of this diagram show the main legislation needed to assess the liability of Chump and Flash.

ANSWER

THEFT

Whilst Chump may be guilty of an offence of poaching under the Game Acts and Poaching Acts (see Sched 1 to the Theft Act 1968), he is not guilty of theft.

The common law rule that wild creatures could not be stolen because they were not regarded as property is preserved by s 4(4) of the Act. This provides that a person cannot steal a wild creature unless it has been reduced into possession by or on behalf of another person and possession of it has not since been lost or abandoned. The owner of the land on which the animal is found is protected by the criminal law relating to poaching, but not by the law of theft.[16]

Neither may Chump be convicted of an offence criminal damage contrary to s 1 of the Criminal Damage Act 1971. The definition of 'property' in s 10 of the 1971 Act is very similar in this respect to the definition in s 4(4) of the 1968 Act.

As, however, the rabbit has been reduced into, and remains in, the possession of Chump, it is capable of being stolen from him. Therefore, as the facts indicate that Flash had a dishonest intention to permanently deprive, he is guilty of stealing the rabbit from Chump.

The maximum punishment for theft is seven years' imprisonment (s 7 of the 1968 Act, as amended by s 26 of the Criminal Justice Act 1991).

BURGLARY

Section 9(1)(a) of the Theft Act 1968 provides that a person is guilty of burglary if he enters any building as a trespasser intending to commit one of a number of offences including theft and, by virtue of s 9(3), Chump's houseboat – an 'inhabited vessel' – is a building for the purposes of this offence.

As a matter of civil law, a person enters as a trespasser if he enters without the possessor's consent. For the purposes of burglary, the prosecution must prove, in addition, that at the time of entry, the accused knew that he was entering without permission or was reckless with respect to that fact (*Collins* (1973)).

As Flash knew of the facts that made his entry a trespass, he entered with the appropriate *mens rea*.[17]

16 The rabbit becomes property capable of being stolen only when it was reduced into possession by Chump.

17 It is not necessary to prove that D knows the legal basis upon which his entry is trespassory; he need not know the law of tort! It is enough that he knows (or is reckless in respect of) the facts that make his entry trespassory.

The penalty for burglary in respect of a dwelling is a term of imprisonment not exceeding 14 years (s 9(3)(a)).

He may also be guilty of burglary contrary to s 9(1)(b). This subsection provides that a person is guilty of burglary if, having entered any building as a trespasser, he steals anything in the building or inflicts or attempts to inflict grievous bodily harm on any person in the building.

The ingredients of liability – that D entered as a trespasser and that, at the time of the theft, he knew or was reckless as to the facts which made his entry a trespass – were present when he appropriated the rabbit.

He also may have committed burglary under s 9(1)(b) when he struck Chump on the head. The facts of the problem disclose neither the extent of any injuries suffered by Chump nor Flash's *mens rea*. To be guilty under s 9(1)(b), the injuries sustained must be serious (*Smith* (1959); *Saunders* (1985)).

As far as the *mens rea* requirement is concerned, the Court of Appeal in *Jenkins* (1983) appeared to accept that, for the purposes of s 9(1)(b) of the **Theft Act 1968**, the infliction of grievous bodily harm need not, in itself, amount to an offence of any kind. If this is correct, the prosecution do not have to prove that the accused inflicted grievous bodily harm with the *mens rea* necessary for a conviction under either s 18 or s 20 of the **Offences Against the Person Act 1861**. (In 1984, the House of Lords allowed Jenkins' appeal on another ground and made no comment on this issue.) The better view, it is submitted, is that the serious offence of burglary requires a *mens rea* beyond that relating to the trespassory entry and that the prosecution are required to prove that D's conduct amounted to an offence under either s 18 or s 20 of the **Offences Against the Person Act 1861**.

The s 18 offence – causing grievous bodily harm with intent – carries a maximum penalty of life imprisonment. The *mens rea* requirement is an intention to cause grievous bodily harm. For the offence under s 20 – which carries a maximum punishment of five years' imprisonment – the prosecution must prove that Flash foresaw the risk of causing some harm, albeit not serious harm (*Savage; Parmenter* (1991)).

If Flash intended grievous bodily harm, but the injuries sustained were less than serious, he may be convicted of an attempt to cause grievous bodily harm contrary to s 1(1) of the **Criminal Attempts Act 1981**. An attempt to cause grievous bodily harm is also a specified offence for the purposes of burglary contrary to s 9(1)(b) of the **Theft Act 1968**.

ASSAULT OCCASIONING 'ACTUAL BODILY HARM'

If the injuries sustained are not serious, Flash may be guilty of the lesser offence of assault occasioning actual bodily harm contrary to s 47 of the **Offences Against the Person Act 1861**. The maximum punishment for this offence is five years' imprisonment.

'Actual bodily harm' means 'any hurt or injury calculated to interfere with the health or comfort of the victim', provided it is more than transient or trifling (*Miller* (1954)). There is no need for a physically discernible injury (*Reigate Justices ex p Counsell* (1983)).

It is unnecessary to prove that the accused intended or was reckless with respect to causing actual bodily harm (*Savage; Parmenter*). The offence is committed where, as in this case, D intentionally (or recklessly) applies unlawful force to another, V, who, as a consequence, suffers harm, as defined above.

Assault occasioning actual bodily harm is not a specified offence for burglary under s 9(1)(b).

AGGRAVATED BURGLARY

Finally, it is proposed to consider whether Flash committed the offence of aggravated burglary contrary to s 10(1) of the Theft Act 1968.

Section 10(1) provides that it is an offence, punishable with a maximum of life imprisonment (s 10(2)), if a person commits any burglary and at the time has with him, among other things, any 'weapon of offence'.

Provided Flash intended to use the stick to cause injury to or incapacitate Chump, then it was a 'weapon of offence' (s 10(1)(b)).

However, to be guilty of the offence under s 10, the accused must have the article with him at the time of committing the burglary. Where the accused is charged with burglary contrary to s 9(1)(a), this is the time of the trespassory entry. Where the charge is burglary contrary to s 9(1)(b), the relevant time is the time of commission of the specified offence.[18]

Clearly, Flash did not commit aggravated burglary at the moment of entry. Did he commit aggravated burglary when he picked up the stick and struck Chump?

Smith and Hogan suggested that, by analogy with decisions concerning s 1 of the Prevention of Crime Act 1953 (possession of an offensive weapon), 'has with him' should be interpreted to imply a degree of continuous possession (see, for example, *Ohlson v Hylton* (1975)). In *Kelly* (1992), however, the Court of Appeal held that s 1 of the 1953 Act and s 10 of the 1968 Act are directed at entirely different mischiefs. Potts J, delivering the judgment of the court, stated that whereas the former is directed at the carrying of a weapon with intent to use it if the occasion arises, the latter is directed at the actual use of articles which aggravate the offence of simple burglary. Thus, the spontaneous and temporary possession of a weapon of offence will suffice for liability under s 10(1).

18 Note the different times at which each of the forms of burglary is committed.

Similarly, for the offence of going equipped contrary to s 25 of the 1968 Act, as amended, the Divisional Court appears to have decided that it was sufficient that D had the article with him immediately prior to the commission of a burglary or theft (*Minor* (1988)). Thus, Flash may be convicted of going equipped with the stick, provided he intended to use it to cause Chump grievous bodily harm. He was not at his place of abode and he had (although only for a matter of moments) the article for use in the course of a burglary. In *Ellames* (1976), the Court of Appeal held that the intention to use the article must relate to the future. Presumably, therefore, there can be no liability for the offence under s 25 in relation to the theft of the rabbit.

> ## Common Pitfalls
> The distinction between the two forms of burglary – one contrary to **s 9(1)(a)** and the other contrary to **s 9(1)(b)** – is frequently misunderstood by candidates and answers are often poorly structured as a result. It is of crucial importance that you can explain the ingredients of each of the two forms and apply them systematically to problems like the instant one.

QUESTION 41

George agreed to paint Liam's flat for £500. Liam gave George an advance of £50. Having painted the flat, George was given a roll of notes by Liam's wife, Margaret, in payment. George put the money in his pocket without counting it. When he got home, he discovered that Margaret had given him £500. George decided to keep the excess. Later that evening, Liam, having discovered his wife's mistake, visited George to request the return of the £50. George was not at home but his wife, Lucy, who was aware that George had been overpaid, persuaded Liam that her husband had been given £450 by Margaret.

▶ Discuss the criminal liability of George and Lucy.

How to Answer this Question

This problem is fairly intricate. It involves liability for theft contrary to s 1 of the **Theft Act** 1968, handling contrary to s 22 of the Theft Act 1968 and fraud contrary to s 1 of the **Fraud Act** 2006. The most important issues are:

❖ the meaning and application of 'dishonesty' for the purposes of theft;
❖ property obtained by another's mistake – s 5(4) of the 1968 Act;
❖ accessorial liability – whether assistance was given at the time of the offence.

Applying the Law

George's liability

| Theft – s1(1) Theft Act 1968 |

| The 'later assumption principle' – s3(1) Theft Act 1968 |

| Property belonging to another – property got by another's mistake – s5(4) Theft Act 1968 |

| Dishonesty – s2(1) Theft Act 1968 |

| Dishonesty – *Ghosh* (1982) |

| Conspiracy – s1(1) CLA 1977 |

Lucy's liability

| Theft – s1(1) Theft Act 1968 |

| Secondary liability |

| Handling – s22 Theft Act 1968 |

| Fraud – s1(1) Fraud Act 2006 |

| Conspiracy – s1(1) CLA 1977 |

This two part diagram highlights the main legislation and principles to apply in your answer.

ANSWER

THEFT CONTRARY TO s1(1) OF THE THEFT ACT 1968

Theft is defined as the 'dishonest appropriation of property belonging to another with the intention of permanently depriving the other of it'.

George did not commit theft when Liam's wife handed over the money. Clearly, as he was unaware of the extra £50, he did not dishonestly appropriate it. He may have been guilty of theft, however, when, on discovering that he had been overpaid in error, he decided to keep the excess. Although he originally came by the property innocently, appropriation is defined to include any later assumption of a right to property by 'keeping or dealing with it as owner' (s3(1)). George, by keeping the £50, appropriated it.

Did he, however, appropriate 'property belonging to another'?

Section 5(1) provides that 'property shall be regarded as belonging to any person having possession or control of it or having in it any proprietary right or interest'.

Section 5(4) provides that where a person gets property by another's mistake, and is under a legal obligation to make restoration (in whole or in part) of the property, then the property (or part) shall be regarded as belonging to the person entitled to restoration.

Where D is overpaid in error, although, as a matter of civil law, the ownership in the money passes to him, he is under a quasi-contractual legal obligation to make restoration (*Moynes v Coopper* (1956); *Davis* (1989)). Therefore, for the purposes of theft, the £50 belonged to another. It is not clear whose money was used to pay George, but, as far as George's liability is concerned, it is immaterial whether it belonged to Liam or Margaret. See also *Hale* (1978).

It may be unnecessary for the prosecution to rely on s 5(4) to attribute a 'notional' proprietary interest to Liam or his wife. In *Chase Manhattan Bank NA v Israel-British Bank (London) Ltd* (1981), it was held that where an action will lie to recover money or other property paid or transferred under a mistake of fact, the payer or transferor retains an equitable proprietary interest. Applying this rule to the law of theft, the Criminal Division of the Court of Appeal in *Shadrokh-Cigari* (1988) held that the property paid in such circumstances is property belonging to another within s 5(1). (Cf *Westdeutsche v Islington London Borough Council* (1996), in which the House of Lords held that receipt of money by another's mistake might not always give rise to a trust.)

Therefore, either by virtue of s 5(4) or the rule in *Chase Manhattan* and provided the remaining conditions of theft are satisfied, George may be convicted of stealing the £50.

Section 5(4) provides that an intention not to make restoration is to be regarded as an intention to permanently deprive. Thus, the only point remaining which requires consideration is whether George was dishonest in keeping the excess.

Section 2(1) of the 1968 Act provides that certain beliefs are, as a matter of law, honest beliefs. Where one of these beliefs is alleged, the judge must instruct the jury that the defendant is to be acquitted if he had or may have had one of the defined states of mind. The reasonableness of the belief is not legally relevant. The only issue is whether it was genuinely held but, of course, the unreasonableness of a belief is some evidence that it was not genuinely held (*Holden* (1991)).

When George discovered the extra £50, he may have believed that it was a bonus or tip, in which case his decision to keep it would, by virtue of s 2(1)(b), be an honest one. Alternatively, he may have been aware that Liam or Margaret made a mistake but believed that, despite the mistake, he was legally entitled to keep the money, in which case he would be able to take advantage of s 2(1)(a). This provides that a person is not dishonest if he believes, albeit mistakenly, that he has, in law, the right to deprive the other of the property.

If George was aware that he had no legal right to retain the money, but alleges that he believed he was morally entitled to retain it, then, according to the Court of Appeal in *Price* (1989) and *O'Connell* (1992), the issue of his dishonesty should be left to the jury, instructed in accordance with the principles expounded in *Ghosh* (1982).

The jury must decide whether, according to the ordinary standards of decent and honest people, keeping the extra money was dishonest. If it was not dishonest by those standards, the prosecution fails.

If, on the other hand, the jury decide that it was dishonest according to those standards, then they should consider whether George realised that keeping the money was, by the above standards, dishonest. If he did not realise that, then the prosecution fails.[19]

ACCESSORIAL LIABILITY

Provided that George was dishonest and is guilty of theft, his wife Lucy may be guilty as an accomplice to the theft. By virtue of s 8 of the Accessories and Abettors Act 1861, a person who aids, abets, counsels or procures the commission of an offence is liable to be tried and punished for that offence as a principal offender.

Lucy may have aided the commission of the theft.

Although accessorial liability attaches only where assistance is given before the conclusion of the offence (*King's Case* (1817)), it could be argued that where, as in this case, the appropriation consists of 'keeping or dealing with the property as owner', the act of theft is a continuing one. If so, the question whether George was still in the course of committing the offence is, presumably, a question of fact for the jury (see *Atakpu and Abrahams* (1994); *Hale* (1978)).[20]

The fact that George was unaware of Lucy's assistance is, it is submitted, immaterial (Think Point (1)).

---

19 Where D innocently receives property by mistake and then later becomes aware of the mistake and decides to keep the property, it is necessary to consider not only whether the property belongs to another by virtue of s 5(4) but also whether he dishonestly appropriated the property when he decided to keep it.

20 Where there is no authority directly on a point consider and make reference to the closest analogous situations.

With respect to the *mens rea*, the prosecution must prove that Lucy intended to assist and that she knew the essential matters, that is, the circumstances which must be proved in order to constitute the offence (*Johnson v Youden* (1950)). The facts of the problem clearly support this conclusion. She had been informed that her husband had been overpaid and was aware that this was in error.

In addition, it must be shown that Lucy was either aware that George was acting with *mens rea*, that is, that he was dishonest as discussed above or, if she did not know that, she was aware that he may have been acting dishonestly (*Carter v Richardson* (1976)).

HANDLING

If the theft was concluded prior to Lucy's involvement, then, as explained above, there can be no accessorial liability. In those circumstances, however, Lucy – assuming she knows or believes the money to be stolen – could be convicted of handling stolen goods contrary to s 22 of the Theft Act 1968. Lucy assisted George to retain the stolen money by persuading Liam that no money was owing (see *Kanwar* (1982)).

CONSPIRACY

There is no question of liability for conspiracy (even if George and Lucy had dishonestly agreed to keep the money). By virtue of s 2(2) of the Criminal Law Act 1977, a person is not guilty of statutory conspiracy if the only other person with whom he or she agrees is his or her spouse. The same rule applies to common law conspiracy to defraud (*Mawji* (1957)).

FRAUD – s 1(1) OF THE FRAUD ACT 2006

Lucy may be guilty of fraud contrary to s 1(1) of the Fraud Act 2006 in the form of a fraud by false representation (s 2). Clearly, she made a false representation when she told Liam that George had received only £450.

The offence requires proof of a dishonest intention to make a gain or cause loss in money or other property. It is sufficient that D intends to make a gain for another (s 2(b)(i)) and, by s 5(3), 'gain' includes a gain by keeping what one has. Similarly 'loss' includes a loss by not getting what one might get, as well as parting with what one has (s 5(4)).

Dishonesty is not defined in the Fraud Act; the jury should be directed in accordance with the *Ghosh* principles (as discussed above) (Think Point (2)).

Think Points

1   The Court of Appeal in *Attorney General's Reference (No 1 of 1975)* (1977) stated that D may 'procure' the commission of an offence even though the principal is unaware of D's involvement. The court stated, *obiter*, that the other forms of

accessorial liability will almost inevitably involve the knowledge of the principal. Lord Widgery said that he found it difficult to think of a case of aiding, abetting or counselling when the parties have not discussed the offence which they have in mind. However, the court did not expressly state that the knowledge and/or agreement of the principal is a prerequisite of liability for the aider. Lord Widgery also stated that the words 'aid, abet', etc, should be given their ordinary meaning. It is submitted that the ordinary meaning of the word 'aid' does not imply consensus.

2 In *McAleer* (2002), the Court of Appeal held that where D claims that he believed he was acting honestly because of a claim of right, a full *Ghosh* direction may not be necessary, but the judge must make it clear that they must acquit if D might have believed he was entitled to the property.

QUESTION 42

Tony, the tenant of 23 Railway Cuttings:

(a) removed the lead from the roof;
(b) dug up a rose bush in the garden and gave it to his uncle, Sidney;
(c) offered to sell the living-room fireplace to his friend, Hattie. She declined the offer;
(d) picked mushrooms from a neighbouring field intending to sell them to Luigi, the owner of a local restaurant; and
(e) agreed that his girlfriend, Lolita, could take a cherry tree growing in the garden when she visited the following day.

Tony knew that his landlord would not have approved of any of the alterations or planned alterations to the house or garden. Discuss the criminal liability of the parties.

How to Answer this Question

The following points need to be discussed:

❖ theft of 'things forming part of the land';
❖ an 'offer to sell' as appropriation;
❖ conspiracy where one party is 'exempt';
❖ attempting the impossible; and
❖ the wider meaning of property for the purposes of criminal damage.

The principal authorities are: s 4(2) of the Theft Act 1968; s 1 of the Criminal Attempts Act 1981; s 1 of the Criminal Law Act 1977.

Answer Structure

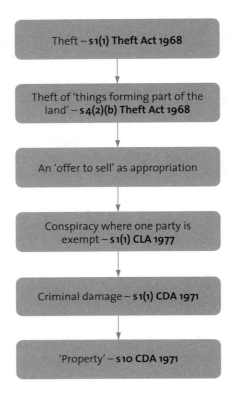

Theft – s1(1) **Theft Act 1968**

Theft of 'things forming part of the land' – s4(2)(b) **Theft Act 1968**

An 'offer to sell' as appropriation

Conspiracy where one party is exempt – s1(1) **CLA 1977**

Criminal damage – s1(1) **CDA 1971**

'Property' – s10 **CDA 1971**

ANSWER

The situations in which a person may be convicted of theft where they have appropriated 'something forming part of the land' are defined in s 4(2)(b) and 4(2)(c) of the Theft Act 1968. Section 4(2)(c) is somewhat narrower than s 4(2)(b). Whereas the non-possessor can be guilty of stealing anything forming part of the land, a tenant can be guilty only where he appropriates a fixture or structure.[21]

PARTS (A) AND (B)

Tony, by virtue of s 4(2)(c), may be convicted of stealing the lead contrary to s 1 of the Theft Act 1968, but he is not guilty of stealing the rose bush. Consequently, his Uncle Sidney cannot be guilty of handling stolen goods contrary to s 22 of the 1968 Act. The goods are not stolen goods.

---

21 Explaining the relevant rules in outline before discussing a number of scenarios in detail can be effective and time-saving.

PART (C)

With respect to the fireplace, s 4(2)(c) of the Theft Act 1968, unlike s 4(2)(b), does not require that the fixture be severed to amount to an appropriation of property; in *Pitham and Hehl* (1976), the Court of Appeal held that an offer to sell is an assumption of the owner's right to sell and hence an appropriation. Thus, provided, as the facts imply, Tony had a dishonest intention to permanently deprive, he may be convicted of theft.

Pitham and Hehl has been criticised by a number of commentators. Professor Williams argues that the purported exercise of a power is not an assumption of a right of the owner. He points out that a person who purports to sell property belonging to another does not commit a civil wrong against the owner if there is no subsequent taking of possession and, thus, there is no reason why he should be convicted of stealing it. Professor Williams contends that it is 'jurisprudentially preposterous' to say that a person may be guilty of theft merely by making an offer. He contends that the error in the reasoning of the Court of Appeal lies in their failure to distinguish between the rights of an owner, such as the right to possession, and the powers of an owner, including the power to sell. Only an assumption of the 'rights' of an owner is an appropriation.[22]

Tony may be guilty of fraud – by false representation – contrary to s 1(1) of the Fraud Act 2006. This requires proof of dishonesty and an intention to make a gain in terms of money or other property or an intention to cause loss to another or expose another to a risk of loss in terms of money or other property. Clearly, these ingredients are satisfied in this case.

A fraudulent representation is an assertion which is untrue or misleading and which the person making it knows is or might be untrue or misleading (s 2(2)). It may be express or implied by conduct (s 2(4)). Where a person offers goods for sale, he impliedly represents that he has a right to sell those goods (see *Edwards* (1978)), but the facts of the problem are unclear as to whether Tony made such a representation. He may have made it clear to Hattie that he had no right to sell the fireplace, in which case there would be no liability for fraud.[23]

PART (D)

Although, in general, a person who picks wild mushrooms or flowers from wild plants growing on another's land is, by virtue of s 4(3) of the Theft Act 1968, excepted from the

---

22 Although a critique of the law is not necessary when answering most problem questions, it can reveal depth of understanding and is appreciated by examiners. But do not spend so much time in evaluating the law that you are left with insufficient time to explain and apply it!

23 It goes without saying that the facts of questions should be read carefully and the temptation to unconsciously project facts into the question should be resisted. Always make clear the assumptions upon which your answer is based.

provisions of s 4(2)(b), the exception does not apply where it is done for reward or sale or other commercial purpose.

It is, however, arguable that an isolated small-scale case of picking and selling mushrooms does not amount to theft. The wording of the section implies that only if D is in the business of selling mushrooms might he be convicted of stealing them.

PART (E)

Tony and Lolita may be guilty of statutory conspiracy to steal contrary to s 1(1) of the Criminal Law Act 1977.

The relevant part of the section provides that a person is guilty of conspiracy if he agrees with another that a course of conduct shall be pursued which, if carried out, would necessarily amount to the commission of an offence by one of the parties to the agreement.

There is no requirement that both parties are capable of committing the agreed offence as principal. Tony and Lolita made an agreement to dig up the tree which, if carried out, would amount to the commission of an offence by one of them (Lolita) and that constitutes a conspiracy (see also *Whitchurch* (1890) and *Duguid* (1906)). The fact that s 4(2) would exempt Tony from liability as a perpetrator does not exempt him from liability for conspiracy, and the exemptions to liability for conspiracy in s 2 of the 1977 Act are not relevant.

If Lolita had carried out the agreement, Tony would have been guilty as an accomplice (*Sockett* (1908)).

The above analysis is based on the assumption that Lolita had a dishonest intent. If, however, she mistakenly believed that Tony had the authority to allow her to remove the tree, then her intended taking of the tree would not be 'dishonest' (s 2(1)(a) of the Theft Act 1968). And, as both parties to the agreement are required to act with the relevant *mens rea*, there would be no conspiracy (s 1(1) and 1(2) of the 1977 Act).

CRIMINAL DAMAGE

The definition of 'property' for the purpose of criminal damage is contained in s 10 of the Criminal Damage Act 1971. It is broadly similar to the definition in s 4 of the Theft Act 1968, except that criminal damage can be committed in respect of land or a building.

Thus, Tony may be convicted of criminal damage contrary to s 1(1) of the 1971 Act for damaging the roof and digging up the rose bush.

The *mens rea* requirement, which appears to be satisfied in both cases, is intention or recklessness with respect to the risk of damage.

As he knew his landlord did not approve of alterations, he cannot take advantage of the defence of 'lawful excuse' in s 5(2)(a) of the 1971 Act.

As far as their liability for conspiracy is concerned, s 5(2)(a) of the 1971 Act provides that D has a lawful excuse if he damages property with the consent of a person who D mistakenly believed was entitled to consent. Thus, there would be no conspiracy if Lolita mistakenly believed that Tony was entitled to authorise the removal of the cherry tree, as no offence would have been committed if the agreement had been carried out in accordance with their intentions. It is immaterial whether this belief is justified or not so long as it is honestly held (s 5(3); *Jaggard v Dickinson* (1981)).

Finally, the mushrooms cannot be the subject matter of criminal damage (s 10(1)(b) of the 1971 Act).

Aim Higher ★

This question involves the meaning of 'property' for the purposes of the **Theft Act 1968** and, in particular, the situations in which a person may be guilty of theft contrary to **s 1** where they appropriate things forming part of the land. A detailed knowledge of **s 4** of the Act is required.

QUESTION 43

The acquisition of an indefeasible title to property is capable of amounting to a dishonest appropriation of property belonging to another for the purposes of s 1(1) of the Theft Act 1968.

▶ Explain and discuss.

How to Answer this Question

This question calls for an analysis of the series of cases concerning liability for theft where D receives property by way of gift. If a person of full capacity makes a gift to another then, in the absence of fraud or coercion, full ownership in the property transfers to the recipient. As the *actus reus* of theft involves the 'appropriation of property belonging to another', it would seem to follow that the recipient could not be guilty of theft even if his behaviour in accepting the gift was, for some reason, morally reprehensible. That was the conclusion reached by the Court of Appeal in *Mazo* (1997), but not by the House of Lords in *Hinks* (2000). Other relevant authorities include:

❖ *Hopkins and Kendrick* (1997);
❖ *Lawrence* (1982);
❖ *Gomez* (1993); and
❖ *Morris and Anderton v Burnside* (1983).

Answer Structure

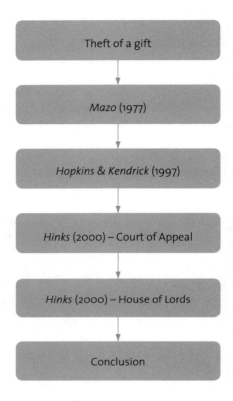

ANSWER

In 1996, Karen Hinks became friendly with John Dolphin, a man of limited intelligence, and between April and November 1996, accompanied him to his building society where he withdrew practically all his savings, a total of £60,000, and gave her the money. She then deposited the money in her own account. Hinks was charged with theft, contrary to s 1(1) of the Theft Act 1968, in respect of the sums of money deposited in her account. At her trial, a consultant psychiatrist described Dolphin as naive and trusting, but nonetheless capable of appreciating the concept of ownership and of divesting himself of property.[24]

The defence submitted that the sums of money were gifts from Mr Dolphin and that, the ownership in the money having passed to Hinks, there was no case to answer. Counsel

24 Answering this question requires a detailed analysis of five or six important cases. As the issues are complex an excellent understanding of each is necessary.

argued that there is no 'appropriation of property belonging to another' if, in the absence of fraud or coercion, the owner, with full capacity, consents to or authorises the transfer of property. The submission was rejected by the judge. The judge directed the jury that even if the gifts were valid, the appellant was guilty of theft provided that her conduct fell short of the standards of ordinary and decent people and the appellant realised this. Appropriation, the judge said, included 'a straightforward taking or transfer of … property', whether by gift or otherwise.

The jury returned a unanimous verdict of guilty.

Hinks, relying in part on the decision of the Court of Appeal in *Mazo* (1997), appealed against her conviction on the grounds, *inter alia*, that the recipient of a valid gift could not be guilty of theft.

Mazo had received gifts from S, an elderly lady whose mental faculties were deteriorating. It was held that the receipt of valid gifts made *inter vivos* could not amount to theft even if the recipient was dishonest. As the trial judge had not directed the jury to consider whether S had the capacity to make the gifts, the defendant's conviction was quashed. A taking with consent would amount to theft only where the recipient did not get an indefeasible title.

However, the decision of the Court of Appeal in *Hopkins and Kendrick* (1997) cast doubt on *Mazo*.

Hopkins and Kendrick were managers of a residential home for the elderly. The victim, Mrs Clare, who was 99 years of age and virtually blind, had moved into the home in 1991. Her affairs were looked after by her daughter until the daughter's death in November 1992, whereupon the appellants took control of them. A large number of cheques were drawn on her account and, after obtaining power of attorney, they liquidated her financial assets, transferring the proceeds into a building society account. The account was set up in the names of the victim and the two appellants, but only one signature was necessary for the drawing of a cheque. The appellants cashed a number of cheques. The appellants contended that they had acted throughout on her instructions and that some of the payments were for the benefit of the victim and others were gifts from her. The appellants were charged with conspiracy to steal and were convicted.

The appellants appealed on the grounds that, following *Mazo*, the judge should have directed the jury that if the donor had the capacity to make the gifts or to consent to the transfer of property, there was no appropriation and hence no theft. The Court of Appeal dismissed the appeal, holding that the submission was 'bold and surprising' and in conflict with the decisions in *Lawrence* (1982) and *Gomez* (1993) (discussed below).

Despite this, the court considered it necessary to distinguish *Mazo*. There was clear evidence in *Hopkins and Kendrick* that the victim lacked the capacity to make a gift.

Ebsworth J said:

> The judge, in summing up, in our view, made it wholly clear to the jury, for the purposes of the law, what the evidence was in relation to the level of mental capacity. There is nothing in the summing up, and nothing in the evidence, as it appears from the summing up, which could have resulted in a jury being confused as to whether Mrs Clare was somebody who is just 'not quite up to it', with reduced mental capacity, which was what was said of S, or lacking the capacity to manage her affairs. There is, both for reasons of a strict reading of the law and, in our judgment, on the way in which it was put to the jury, no basis upon which there was either a misdirection or anything which could have rendered the verdict of the jury unsafe.

Professor Smith points out that 'an instruction to convict only if [the victim] lacked the capacity to manage her own affairs was … unnecessary if *Mazo* was wrong' (see the commentary on the decision in the *Criminal Law Review*, 1997, p 360).

The approach in *Mazo* has much in its favour. It removes a potential inconsistency between the civil law and the criminal law. Professor Smith comments:

> If the gifts in these cases were valid in the civil law – neither void nor voidable for fraud, duress, undue influence or any other reason – the donees acquired an absolute, indefeasible title to the property. If it were seized from them by the police, they, not the donors or anyone else, would be entitled to recover it. They would have an action in conversion against the police – or the donor, if the police returned the property to her. It is submitted then that the question in both *Mazo* and *Hopkins and Kendrick*, in the absence of proof of deception, duress or undue influence, was whether P was competent to make the disposition she did.
>
> *The Law of Theft*, 8th edn, 1997, p 19

HINKS (2000) – THE DECISION OF THE COURT OF APPEAL

The Court of Appeal in *Hinks* (2000) preferred the approach in *Hopkins and Kendrick* to that in *Mazo* and dismissed the appeal. Rose LJ thought that Professor Smith's analysis was flawed and stated that 'civil unlawfulness is not a constituent of the offence of theft'. His Lordship concluded that an appropriation may occur even though the owner has consented to the property being taken. It followed that the receipt of a gift was capable of amounting to an appropriation and that the state of mind of the donor was irrelevant. Rose LJ observed that it was important not to conflate the two distinct ingredients of appropriation and dishonesty. Belief or lack of belief that the owner consented to the appropriation was relevant to dishonesty, but not to the issue of whether there had been an appropriation of property belonging to another.

Hinks appealed to the House of Lords, the Court of Appeal having certified that a question of law of general public importance was involved in its decision, viz:

> Whether the acquisition of an indefeasible title to property is capable of amounting to an appropriation of property belonging to another for the purposes of s 1(1) of the Theft Act 1968.[25]

HINKS – THE DECISION OF THE HOUSE OF LORDS

The House of Lords (Lords Hutton and Hobhouse dissenting) dismissed the appeal. It was immaterial whether the gifts to the appellant were valid or not. Appropriation is a neutral concept and thus a person could appropriate property belonging to another even though that other person had made an indefeasible gift of it.

Lord Steyn, speaking for the majority, reviewed the previous decisions of the House of Lords concerning the issue of consent and appropriation – *Lawrence*; *Morris and Anderton v Burnside* (1983) and *Gomez* – and concluded that the decisions in *Lawrence* and *Gomez* were binding upon the House.

Lawrence – the first case to deal with the issue – involved an Italian student, Mr Occhi, who arrived at Victoria station and asked Lawrence, a taxi driver, to take him to an address in Ladbroke Grove. The appellant told the student that the fare would be expensive. Mr Occhi got into the taxi and offered £1. Lawrence took the money tendered but said that it was not enough and, with Mr Occhi's permission, removed a further £6 from his open wallet. He then took Mr Occhi to his destination. The proper fare for the journey was approximately 50 pence. Lawrence appealed against his conviction 'of theft of the approximate sum of £6'. He contended that as he had taken the money with the consent of the student, he had not stolen it. The House of Lords, dismissing his appeal, held that s 1(1) was not to be construed as though it contained the words 'without the consent of the owner'.

In *Morris and Anderton v Burnside*, the appellants had taken goods from the shelf in a supermarket, removed the correct price label and attached a lower one. One was arrested after he had passed through the checkout paying the lower price; the other was arrested at the checkout before he had paid for the goods. The House of Lords concluded that both were properly convicted of theft. Lord Roskill said that the combination of switching the

---

25 Misunderstandings about the decision in **Hinks** can be avoided by noting carefully the question of law certified by the Court of Appeal. The judgment is a response to that specific question.

labels and removing the items from the shelf amounted to an appropriation. At that point, there was a usurpation or 'assumption of the rights of an owner' within s 3(1) of the Theft Act 1968.

Lord Roskill observed, at p 293:

> If, however, one postulates an honest customer taking goods from a shelf to put in his or her trolley to take to the check-point there to pay the proper price, I am unable to see that any of these actions involves any assumption by the shopper of the rights of the supermarket.

And that:

> In the context of s 3(1) an appropriation in my view involves not an act expressly or impliedly authorised by the owner but an act by way of adverse interference with or usurpation of those rights.

In *Gomez*, D1, an assistant manager of a shop, obtained authority from his manager, P, to supply goods to D2 in return for two cheques. D1 knew that the cheques were worthless. The House (Lord Lowry dissenting) held that although P had authorised the transaction, there was an appropriation of property belonging to another and allowed the prosecution appeal. Lord Keith, speaking for the majority, stated that although the actual decision in *Morris* was correct, it was unnecessary and erroneous to suggest that an authorised act could never amount to an appropriation and that *Morris* could not be regarded as overruling *Lawrence*. Lord Browne-Wilkinson considered the view expressed by Lord Roskill to be flawed, as it introduced the mental state of the owner into the concept of appropriation. In his opinion, the word 'appropriation' related purely to the act done by the accused.

The Court of Appeal in *Mazo* concluded that *Gomez* was restricted to cases where the consent of the owner was induced by fraud, deception or a false representation. A taking with consent only amounted to theft where the recipient did not get an indefeasible title. However, Lord Steyn in *Hinks* considered that although the certified question in *Gomez* referred to situations where the consent had been induced by fraud, the majority judgments did not differentiate between cases involving deceit and those which did not.

Lord Steyn added that the tension between the civil and criminal law was not so important as to justify a narrowing of the definition of appropriation. Such a course would unjustifiably restrict the scope of the law of theft. Nor was he persuaded by counsel's submission that the decision would lead to 'absurd and grotesque' results. The requirement that the appropriation was dishonest would provide adequate protection against injustice.

DISHONESTY

Section 2(1) of the Theft Act 1968 defines three states of mind which are, as a matter of law, not dishonest. The list is not exhaustive. Where the statute is silent, the issue of dishonesty is a question of fact for the jury and, in such cases, the jury should be instructed that a defendant is dishonest if what he did fell short of the ordinary standards of reasonable and honest people and he realised that (*Ghosh* (1982)).

Lord Hutton, whilst agreeing with the majority response to the certified question, thought that the direction on the issue of Hinks' dishonesty was materially defective. The instructions had failed to address the issue of capacity as it related to this element of theft and thus there was the danger that the jury might have convicted simply on the basis that the behaviour of the defendant was morally reprehensible.

Section 2(1)(b) of the Theft Act 1968 provides that an appropriation is not to be regarded as dishonest if it is done in the belief that the owner would have consented had he known of the appropriation and the circumstances of it. Clearly, the subsection is intended to apply to situations where the alleged thief mistakenly believed he would have had the owner's consent, but it would be remarkable if it did not also apply to the situation where the recipient of property knew that he, in fact, did have the owner's consent to appropriate the property.

Indeed, in *Lawrence*, Viscount Dilhorne had said that if the appellant had believed that Mr Occhi had known that the fare was excessive and nonetheless agreed to pay it, the element of dishonesty would not have been established.

Lord Hutton observed that a person's appropriation should not be regarded as dishonest if the other person actually gives the property to him and that in cases involving gifts, issues of capacity and deceit are relevant to this element of theft. Provided Mr Dolphin had capacity to make the gifts and Ms Hinks had practised neither fraud nor coercion, the appropriation was not dishonest, irrespective of how deplorable her conduct may have been.[26]

In his dissenting speech, Lord Hobhouse referred to s 2(1)(a) of the Theft Act, which provides that a person is not dishonest if he appropriates property in the belief that he has a legal right to deprive the other of it and pointed out that in the case of a valid gift, the recipient's knowledge that he has such a right must inevitably be relevant to the question of whether he is guilty of theft.

---

26 An answer to this essay question requires consideration of the element of dishonesty in theft and the speeches of the dissenting judges in *Hinks*.

The majority declined to consider the judge's directions on the issue of dishonesty. It had not formed part of the certified question and Lord Steyn felt that the House was not properly informed as to how the issue had been dealt with at trial. Nonetheless, His Lordship considered a number of hypothetical situations involving the transfer of an indefeasible title to property in which the transferor acted under a misapprehension of which the recipient was aware. His Lordship remarked at p 843 that:

> ... a jury could *possibly* find that the acceptance took place in the belief that the transferee had the right in law to deprive the other of it within the meaning of s 2(1)(a) of the 1968 Act [emphasis added].

Does this mean that a defendant who fails to appreciate that he is in law entitled to the property transferred to him might be guilty of theft?

It surely cannot be correct that, whilst a defendant who mistakenly believes that he has a legal right to property that he appropriates is exonerated, a defendant who mistakenly believes that he has no legal right to a gift is guilty of stealing it, provided the jury conclude that his acceptance of the gift was morally reprehensible.

PROPERTY BELONGING TO ANOTHER

Lord Hobhouse noted at p 854 that although the House of Lords and the Court of Appeal have warned on a number of occasions against introducing complex questions of civil law into the law of theft:

> [T]he truth is that theft is a crime which relates to civil property and, inevitably, property concepts from the civil law have to be used and questions answered by reference to that law.

Section 1(1) of the Theft Act 1968 requires that the property belonged to another at the time of the appropriation and s 5 of the Act defines and qualifies the expression 'belonging to another' by reference to a number of civil law concepts. Thus, in some cases of theft, it will be necessary to have recourse to the civil law to determine whether the relevant property belonged to the alleged victim or the defendant. If the transferor has validly transferred ownership and possession to the defendant and retains no equitable or restitutionary rights, no keeping or dealing with the property by the defendant can amount to theft, irrespective of whether he is dishonest and whether he is regarded as appropriating it (Think Point (1)).

CONCLUSION

Hinks is the fourth case in which the House has considered whether an act of appropriation requires an unlawful assumption of the rights of an owner and it is the third in which it has concluded that it does not. Despite the strength of the arguments to the contrary and despite the intention of the framers of the Theft Act 1968, every acquisition of property amounts to an appropriation. A person appropriates property when he accepts a valid gift.

Think Point

1   Lord Steyn believed that eliminating the need for an explanation of the civil law in respect of appropriation was 'a great advantage in an overly complex corner of the law'. Civil unlawfulness, it seems, is not a constituent of this element of theft. But if Lords Hutton and Hobhouse are correct, and it is submitted that they are, the judge may have to explain the relevant civil law issues to the jury when instructing them to consider whether the appropriation was dishonest and whether the property belonged to another at the time of the appropriation.

QUESTION 44

Dodger was a pickpocket. He entered a branch of the MidWest bank and waited for a customer to make a large withdrawal of cash. Mrs Pendlebury entered the bank and withdrew £500. She put the money in an envelope and put the envelope into her bag. Whilst she was distracted, Dodger picked the envelope from her bag. Mrs Pendlebury realised what had happened and screamed for assistance. Dodger dropped the money and ran out of the bank. Trevor, an employee of the bank, tried to block Dodger's escape. Dodger pushed Trevor who fell and suffered a slight injury.

▶   Discuss Dodger's criminal liability.

How to Answer this Question

This question involves a number of offences contrary to the Theft Acts of 1968 and 1978. Although it does not raise any particularly difficult issues, it is important to be methodical about answering this question. It is advisable in a question of this type for your answer to mirror the sequence of events.

Particular issues to be considered are:

- ❖   Burglary: did D 'enter the bank as a trespasser'?
- ❖   Robbery: was force used in order to steal?
- ❖   Assaults: only minor injuries are suffered and therefore only liability under s 47 of the Offences Against the Person Act 1861 needs to be considered.

Applying the Law

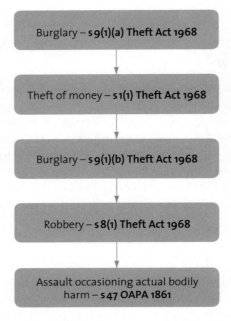

This diagram highlights the main principles you need to discuss in your answer.

ANSWER[27]

BURGLARY (s 9(1)(a))

Dodger may be convicted of burglary contrary to s 9(1)(a) of the Theft Act 1968. This provides that a person commits burglary if he enters a building as a trespasser with intent to commit one of a number of specified offences, including theft (s 9(2)).

A person enters as a trespasser if he enters without consent or permission. Although there is an implied permission to enter a bank, this is restricted to particular lawful purposes. As Dodger entered the building intending to steal, he entered in excess of the implied permission (*Jones and Smith* (1976)) and, as he knew of the facts that made his entry trespassory, he entered with the appropriate *mens rea* (*Collins* (1973)).

Dodger did not intend to steal specific property from a particular individual when he entered the bank. This, however, does not present a problem. A person may be convicted

---

27   When answering questions raising issues in respect of a number of property offences it is generally a good strategy to deal with the incidents chronologically.

of burglary contrary to s 9(1)(a) if he intended to steal something in the building, even though, at the time of entry, he had no specific item in mind. In *Attorney General's References (Nos 1 and 2 of 1979)* (1979), it was held that an intention to steal, conditional on there being money in the building, would suffice for burglary. The indictment should be framed in general terms alleging an 'intent to steal' without reference to specific property or victim.

THEFT

When Dodger took the money from Mrs Pendlebury's bag, he committed theft contrary to s 1 of the Theft Act 1968. In *Corcoran v Anderton* (1980), two youths snatched a bag from a woman. The Divisional Court held that the appropriation took place at the moment they snatched it from her grasp.

The fact that Dodger did not manage to keep possession of the money makes no difference to his liability. Theft requires an intention to permanently deprive; there is no requirement of permanent deprivation in fact.

BURGLARY (s 9(1)(b))

At this point, he also committed burglary contrary to s 9(1)(b) of the 1968 Act. This provides that a person is guilty of burglary if, having entered a building as a trespasser, he commits one of a number of specified offences, including theft.

It must be shown that the defendant entered as a trespasser (see discussion of this point, above) and that at the time of the theft he knew or was at least reckless with respect to the facts that made his entry trespassory (*Collins*).

ROBBERY

Robbery under s 8 of the Theft Act 1968 requires the use or threat of force on any person in order to steal. There is no evidence in this case that he used force on Mrs Pendlebury when he stole the envelope from her bag. Furthermore, although for the purposes of robbery the force may be used on any person and not necessarily the person from whom the property was stolen, the force used against Trevor, it is submitted, would not suffice for robbery. Section 8 requires that the force is used 'immediately before or at the time of the theft' and 'in order to steal'. Dodger applied force to Trevor after the theft and did so in order to escape and not to steal (see *James* (1997)).

In *Hale* (1978), it was said that an appropriation is a continuing act and that a person may be guilty of robbery when he uses force as he makes off with the property. The Court of Appeal held that the question of whether the theft has come to an end is one for the jury (see also *Atakpu and Abrahams* (1994)). In *Hale*, however, the defendants still had possession of the property as they made their getaway. In the case of Dodger, the theft clearly came to an end when he dropped the envelope.[28]

ASSAULTS

Dodger may be convicted of an assault occasioning actual bodily harm contrary to s 47 of the Offences Against the Person Act 1861. The section requires that the defendant committed an assault or a battery which resulted in actual bodily harm (*DPP v Little* (1991)).

When Dodger pushed Trevor in order to escape, he committed a battery. A battery is the intentional or reckless infliction of unlawful personal force on any person (*Faulkner v Talbot* (1981)).

'Actual bodily harm' was defined in *Miller* (1954) to include any hurt or injury which interferes with the health or comfort of the victim and this would include minor bruising.

Although the *actus reus* of the offence under s 47 requires that actual bodily harm be occasioned, the House of Lords held in *Savage; Parmenter* (1991) that as far as the *mens rea* for the offence is concerned, it is not necessary to prove that the accused intended or foresaw actual bodily harm; all that is required is intention or recklessness with respect to the application of force.

Thus, as he intentionally applied force to Trevor, and Trevor suffered actual bodily harm as a result, Dodger may be convicted of the offence under s 47, punishable with a maximum of five years' imprisonment.

There is no liability under either s 18 or 20 of the 1861 Act. Both offences require that D either wounded or inflicted or caused grievous (ie serious) bodily harm. To amount to a 'wound', the inner and outer skin must be broken (*JCC (A Minor) v Eisenhower* (1984)) – a bruise is not a wound – and the injuries suffered by Trevor were not serious.

DISHONESTY

The facts raise no issue of dishonesty and so this element has not been discussed. However, it is, of course, an ingredient of the *mens rea* for each of the Theft Act offences.[29]

---

28 Where appropriate, identify those facts that distinguish the facts of a problem from those of a decided case. Legally significant distinctions are often difficult to draw so reflect carefully when doing so.

29 It is a waste of valuable examination time to discuss, in any depth, elements of liability about which the facts of the problem do not raise 'live' issues. Noting the requirement of dishonesty for the offences discussed is sufficient.

QUESTION 45

George was an assistant in a shop selling computers. One day, Arnold visited him at the shop and told him that unless George gave him a laptop, he would tell Malcolm to go round to George's house and beat up his wife when she returned from her mother's. George took a laptop from the shelf and gave it to Arnold.

Arnold swapped the laptop with his friend, Barry, for a DVD player which Barry had lawfully purchased. Barry knew that the laptop was stolen, but did not reveal that he knew to Arnold.

Barry sold the laptop for £280 to Charlie, a bona fide purchaser.

Later that evening, Charlie learned how Arnold had come by the laptop. Although he knew he was not entitled to, Charlie sold the laptop for £300 to Eric, a bona fide purchaser.

Arnold, who had become bored with the DVD player, sold it to David. David was aware of the circumstances by which Arnold had come by the DVD player.

▶ Discuss the liability of George, Arnold, Barry, Charlie, and David.

How to Answer this Question

This problem centres on the law relating to handling stolen goods, an offence contrary to s 22 of the Theft Act 1968. It also raises issues concerning:

- ❖   theft (s 1);
- ❖   robbery (s 8);
- ❖   blackmail (s 21);
- ❖   procuring the execution of a valuable security (s 20(2)); and
- ❖   attempt (s 1 of the Criminal Attempts Act 1981).

Answer Structure

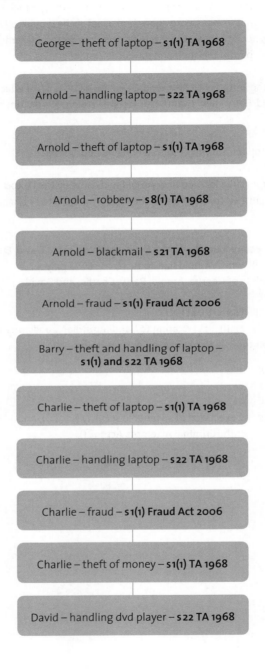

George – theft of laptop – s1(1) TA 1968

Arnold – handling laptop – s22 TA 1968

Arnold – theft of laptop – s1(1) TA 1968

Arnold – robbery – s8(1) TA 1968

Arnold – blackmail – s21 TA 1968

Arnold – fraud – s1(1) Fraud Act 2006

Barry – theft and handling of laptop – s1(1) and s22 TA 1968

Charlie – theft of laptop – s1(1) TA 1968

Charlie – handling laptop – s22 TA 1968

Charlie – fraud – s1(1) Fraud Act 2006

Charlie – theft of money – s1(1) TA 1968

David – handling dvd player – s22 TA 1968

ANSWER

GEORGE

THEFT

George may be charged with theft contrary to s 1(1) of the Theft Act 1968. He may, however, be able to take advantage of the defence of duress. There is an evidential burden on the accused in respect of the defence, but the burden of disproving it lies with the prosecution (*Gill* (1963)).

The defence excuses where the defendant was, or may have been, compelled to commit an offence because he had good cause to fear that if he did not do so, he would be killed or would suffer serious injury and a sober person of reasonable firmness sharing the characteristics of the accused would have responded in a similar fashion (*Graham* (1982); *Howe* (1987); *Hasan* (2005)). The characteristics of the defendant which may be attributed to the reasonable person include age and sex and, if appropriate, serious physical disability or recognised psychiatric conditions such as post-traumatic stress disorder. However, the mere fact that the accused is more pliable, vulnerable, timid or susceptible to threats than a normal person are not characteristics with which it is legitimate to invest the reasonable/ordinary person (*Bowen* (1996); see also *Hegarty* (1994); *Horne* (1994); *Hurst* (1995); and *Flatt* (1996); cf *Emery* (1993)).

In *Ortiz* (1986), the Court of Appeal held that threats to seriously injure one's spouse might amount to duress.

The difficulty that George may have in successfully pleading the defence relates to the immediacy of the threat. In *Hasan* (2005), the House of Lords held that if there was an opportunity which D might reasonably have taken in order to avoid committing the crime then the defence will fail. Lord Bingham expressed disapproval of the judgment in *Hudson and Taylor* (1971) and stated that it should be made clear to the jury that if the threat against the defendant or his family or a person for whom he reasonably feels responsible is not such as he reasonably expects to follow immediately or almost immediately on his failure to comply, there may be little if any room for doubt that he could have avoided committing the crime charged either by going to the police or by some other means.

The question is one for the jury who, in deciding whether an opportunity was reasonably open to the defendant, should have regard to all the circumstances and to any risks to which he might have exposed either himself or his wife (see also *Cole* (1994)).

If George's plea is successful, then he will be absolved of criminal liability. If not, then the threats may be regarded as a factor in mitigation.

ARNOLD

HANDLING

If George's plea of duress is unsuccessful, then Arnold may be guilty of handling stolen goods contrary to s 22(1) of the 1968 Act. However, a receiver is guilty of handling only if he dishonestly received them otherwise than in the course of the stealing. The stipulation is a reference to the offence of theft by virtue of which the goods originally became stolen.

Was the theft complete at the time Arnold received the laptop?

In *Pitham and Hehl* (1976), it was held that theft is an instantaneous occurrence complete at the moment the goods are first appropriated. This decision is unlikely to be followed as it would mean that the phrase 'in the course of the stealing' was of no effect. It is submitted that a better approach is to be found in the decisions of the Court of Appeal in *Atakpu and Abrahams* (1994) and *Hale* (1978), in which it was held that an appropriation continues as long as the thief is 'on the job' – a question for the jury.[30]

THEFT

Irrespective of whether he is guilty of handling, Arnold is guilty of theft contrary to s 1 of the Act. He dishonestly appropriated property belonging to another with the intention of permanently depriving the other of it.

ROBBERY

Although Arnold has stolen and employed threats in order to steal, he cannot be guilty of robbery contrary to s 8 of the Theft Act 1968, because he did not 'put or seek to put any person in fear of being then and there subjected to force'. George was not in fear of being subject to force. Neither was his wife. She was not present at the time the threats were made (*Taylor* (1996)).[31]

BLACKMAIL

Arnold may, however, be guilty of blackmail contrary to s 21 of the Theft Act 1968. The *actus reus* consists of a 'demand with menaces'. He made a 'demand' when he instructed George to give him a laptop.

'Menaces' includes threats of any action detrimental or unpleasant to the person addressed, provided that it would have moved an ordinary person of normal stability and courage to accede unwillingly to the demand (*Thorne v Motor Trade Association* (1937); *Clear* (1968)).

---

30 Acknowledge where decisions are conflict and, if possible, express a view as to the better approach.
31 Note carefully the wording of s 8 of the Theft Act 1968.

The question of whether a threat amounts to a menace is one for the jury to decide. One might reasonably expect them to conclude that a threat to beat up a man's wife would move him to accede unwillingly to a demand to hand over property.

It is immaterial that the threat related to action to be taken by Malcolm and not Arnold, the person making the threat (s 21(2)). Nor does it matter that the victim of the blackmail, George, was not the individual at whom the threatened action was directed.

The requirement that the demand was made with a 'view to gain' in terms of property is satisfied (s 34(2)(a)).

Whether or not the demand with menaces was unwarranted is a question of *mens rea*. There is nothing in the facts to suggest that Arnold believed that he had reasonable grounds for making the demand and that the menaces were a proper means of reinforcing the demand, and therefore it would appear that he is guilty of blackmail (and see *Harvey* (1981)).

FRAUD

Arnold is guilty of fraud contrary to s 1(1) of the Fraud Act 2006.

The form of the offence defined in s 2 of the Act – fraud by false representation – requires that D, dishonestly and with intent to make a gain or cause or expose another to a loss, makes a false representation. A representation may be express or implied (s 2(4)) and in *Edwards* (1978) it was held that a person who sells goods impliedly represents that he has a right to sell.

It is immaterial that Barry knew that the laptop was stolen. The offence of fraud does not require proof that anyone was deceived by the false representation.

BARRY

THEFT AND HANDLING

As he knew it was stolen, Barry is guilty of theft of the laptop contrary to s 1 and handling stolen goods contrary to s 22 of the Theft Act 1968.

FRAUD

He is also guilty of an offence of fraud – by false representing to Charlie that he had a right to sell the laptop – as discussed above.

CHARLIE

THEFT OF THE LAPTOP

Charlie, as he was bona fide, was not guilty of theft when he took possession of the laptop. Nor, on discovering that it was stolen, was he guilty of theft by 'keeping or dealing with it as owner'. Section 3(2) provides an exception to the later assumption principle in s3(1). The subsection protects – from a conviction for theft – the innocent purchaser of stolen goods who later discovers they are stolen and decides to keep them or otherwise dispose of them.[32]

HANDLING

As he had no *mens rea* when he took possession, he cannot be convicted of handling by receiving. Nor did he commit handling when he sold it. In *Bloxham* (1983), it was held that a person who sells stolen goods on his own behalf does not undertake or assist in the realisation or disposal by or for the benefit of another. The House of Lords held that a person who sells an article does not assist the buyer to dispose of it, since the buyer does not dispose of it, nor does the seller undertake the realisation or disposal for the benefit of another as he sells it for his own benefit. The buyer benefits from the purchase, but not from the realisation.[33]

FRAUD

Charlie is, however, guilty of fraud – by falsely representing that the goods were his to sell (see the discussion above). Section 3(2) does not affect the principles of civil law concerning ownership, nor does it provide protection from the offence in s1 of the Fraud Act 2006.

THEFT OF THE £300

He is also guilty of stealing the £300 contrary to s1 of the Theft Act 1968. The money was property belonging to another which he appropriated with a dishonest intention to permanently deprive (Think Point (1)).

DAVID

HANDLING STOLEN GOODS

By virtue of s24(2), the DVD player amounted to 'stolen goods', since it directly represented the goods originally stolen (the laptop) in the hands of the thief (Arnold) as the proceeds of a disposition of them. As he was aware of the circumstances – and as there is nothing in the facts to suggest he is not dishonest – he is guilty of handling by receiving.

Think Point

1   It is possible that Charlie thought that, despite everything, selling the recorder was not dishonest, in which case it is a matter for the jury directed in accordance with *Ghosh* (1982).

---

32   Explaining the effect of **s3(2)** is best achieved by noting that it is an exception to 'the later assumption principle' in **s3(1).**

33   Note carefully the wording of **s22** of the **Theft Act 1968**.

Aim Higher ★

This question raises liability for a large number of offences and there are many parties. Only a well planned answer is likely to deal with the issues effectively. Deal with each party separately and within that structure consider each of the offences they may have committed.

QUESTION 46

PART (A)

Albert approached Mrs Bennett as she was walking in the park with her six-month-old baby, Edgar. Albert threatened to hurt Edgar unless Mrs Bennett handed over some money. Mrs Bennett took £50 from her purse and gave it to Albert.

▶ Discuss Albert's criminal liability.

PART (B)

Michael was owed £30 by Thomas. When Michael asked for the return of the money owing, Thomas told him that he was unable to pay until the end of the month. Angered by this, Michael told Thomas that unless he handed over his watch in satisfaction of the debt he would beat him up. Reluctantly, Thomas handed over the watch.

▶ Discuss Michael's criminal liability.

How to Answer this Question

The principal issues are:

- ❖ robbery contrary to s 8 of the Theft Act 1968;
- ❖ blackmail contrary to s 21;
- ❖ the meaning of 'puts or seeks to put any person in fear of being then and there subjected to force' in s 8;
- ❖ the meaning of 'menaces' in s 21; and
- ❖ the difference between the meaning of 'dishonesty' for the purposes of theft and 'unwarranted' for the purposes of blackmail.

Answer Structure

(a)

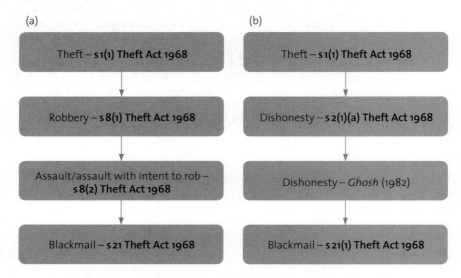

(b)

The two flow charts above highlight the legislation you need to consider in your answer.

ANSWER -

PART (A)

THEFT

Albert has committed theft of the £50 contrary to s 1 of the Theft Act 1968, an offence carrying a maximum of seven years' imprisonment (s 7, as amended by s 26 of the Criminal Justice Act 1991). Although Mrs Bennett handed him the money, he 'appropriated property belonging to another' and he did so dishonestly, intending to steal.

ROBBERY

A person is guilty of robbery contrary to s 8 if he steals and, immediately before or at the time of doing so, and in order to do so, he uses force on any person or puts or seeks to put any person in fear of being then and there subjected to force. The offence is punishable with life imprisonment (s 8(2)).

However, although for the purposes of robbery, threats of force used on any person in order to steal will suffice, s 8 requires that the accused puts or seeks to put that person in fear of being then and there subject to force. This requirement is not satisfied in the current problem. Albert did not put nor seek to put Mrs Bennett in fear of being subject to force because the threat was to hurt Edgar. Neither did he put, nor presumably seek to put, Edgar in fear of being subject to force, as Edgar was, of course, unaware of Albert's threats (see *Taylor* (1996)).[34]

For similar reasons, Albert may not be convicted of common assault contrary to s 39 of the Criminal Justice Act 1988 nor assault with intent to rob contrary to s 8(2) of the Theft Act 1968. A person is guilty of an assault if he intentionally or recklessly causes another to apprehend immediate and unlawful personal violence. In other words, the victim must anticipate the application of immediate and unlawful force to his body. For the reasons explained above, neither Mrs Bennett nor Edgar apprehended such force (*Fagan v Metropolitan Police Commissioner* (1969)).

BLACKMAIL

Section 21 of the Theft Act 1968 provides that a person is guilty of blackmail if, with a view to gain for himself or another or with intent to cause loss to another, he makes any unwarranted demand with menaces. Blackmail is an offence triable only on indictment and punishable with imprisonment for a maximum of 14 years (s 21(3)).

Albert has made a demand for £50.

A 'menace' includes threats of any action detrimental or unpleasant to the person addressed. It is not restricted to threats of violence directed at the victim of the demand (*Thorne v Motor Trade Association* (1937)). Provided the threat is of such a nature and extent that the ordinary person of normal stability and courage would be influenced to accede unwillingly to the demand, the threat amounts to a menace (*Clear* (1968)).

Albert's threat to hurt Edgar would appear to amount to a menace. It is an issue for the jury, but one might reasonably expect them to conclude that a threat to hurt a baby would move a mother to accede unwillingly to a demand to hand over money.[35]

A blackmail demand must be made with a view to gain or intent to cause loss in terms of money or other property (s 34(2)(a)). In this case, Albert made the demand with a view to gain money.

Provided the prosecution can prove that Albert either did not believe that he had reasonable grounds for making the demand or that he did not believe that the menaces were a proper means of reinforcing the demand – and, from the facts, there appears to be

---

34 Read **s 8(1)** carefully. It is not enough that a person is put in fear. They must be put in fear that they will be subjected to force.

35 Provided it is acknowledged that the question is one for the jury it is permissible to volunteer an opinion whether the threat amounts to a menace. But note the way in which the submission is expressed.

no reason to doubt this – Albert's demand with menaces was 'unwarranted' and he may be convicted of blackmail (see below for a fuller discussion of the meaning of 'unwarranted').

PART (B)

THEFT

Michael has committed the *actus reus* of theft; that is, he has 'appropriated property belonging to another'.

If, however, he genuinely, albeit mistakenly, believed that he was legally entitled to take the watch in satisfaction of the debt then, in accordance with s 2(1)(a) of the Theft Act 1968, his appropriation was not dishonest and therefore he did not commit theft. Furthermore, if Michael believed he had the legal right to deprive, he cannot be convicted of either theft or robbery even if he knew that he had no legal right to use or threaten force (*Robinson* (1977)).[36]

Section 2(1)(a) is limited to the situation where the accused believes he has a legal right to deprive another of property. If Michael knew that he had no legal right to the watch but considered himself to be morally entitled to take it, then the question of his dishonesty falls to the jury directed in accordance with the test expounded by the Court of Appeal in *Ghosh* (1982).

According to the Court of Appeal, the jury should be instructed, first, to determine what the accused's beliefs and intentions were and then, having done so, to decide whether what the accused did was dishonest according to the ordinary standards of reasonable and honest people. If they were not dishonest according to those standards, the prosecution fails.

However, if the accused's actions were dishonest according to the ordinary standards of reasonable and honest people, the jury must consider whether the accused realised that what he did was dishonest according to those standards. If the accused did not realise that, then he was not dishonest and the prosecution fails.

If the jury conclude that Michael was not dishonest, then he is neither guilty of theft nor robbery. On the other hand, if the court concludes that he was dishonest, he will be guilty of theft and, as he put Thomas in fear of being subjected to force, in order to steal, he will also be guilty of robbery.

---

36 Robbery is an aggravated form of theft. It is important therefore to consider whether all the elements of theft are satisfied.

BLACKMAIL

Michael made a demand with menaces (as explained above) when he threatened to beat up Thomas unless he paid the money owing.

In addition, he acted with a view to gain. In *Parkes* (1973), it was held that the repayment of a debt is a gain. Whether he is guilty of blackmail will therefore depend upon whether his demand with menaces was 'unwarranted'.

This is a question of *mens rea*. The onus is on the prosecution to prove either that Michael did not believe that he had reasonable grounds for making the demand for the return of the money or that he did not believe that the use of the threat to beat up Thomas was a proper means of reinforcing the demand.

Michael might have believed he had reasonable grounds for making the demand but, unless he also believed that the threat employed was morally and socially acceptable, he will be guilty of blackmail. The test is subjective, but the word 'proper' refers to general standards. A person believes a threat to be 'proper' not merely by believing that it is in accordance with his own standards. The test is whether he believes that the use of the threat would be regarded as proper by people generally (Think Point (1)).

In *Harvey* (1981), the Court of Appeal held that, in general, where the accused knew that the act threatened was unlawful, it will not be possible for him to contend that he thought it was proper. Therefore, it is unlikely that Michael's demand with menaces was 'warranted' and, thus, he may be convicted of blackmail (see also *Harrison* (2001)).[37]

Think Point

1   But see *Lambert* (1972), where it was accepted that menaces were warranted if D believed that by his own standards what he threatened was proper.

QUESTION 47

Plug went into a supermarket intending to do some shopping and to steal some goods if the opportunity presented itself. Plug put a bottle of sherry in the trolley provided by the supermarket intending to conceal it in a large inside pocket of his coat pocket at a later stage and remove it from the shop without paying for it. Continuing with his shopping,

---

37 It has been held that the word 'proper' involves reference to generally held standards. Thus the question whether a demand with menaces was unwarranted is not resolved by reference to the standards of the defendant.

Plug took a bottle of wine from its shelf. He intended to pay for the wine. He then decided to return the sherry to the shelf as he had no opportunity to put it in his pocket and he did not want to buy it. At the checkout, the shop assistant rang up the price marked on the bottle of wine. At that point, Plug realised that the wine had been underpriced, but he chose to say nothing. In addition, the assistant gave Plug too much change. Plug did not notice the excess until after he had left the supermarket.

How to Answer this Question

The principal issues are:

- ❖ burglary contrary to s 9(1)(a) and (b) of the Theft Act 1968;
- ❖ theft contrary to s 1(1);
- ❖ 'property got by another's mistake' – s 5(4).

The principal authorities are: *Gomez* (1993); *Jones and Smith* (1976); *Collins* (1973).

Applying the Law

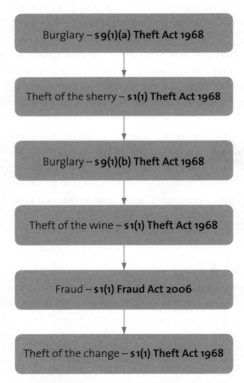

This diagram demonstrates the legislation needed to answer this question effectively.

ANSWER

BURGLARY – s 9(1)(a) OF THE THEFT ACT 1968

By virtue of s 9(1)(a) and 9(2) of the Theft Act 1968, a person is guilty of burglary if he enters a building as a trespasser intending to commit one of a number of specified offences including theft contrary to s 1(1) of the Act (Think Point (1)).

The *actus reus* requires proof that D entered a building as a trespasser, that is, he entered without the consent or permission of the occupier. And, in *Jones and Smith* (1976) it was held that a person is a trespasser for the purposes of s 9 if he enters a building in excess of the permission that has been given to him. The decision means that a person who enters a supermarket intending to steal is a trespasser at the moment of entry. The shopkeeper's invitation to enter the premises does not extend to those who enter for the purpose of stealing (Think Point (2)).

In addition it must be proved that D knew, at the time of entry, that his entry was trespassory or he was reckless in respect of that fact (*Collins* (1973)). Clearly, Plug was aware of the facts that made his entry trespassory and was, therefore, guilty of burglary when he entered the supermarket. The fact that he did not, at the time of entry, have specific items in mind does not preclude a conviction for burglary (*Walkington* (1979); *Attorney General's References (Nos 1 and 2 of 1979)* (1980)).[38]

THEFT OF THE SHERRY – s 1(1) OF THE THEFT ACT 1968

Section 1(1) of the Theft Act 1968 provides that a person is guilty of theft if he dishonestly appropriates property belonging to another with the intention of permanently depriving the other of it. The maximum penalty for theft is a term of imprisonment not exceeding seven years (s 7 of the Theft Act, as substituted by s 26 of the Criminal Justice Act 1991).

Section 3(1) of the Theft Act 1968 provides that an 'assumption of the rights of an owner' amounts to an appropriation and in *Gomez* (1993), the House of Lords decided that, a person assumes rights even where he takes possession of goods with the consent or authority of the owner. Thus, a person who removes goods from a supermarket shelf appropriates them and is guilty of theft if the act of appropriation is accompanied by a dishonest intention permanently to deprive. Therefore, Plug stole the sherry when he took it from the shelf. He intended to permanently deprive the supermarket of the sherry and, at the time he appropriated the goods, he was dishonest (see discussion of dishonesty, below). The fact that he returned the sherry is of no consequence. He was guilty of theft at the time he removed the bottle from the shelf (Think Point (3)).[39]

---

38 Note that all the elements of burglary contrary to **s 9(1)(a)** must be present at the moment of entry into the building or part of the building.

39 If D commits an offence nothing that is done after that can affect D's liability.

BURGLARY – s 9(1)(b) OF THE THEFT ACT 1968

Section 9(1)(b) of the Theft Act 1968 provides that a person is guilty of burglary if, having entered a building as a trespasser, he steals anything therein. As his entry into the supermarket was trespassory and he was aware of that Plug is also guilty of this form of burglary (see the discussion above; *Jones and Smith*; *Collins*).

THEFT OF THE WINE – s 1(1) OF THE THEFT ACT 1968

Although Plug 'appropriated' the wine when he took it from the shelf, he did not steal it. At that moment, he lacked the dishonest intent to steal and, it is submitted, there was no theft when he took possession of the bottle after the cashier had rung up the wrong price. In *Dip Kaur* (1981), it was held that a mistake as to price does not render a contract void. The ownership in the goods transfers to the buyer who, therefore, cannot be said to appropriate property *belonging to another* when he pays for and takes possession of the goods.

Doubt was cast on the decision in *Kaur* by Lord Roskill in *Morris*. His Lordship did not fully explain why he considered *Kaur* to be wrongly decided, but said that he did not consider fine points of civil law regarding void and voidable contracts to be relevant issues as far as theft was concerned. In *Hinks* (2000), the House of Lords adopted a similar point of view. Speaking for the majority, Lord Steyn said that there were great advantages, in a theft trial, in not having to explain 'complex' civil law concepts to the jury.

It is respectfully submitted that this approach is misguided. It is not possible to avoid recourse to the civil law when the facts raise the issue of whether the property belonged to another at the time of the alleged appropriation. In *Walker* (1984), the Court of Appeal allowed D's appeal against conviction for theft where the trial judge had failed to direct the jury with respect to the relevant issues of civil law contained in the Sale of Goods Act 1979.

In addition, although the point was not argued in *Kaur,* Plug may contend that taking incorrectly priced goods is not dishonest.

If Plug mistakenly believed that he had a right in law to take the wine at the price indicated, then, as a matter of law, it was not appropriated dishonestly (s 2(1)(a)). Alternatively, even if he knew that he had no legal right to the wine at the wrong price, he may raise evidence that he believed that, by ordinary standards, it was not dishonest to take advantage of a pricing error made by a supermarket. (*Roberts* (1987)).[40]

If so, the judge should direct the jury to decide whether *according to the standards of reasonable and honest people* what was done was dishonest. If it was not dishonest according to those standards, the prosecution fails. If it was dishonest according to those standards, then the jury must consider whether the prosecution have proved that the

40 **Section 2(1)** should be considered before turning to the *Ghosh* test.

defendant himself realised that what he was doing was, *by the above standards*, dishonest. If the defendant did not know that, the prosecution fails (*Ghosh* (1982) (Think Point (4)).

FRAUD – s1 OF THE FRAUD ACT 2006

Did Plug commit an offence of fraud contrary to s1 of the Fraud Act 2006 in respect of the underpriced wine?

There are two forms of the offence of relevance to this question: fraud by false representation, defined by s2 of the Act and fraud by failing to disclose information (s3). Both require proof of dishonesty and an intention to make a gain or an intention to cause loss to another in terms of money or other property. Although he did intended to make a gain it is submitted, for the following reasons, that Plug is not guilty of fraud:

FRAUD BY FALSE REPRESENTATION

A representation may be express or implied (s2(4)) but simple non-disclosure does not amount to a representation. In *Dip Kaur* the Divisional Court held that D had not practised a fraud to obtain the goods and that in general, silence does not constitute fraud (Think Point (5)).

FRAUD BY FAILING TO DISCLOSE INFORMATION

This form of fraud requires proof that D failed to disclose information which he was under a legal duty to disclose. Although a shopper may be under a moral obligation not to take advantage of a pricing error there is no legal duty to disclose the error. The framers of the Act and the Law Commission intended that this form of the offence should apply where a duty arose by virtue of a statute or there was a fiduciary relationship between the parties. Neither of these situations applies in this case (Think Point (6)).[41]

THEFT OF THE CHANGE

Plug did not steal the excess change when he was given it by the cashier. At that time, he was unaware of the excess and, therefore, he did not dishonestly appropriate it. However, he may be guilty of theft when, on becoming aware of the shop assistant's mistake, he decided to keep the excess change. First, s3(1) provides that, even if the original taking was innocent, a later assumption of a right to property by keeping or dealing with it as owner will amount to an appropriation. Secondly, although, as a matter of common law, the ownership in the money passed to Plug on delivery, the excess change is regarded, for the purposes of theft, as belonging to the supermarket; the conditions in s5(4) apply: the money was 'got by another's mistake' and Plug is 'under a [quasi-contractual] obligation to make restoration'.

---

41 Liability for fraud in breach of s4 applies only where D is under a legal duty to disclose. It is not sufficient that D was under a moral duty.

Plug may contend that keeping excess change is not dishonest. The issues relating to the question of dishonesty are discussed above.

Think Points

1   The penalty for burglary in a building other than a dwelling place is a term of imprisonment not exceeding 10 years (s 9(3)(a), as substituted by s 26(2) of the Criminal Justice Act 1991).

2   Williams, G, *Textbook of Criminal Law*, 2nd edn, 1983, p 848.

3   The question certified for the decision of the House of Lords in *Gomez* was as follows:

When theft is alleged and that which is alleged to be stolen passes to the defendant with the consent of the owner, but that consent has been obtained by a false representation, has: (a) an appropriation within the meaning of s 1(1) of the Theft Act 1968 taken place; or (b) must such a passing of property necessarily involve an element of adverse interference with or usurpation of some right of an owner?

It is therefore arguable that the *ratio* of the majority is restricted to the situation where the defendant practises a deception to obtain possession or ownership of the article.

Gomez was applied in *Atakpu and Abrahams* (1994), but, in that case too, the property was obtained by virtue of false representations made by the defendants.

In *Hinks*, however, Lord Steyn said that although the certified question in *Gomez* referred to the situation where consent has been obtained by fraud, the majority judgments did not 'differentiate between cases of consent induced by fraud and in any other circumstances. The *ratio* involves a proposition of general application'.

4   It was decided in *Hyam* (1997) that, where a direction on dishonesty is necessary, the exact words used in *Ghosh* should be followed.

5   *DPP v Ray* (1974) is distinguishable from the present facts. In that case, the restaurant customer was taken to impliedly represent, on ordering a meal, that he intended to pay for it, a representation which he continued to make throughout. Similarly in *Firth* (1990) the D referred patients to a hospital for treatment. He did not inform the hospital that they were private patients obliged to pay for the treatment. He was convicted of the offence, since repealed, of evading liability by deception. This was not a case of mere silence. D had induced the hospital to assume that the patients were entitled to be treated under the NHS. A shopper, on

the other hand, does not impliedly represent the accuracy of the prices displayed on goods for sale. Nor, if he remains silent, does he do anything positive to induce a false belief in the accuracy of the price.

6   The Law Commission, *Fraud,* Law Com No. 276, (2002) paras 7.28–7.29

Common Pitfalls

It is very important to consider liability for each incident separately. Follow the sequence of events and address the issues raised as they arise. Use clear headings to structure the answer.

QUESTION 48

Charlie was passing Slim's house when he heard a voice inside calling him. Believing he had been invited in and as the door was open he went into the house. On entering the living room, he noticed, on a perch, Johnny, a parrot, and realised that it had been the parrot which had been calling out his name. Irritated by Johnny's continual shrieking, Charlie took out his penknife and cut its throat. Johnny uttered a short sigh and fell off his perch, dead.

Charlie decided to look around the room to see if there was anything worth taking. He noticed a bookcase full of what appeared to be first editions. To his surprise, he noticed a copy of *Dead Men Don't Eat Quiche* by Rancy Blooter. Charlie picked up the book to have a look at it. He was astonished to discover from the dedication inside the front cover that this was the very copy which Rancy had signed for Charlie at the Crime Detective Book Fair and which he had lost on the train journey back from that event. He put the book in his bag, took a couple of DVDs from a rack and, treading heavily on Johnny, made his way out of the house.

▶   Discuss Charlie's criminal liability.

How to Answer this Question

This question involves consideration of liability for offences of criminal damage, theft and burglary.

The principal issues are:

❖   the meaning of property for the purposes of criminal damage and theft;
❖   the requirement, for theft, that property belongs to another at the time of the appropriation;

❖   the requirement for burglary that D knew or was reckless that his entry was trespassory.

Applying the Law

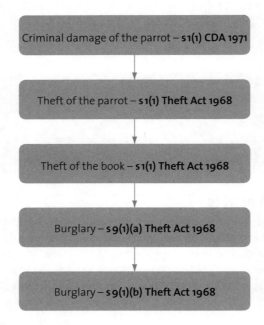

Criminal damage of the parrot – s1(1) **CDA 1971**

Theft of the parrot – s1(1) **Theft Act 1968**

Theft of the book – s1(1) **Theft Act 1968**

Burglary – s9(1)(a) **Theft Act 1968**

Burglary – s9(1)(b) **Theft Act 1968**

This flow chart highlights the relevant legislation you need for your answer.

ANSWER

CRIMINAL DAMAGE

It is an offence, contrary to s1(1) Criminal Damage Act 1971, to damage or destroy property belonging to another intentionally or recklessly and without lawful excuse.

By s10 of the Act property includes wild creatures which have been tamed or are ordinarily kept in captivity and thus the parrot Johnny was property belonging to Slim and its intentional destruction amounts to an offence of criminal damage by Charlie.

THEFT

Charlie may also be guilty of theft of the parrot. Theft is defined in s1(1) Theft Act 1968 as the dishonest appropriation of property belonging to another with the intention of permanently depriving the other of it. Taking an identical approach to that taken in the law of criminal damage, pet animals are also property belonging to another for the purposes of theft (s 4(4)).

'Appropriation' is defined in s 3(1) of the Act as requiring an assumption of the rights of an owner. Although property is most commonly appropriated by taking possession of it the concept is wide enough to include the destruction of property belonging to another. Clearly, Charlie was dishonest and intended permanently to deprive the owner of the property – the living pet parrot.[42]

He is not guilty, however, of stealing the copy of *Dead Men Don't Eat Quiche*. Firstly, the book does not belong to another. Even if Slim found the book and honestly retained possession believing that the owner could not reasonably be found the ownership of the item remained with Charlie. And, although s 5(1) protects the interest in property of a possessor, a finder of a thing does not acquire an absolute property or ownership in the thing, and acquires no right to keep it against the true owner (*Parker v British Airways Board* (1982)). The decision in *Turner (No.2)* (1971) which held that D may be regarded as appropriating property in the possession of another who had no right to retain it against D has been heavily criticised and is unlikely to be followed (see *Meredith* (1973)).[43]

In addition, Charlie does not appropriate the book with a dishonest intent. Section 2(1)(a) provides that a person who appropriates property in the belief that he has a legal right to deprive does not appropriate the property dishonestly. Thus he is not guilty of stealing the book but he is guilty of stealing the DVDs.

BURGLARY

Charlie did not commit burglary under s 9(1)(a) Theft Act 1968 when he entered the house. Although he entered the house without the permission of the occupier, he believed that he had been invited in. Burglary under s 9(1)(a) requires proof that D entered the building, knowing at the time of entry the facts that made the entry trespassory or being reckless as to whether the entry was without the occupier's consent (*Collins* (1973)). In addition he did not, at the time of entry, intend to commit one of the ulterior offences in s 9(2) of the Act.

He may, however, be guilty of offences contrary to s 9(1)(b) when he committed theft of the parrot and the DVDs. The subsection provides that a person is guilty of burglary if, having entered any building or part of a building as a trespasser, he steals or attempts to steal anything in the building or that part of it or inflicts or attempts to inflict on any person therein any grievous bodily harm.

---

42 Any assumption of the rights of an owner will suffice for theft.
43 The decision in *Turner (No.2)* is criticised because the decision of the Court of Appeal was based on the premise that the repairer was a mere bailee at will and a mere bailee at will has no right to possession against the owner.

It is not clear, however, whether it is sufficient for s 9(1)(b) to prove that D was aware, *at the time he committed the ulterior offence*, that he had entered as a trespasser or was reckless in respect of that fact or whether it is necessary to prove that he was aware or was reckless that his entry was trespassory *at the time of entry*. Most commentators take the view that knowledge or recklessness at the time of the ulterior offence (Think Point (1)) suffices but the analysis of the decision of the Court of Appeal in *Collins* would suggest that for both forms of burglary – that under s 9(1)(a) and that under s 9(1)(b) – it must be proved that D knew or was reckless at the time of entry that the entry was trespassory.

In *Collins*, Edmund Davies LJ, delivering the judgment of the court, stated that for the purpose of s 9 of the Theft Act a person entering a building does not enter as a trespasser if he enters without knowledge that he is trespassing and is not reckless as to whether or not he is unlawfully entering.[44]

If this approach is the correct one to s 9(1)(b) Charlie did not, for the purposes of burglary, enter the building as a trespasser and therefore is not guilty under s 9(1)(b) even though, at the time of the thefts, he was aware that his entry was without permission or consent.

Think Point

1   See for example J. C. Smith, *The Law of Theft*, London, Butterworths, 1997 para 11–25.

QUESTION 49

PART (A)

Stanley, a schizophrenic, received what he believed were instructions from 'God' to destroy all 'places of sin'. Stanley explained to 'God' that it was a crime in England to destroy property. 'God' reassured Stanley that if he did as he was instructed, no human life would be endangered and informed him that unless Stanley set about the task immediately, the towns of England would be destroyed in alphabetical order. Stanley, who lived in Accrington, responded straightaway. He went out and threw a petrol bomb through the window of a betting shop. The shop was completely destroyed. Although there were a number of people in neighbouring buildings, no one was injured.

▶   Discuss Stanley's criminal liability.

---

44 It is important to remember that for both s 9(1)(a) and s 9(1)(b) the entry must be trespassory.

PART (B)

Optic lived at No 11 Acacia Avenue. One night, he arrived home drunk. By mistake, he attempted to get into No 13. As his key failed to open the door, he assumed that the lock was broken. He went to the back of the house and, to gain entry, smashed the window of the back door.

▶ Discuss Optic's criminal liability.

Would your answer differ if No 11 had been the house of one of Optic's friends with whom Optic had been spending a few days?

How to Answer this Question

Although both parts of this question contain elements of liability for criminal damage, they deal with quite different issues. The first part focuses on the defence of insanity. The second part involves analysis of the contrasting treatment of, on the one hand, drunken mistakes going to the *mens rea* and, on the other, drunken mistakes going to a 'defence' of 'lawful excuse'.

The principal issues are:

❖ the meaning of 'recklessness';
❖ the meaning and application of 'lawful excuse' in s 5(2)(b) of the Criminal Damage Act 1971 – protection of property;
❖ the defence of insanity – nature and quality of act; insane delusions; and
❖ the meaning and application of 'lawful excuse' in s 5(2)(a) – belief in consent; mistake induced by drunkenness and s 5(2)(a).

The principal authorities are: *R v G and Another* (2003); *Jaggard v Dickinson* (1981); *Sullivan* (1984).

Applying the Law

(a)

(b)

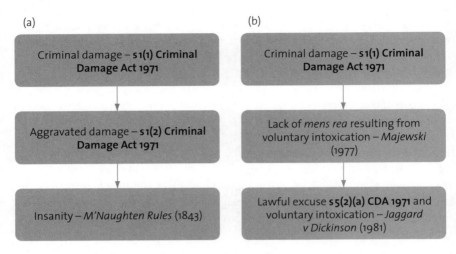

Criminal damage – **s 1(1) Criminal Damage Act 1971**

Criminal damage – **s 1(1) Criminal Damage Act 1971**

Aggravated damage – **s 1(2) Criminal Damage Act 1971**

Lack of *mens rea* resulting from voluntary intoxication – *Majewski* (1977)

Insanity – *M'Naughten Rules* (1843)

Lawful excuse **s 5(2)(a) CDA 1971** and voluntary intoxication – *Jaggard v Dickinson* (1981)

The two parts of this flow chart show the main legislation and principles needed to answer this question.

ANSWER

PART (A)

CRIMINAL DAMAGE

Stanley may be charged with criminal damage contrary to s 1(1) of the Criminal Damage Act 1971 ('simple damage') and damaging property being reckless as to whether the life of another would be endangered contrary to s 1(2) ('dangerous damage'). Where an offence is committed by fire, then it is charged as arson (s 1(3)), punishable with life imprisonment (s 4(1)).

Clearly, Stanley committed the *actus reus* of both offences ('property' includes land – s 10(1) of the 1971 Act).

In the case of simple damage, the *mens rea* is satisfied on proof of an intention to damage/destroy property belonging to another or recklessness with respect to doing so. The facts of the problem indicate that he intended to destroy the building.

Section 5(2)(b) of the 1971 Act provides that a person has a lawful excuse for the purposes of 'simple damage' if he destroyed property to protect other property which he believed to be in need of immediate protection. In *Hunt* (1977), however, the Court of Appeal held that whether property was in need of protection involves an objective question – whether in fact the action taken might protect property. *Hunt* was followed in the cases of *Ashford and Smith* (1988), *Hill and Hall* (1989) and *Jones and Others* (2004) (see also *Blake v DPP* (1993)).[45]

Undoubtedly, the court would take the view that destroying a betting shop could not protect Accrington and, thus, Stanley committed 'simple damage' (subject to the defence of insanity discussed below).

For 'dangerous damage', the prosecution would have to prove that Stanley was at least reckless with respect to the prospect of the life of another being endangered. In *R v G and Another* (2003), the House of Lords held that a person acts recklessly within the meaning of s1(2) of the **Criminal Damage Act 1971** when he is aware of a risk that life might be endangered and it is, in the circumstances known to him, unreasonable to take the risk (Think Point (1)).

The facts state that Stanley considered the risk of human life being endangered and acted on the assurance of 'God' that it would not be. As he did not believe there was a risk of life being endangered when he threw the petrol bomb, he was not reckless. However, he may only be entitled to a qualified acquittal on the grounds of insanity.

INSANITY

According to the *M'Naghten Rules* (1843), a person is legally insane if at the time he committed the act he was suffering from:

(a)   a defect of reason caused by disease of the mind;
(b)   (i) as not to know the nature and quality of his act; or (ii) if he did know that, he did not know that what he was doing was wrong.

There is a presumption of sanity in English law. The burden of proving insanity is therefore on Stanley and he must prove his case on a balance of probabilities (*M'Naghten Rules*; *Bratty v Attorney General for Northern Ireland* (1963)).

Whether a condition amounts to insanity is a question of law (*Bratty v Attorney General for Northern Ireland*).

In *Sullivan* (1984), Lord Diplock explained that 'disease of the mind' in the rules refers to an impairment of the faculties of reason, memory and understanding. It is unnecessary to show that the brain is diseased – the disorder may be functional.

---

45   Note that although **s5(2)(b)** is expressed in subjective terms it has been interpreted to involve an objective element.

The condition from which Stanley suffered is clearly capable in law of amounting to a disease of the mind.

The judges in the *M'Naghten* case said that in cases of insane delusion, the defendant is to be considered in the same situation as to responsibility as if the facts were as he perceived them to be. His delusion that 'God' was going to destroy other property unless he destroyed the places of sin falls within this rule. If the facts had been as he believed, he would have had a lawful excuse. He believed that the property was in immediate need of protection (see s 5(2)(b)(i)) and that the means adopted were reasonable, and, therefore, the proper verdict on a charge of simple damage is 'not guilty by reason of insanity'.

As explained above, Stanley lacked the *mens rea* for 'dangerous damage'. However, again, he is entitled only to a qualified acquittal. Where the defendant has put his state of mind in issue, the judge may rule that he has raised the defence of insanity (*Bratty v Attorney General for Northern Ireland*; *Sullivan*). It is submitted that this rule is not limited to cases of automatism and would apply where the defendant, as in this case, alleges a mistake of fact.[46]

As Stanley understood his act to be legally wrong, the case for insanity must be based on the 'nature and quality' limb. This refers to whether Stanley knew what he was doing. It has not been authoritatively decided whether this would apply to the situation where D dismisses a risk that the reasonable man would recognise as 'obvious' but, it is submitted, the foreseeable consequences of an act are an element of the nature and quality of the act – and this interpretation is supported by the rule regarding insane delusions.

Where a defendant is found not guilty by reason of insanity, the judge must make one of a number of orders including a hospital order with or without restrictions on discharge (s 5 of the Criminal Procedure (Insanity) Act 1964, as substituted by Sched 1 to the Criminal Procedure (Insanity and Unfitness to Plead) Act 1991).

PART (B)

Optic may be guilty of 'simple damage' as defined in s 1(1) of the Criminal Damage Act 1971 (see above). He has damaged property, that is, the window belonging to another.

Clearly, he did not intend to damage property belonging to another. Nor, it seems, was he reckless. In *R v G and Another*, it was held that a person is reckless as to whether property belongs to another when he is aware of a risk that it might belong to another. Optic believed the window was his.

---

46 The defence of insanity is most commonly raised in cases where D was an automaton but it is clear that it is not restricted to such cases.

However, if he lacked the *mens rea* as a result of voluntary intoxication, he may be convicted of 'simple damage'. Where D is alleged to have 'recklessly damaged property belonging to another', the offence is one of 'basic intent', and a lack of *mens rea* caused by drunkenness is no defence to a crime of basic intent (*DPP v Majewski* (1977); *Richardson and Irwin* (1999)).[47]

ALTERNATIVE FACTS

In this situation, Optic will have a 'lawful excuse' if he believed that the person whom he believed to be entitled to consent to the damage (that is, his friend) would have consented to the damage (s 5(2)(a) of the 1971 Act).

In similar circumstances, the Divisional Court in *Jaggard v Dickinson* (1981) held that D could rely on her intoxication to explain her mistaken belief. The court considered that the *DPP v Majewski* rule was inapplicable. This was not a case where D's 'drunken mistake' went to the *mens rea*.

The Divisional Court were influenced by the fact that s 5(3) provides that, for the purposes of s 5(2), it is immaterial whether the belief is justified or not so long as it is genuinely held.

Think Point

1   It is not necessary to prove that life was in fact endangered (*Sangha* (1988); *Parker* (1993)).

Common Pitfalls

In answering part (a) it is not enough to state, without explanation, that Stanley is insane. You should explain, by reference to the *M'Naghten Rules* why his delusional state might amount to insanity in law. The most common mistakes in respect of part (b) are based upon a misunderstanding of the different ways in which voluntary intoxication might impact upon criminal liability. The legal treatment of a drunken mistake negativing *mens rea* is quite different from the legal treatment of a drunken mistaken belief in the excusing conditions defined in **s 5(2)** of the **Criminal Damage Act 1971**.

---

47   The rule in **Majewski** applies where D, as a result of voluntary intoxication, commits the *actus reus* of a basic intent offence but lacks the necessary intent for that offence and provides that, despite the lack of intent, D will be convicted of the offence in question.

QUESTION 50

PART (A)

George telephoned Paul and said that if Paul did not destroy some compromising photographs of George with Patti, he would set fire to Paul's shop. In fact, Paul's telephone was faulty, with the result that he did not hear the message.

▶ Discuss George's criminal liability.

PART (B)

John, a farmer, noticed that a large dog, Martha, belonging to Stuart, was attacking his sheep. He asked Ringo, who was shooting grouse in a neighbouring field, if he would lend him his shotgun. Ringo refused. John wrenched the gun from Ringo's grasp and pushed Ringo to the ground. John shot and killed Martha.

▶ Discuss John's criminal liability.

How to Answer this Question

The first part of the question is concerned with the offences of blackmail contrary to s 21 of the Theft Act 1968 and threats of damage to property contrary to s 2 of the Criminal Damage Act 1971. The second part concerns issues of liability for criminal damage and, to a minor extent, battery.

PART (A)

The principal issues are:

❖ whether a 'demand with menaces' is 'made' for the purposes of blackmail if the intended recipient does not hear it (s 21 of the Theft Act 1968);

❖ the meaning and application of 'view to gain' or 'intent to cause loss' in s 21; and

❖ whether a 'threat of damage' is 'made' if the intended recipient does not hear it (s 2 of the Criminal Damage Act 1971).

PART (B)

The principal issues are:

❖ the meaning and application of 'lawful excuse' in s 5(2)(b) of the Criminal Damage Act 1971; and

❖ the availability of the defence of 'duress of circumstances'.

Principal authorities: *Treacy v DPP* (1971); *Clear* (1968); *Harvey* (1981); *Hunt* (1977); *Martin* (1989); *Conway* (1989).

Applying the Law

(a)   (b)

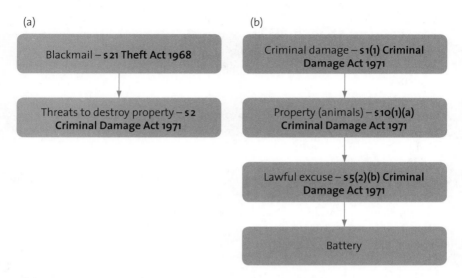

The two parts of this diagram highlight the legislation you need to discuss in your answer.

ANSWER

PART (A)

BLACKMAIL

George may be guilty of blackmail contrary to s 21 of the Theft Act 1968, an offence punishable with a term of imprisonment not exceeding 14 years (s 21(3)).

The *actus reus* of blackmail is a 'demand with menaces'.

In *Treacy v DPP* (1971), the House of Lords held by a majority that a demand contained in a letter is made when it is posted, irrespective of whether it arrives or is read by the person to whom it is addressed. Lord Diplock was influenced by the fact that the person who makes an uncommunicated demand is no less wicked nor less in need of deterrence than the person whose demand is received.

The same may be said of the person who makes an oral communication which is not heard and, thus, it is submitted, George made a demand, viz, that Paul give him the photographs.[48]

---

48 By reference to the principle underlying written communications it is possible to derive a parallel rule for oral communications.

A threat of any action detrimental or unpleasant to the person addressed is capable of amounting to a menace so long as the threat is of sufficient intensity that it would move the ordinary person of normal stability and courage to accede unwillingly to the demand (*Thorne v Motor Trade Association* (1937); *Clear* (1968)). Thus, it is unnecessary to know how Paul would have reacted to the threat to demolish his shop. The question – and it is one for the jury – is whether the ordinary person would be influenced by the threat.

The demand must be made with a 'view to gain' or 'intent to cause loss' in terms of money or other property (s 34(2)(a)). In this case, George intended to cause Paul the loss of property, that is, the photographs.

The prosecution must prove that the 'demand with menaces' was unwarranted. This is a question of *mens rea*. Section 21(1) provides that D's demand with menaces is unwarranted unless D made it in the belief that (a) he had reasonable grounds for making the demand, and (b) the use of the menaces was a proper means of reinforcing the demand.

The facts of the problem suggest that George's demand with menaces was unwarranted. Even if he believed that he had reasonable grounds for demanding the photographs, it is improbable that he believed the use of the menaces was a proper means of reinforcing the demand. If George knew that what he threatened to do was unlawful, his demand with menaces was unwarranted (*Harvey* (1981)).[49]

THREATS TO DESTROY PROPERTY

It is an offence contrary to s 2 of the Criminal Damage Act 1971 to threaten to destroy or damage property belonging to another intending that the person threatened would fear that the threat would be carried out.

There are three main issues: (a) whether, objectively, a threat had been made to another; (b) whether the words and actions amounted to a threat to destroy or damage property in law; and (c) a question of *mens rea*, whether the defendant intended that the person threatened would fear that the threat would be carried out (*Cakmak* (2002)).

The offence is not limited to written threats and, although there is no direct authority on the point, it is submitted that, by analogy to blackmail, a threat is made even if it is not received.[50]

---

49 Although the requirement that the demand with menaces was unwarranted is a question of *mens rea* the word 'proper' involves reference to generally held standards.

50 Where there is no direct authority, make reference to an analogous rule.

PART (B)

CRIMINAL DAMAGE

John may be charged with criminal damage contrary to s 1(1) of the Criminal Damage Act 1971, an offence which, by virtue of s 4, is punishable with a maximum of 10 years' imprisonment.

The offence is committed where D intentionally or recklessly damages property belonging to another.

Tame animals or animals reduced into possession amount to 'property' for the purposes of this offence (s 10(1)(a)). The killing of an animal constitutes destruction of property. Thus, clearly, John committed the *actus reus* of the offence. Similarly, his *mens rea* is not in doubt – John intentionally destroyed property belonging to another.

Section 1(1) provides, however, that no offence is committed if D had a 'lawful excuse'. Section 5(2)(b) provides that D has a lawful excuse if he destroyed the property in order to protect property belonging to himself which he believed to be in immediate need of protection.

For the reasons explained above, the sheep are 'property' belonging to John.

Although the defence in s 5(2)(b) is expressed in 'subjective' terms, the Court of Appeal in *Hunt* (1977) held that the defence will be denied if it is proved that what was done could not amount, objectively, to something done in protection of property.

In this case, the objective requirement is satisfied. If, as the facts imply, John believed that his sheep were in immediate need of protection and he believed that shooting the dog was a reasonable means of protecting his property, then he has a 'lawful excuse'. It is immaterial whether those beliefs were justified. All that matters is that they were genuinely held (s 5(3)).

BATTERY

John may be charged with the battery of Ringo.

Battery is a summary offence. It is committed where a person intentionally or recklessly inflicts unlawful personal violence upon another (*Rolfe* (1952)). The slightest degree of force will suffice (*Cole v Turner* (1704); *Collins v Wilcock* (1984)). The maximum punishment is a fine not exceeding level 5 on the standard scale and/or a term of imprisonment not exceeding six months or both (s 39 of the Criminal Justice Act 1988).

It is clear from the facts that John intentionally applied force. The issue is whether he did so 'unlawfully'.

Section 5(2) of the Criminal Damage Act 1971 only provides a defence of 'lawful excuse' to a charge of criminal damage. It does not apply to other offences. It would appear that there is no other defence of which John may take advantage.

The recognised defence of 'duress of circumstances' applies where D can be said to be acting reasonably and proportionately in order to avoid a threat of death or serious injury to himself or another person (*Martin* (1989)) and, although there is some weak authority for the proposition that a defence of necessity might be available in cases where a lesser danger threatens (see, for example, *Conway* (1989), per Woolf LJ), there is no modern authority in which a threat of damage to property has been recognised as providing an excuse or justification for an offence against the person.[51]

---

51 Good luck in your examinations!

Index